the Unofficial Guide to Managing Time

Dawn E. Reno

IDG Books Worldwide, Inc.
An International Data Group Company
Foster City, CA • Chicago, IL • Indianapolis, IN •
New York, NY

IDG Books Worldwide, Inc.
An International Data Group Company
919 E. Hillsdale Boulevard
Suite 400
Foster City, CA 94404

Copyright © 2000 by Dawn E. Reno

All rights reserved, including the right of reproduction in whole or in part in any form.

This publication contains the opinions and ideas of its author[s] and is designed to provide useful advice to the reader on the subject matter covered. Any references to any products or services do not constitute or imply an endorsement or recommendation. The publisher and the author[s] specifically disclaim any responsibility for any liability, loss or risk (financial, personal or otherwise) which may be claimed or incurred as a consequence, directly or indirectly, of the use and/or application of any of the contents of this publication.

Certain terms mentioned in this book which are known or claimed to be trademarks or service marks have been capitalized.

IDG Books Worldwide, Inc. does not attest to the validity, accuracy or completeness of this information. Use of a term in this book should not be regarded as affecting the validity of any trademark or service mark.

Unofficial Guides are a [registered] trademark of Macmillan General Reference USA, Inc., a wholly owned subsidiary of IDG Books Worldwide, Inc. For general information on IDG Books Worldwide's books in the U.S., please call our Consumer Customer Service department at 800-762-2974. For reseller information, including discounts and previous sales, please call our Reseller Customer Service department at 800-434-3422.

ISBN: 0-02863667-8

Manufactured in the United States of America

10 9 8 7 6 5 4 3 2 1

First edition

For Gail Radley, who knows how important time is to friends.

Acknowledgments

Many people help with the writing of a book, but there are several who went over and above on this one. Special thanks to the librarians at the Deltona Public Library and the University of Central Florida. Thanks to all of the professionals who were contacted with questions or asked for comments, especially Gail Radley, Susan Hubbard, Pat Rushin, KK Wilder, Kathleen Bell, and Judith Hamschemeyer. Special thanks to Randy Ladenheim-Gil, who helped with this book's creation; Kitty Werner, who was responsible for getting me in touch with Randy; and Al McDermid, who held my hand throughout the developmental process. And, finally, as always, my husband, Bobby, who fed me while I was on deadline and withstood some very anxious moments.

Contents

The *Unofficial Guide* Reader's Bill of Rights

We Give You More Than the Official Line

Welcome to the *Unofficial Guide* series of Lifestyles titles—books that deliver critical, unbiased information that other books can't or won't reveal—*the inside scoop*. Our goal is to provide you with the *most accessible, useful* information and advice possible. The recommendations we offer in these pages are not influenced by the corporate line of any organization or industry; we give you the hard facts, whether those institutions like them or not. If something is ill-advised or will cause a loss of time and/or money, we'll give you ample warning. And if it is a worthwhile option, we'll let you know that, too.

Armed and Ready

Our hand-picked authors confidently and critically report on a wide range of topics that matter to smart readers like you. Our authors are passionate about their subjects, but have distanced themselves enough from them to help you be armed and protected, and help make you educated decisions as you go through the process. It is our intent that, from having read this book, you will avoid the pitfalls everyone else falls into and get it right the first time.

Don't be fooled by cheap imitations; this is the genuine article *Unofficial Guide* series from IDG Books. You may be familiar with our proven track record of the travel *Unofficial Guides*, which have more than three million copies in print. Each year, thousands of travelers—new and old— are armed with a brand new, fully updated edition of the flagship *Unofficial Guide to Walt Disney World*, by Bob Sehlinger. It is our intention here to provide you with the same level of objective authority that Mr. Sehlinger does in his brainchild.

Every work in the Lifestyle *Unofficial Guides* is intensively inspected by a team of three top professionals in their fields. These experts review the manuscript for factual accuracy, comprehensiveness, and an insider's determination as to whether the manuscript fulfills the credo in this Reader's Bill of rights. In other words, our Panel ensures that you are, in fact, getting "the inside scoop."

Our Pledge

The authors, the editorial staff, and the Unofficial Panel of Experts assembled for *Unofficial Guides* are determined to lay out the most valuable alternatives available for our readers. This dictum means that our writers must be explicit, prescriptive, and above all, direct. We strive to be thorough and complete, but our goal is not necessarily to have the "most" or "all" of the information on a topic; this is not, after all, an encyclopedia. Our objective is to help you narrow down your options to the best of what is available, unbiased by affiliation with any industry or organization.

In each *Unofficial Guide,* we give you:

- Comprehensive coverage of necessary and vital information
- Authoritative, rigidly fact-checked data
- The most up-to-date insights into trends
- Savvy, sophisticated writing that's also readable
- Sensible, applicable facts and secrets that only an insider knows

Special Features

Every book in our series offers the following six special sidebars in the margins that were devised to help you get things done cheaply, efficiently, and smartly.

1. **Timesaver**—tips and shortcuts that save you time

2. **Moneysaver**—tips and shortcuts that save you money

3. **Watch out!**—more serious cautions and warnings

4. **Bright Idea**—general tips and shortcuts to help you find an easier or smarter way to do something

5. **Quote**—statements from real people that are intended to be prescriptive and valuable to you

6. **Unofficially...**—an insider's fact or anecdote

We also recognize your need to have quick information at your fingertips, and have thus provided the following comprehensive sections at the back of the book:

1. **Seminar Guide**—helpful contact information for attending or setting up time-management seminars for yourself or your company.

2. **Glossary**—definitions of complicated terminology and jargon

3. **Resource Guide**—lists of relevant agencies, associations, institutions, Web sites, etc.

4. **Recommended Reading List**—suggested titles that can help you get more in-depth information on related topics

5. **Index**

Letters, Comments, Questions from Readers

We strive to continually improve the *Unofficial* series, and input from our readers is a valuable way for us to do that.

Many of those who have used the *Unofficial Guide* travel books write to the authors to ask questions, make comments, or share their own discoveries and lessons. For Lifestyle *Unofficial Guides*, we would also appreciate all such correspondence—both positive and critical— and we will make best efforts to incorporate appropriate readers' feedback and comments in revised editions of this work.

How to write us:

Unofficial Guides

Lifestyle Guides

IDG Books

1633 Broadway

New York, NY 10019

Attention: Reader's Comments

About the Author

Dawn E. Reno, author of 14 books, lives in the South with her husband, Robert, and their two cats. For the past thirty years, she has been learning how to manage her time the hard way: by being on deadline!

Currently, she is an Assistant Professor of English/Creative Writing at Lake City Community College and is at work on a new novel and a non-fiction book about the online auction community.

The *Unofficial Guide* Panel of Experts

The *Unofficial* editorial team recognizes that you've purchased this book with the expectation of getting the most authoritative, carefully inspected information currently available. Toward that end, on each and every title in this series, we have selected a minimum of two "official" experts comprising the Unofficial Panel who painstakingly review the manuscripts to ensure the following: factual accuracy of all data; inclusion of the most up-to-date and relevant information; and that, from an insider's perspective, the authors have armed you with all the necessary facts you need—but that the institutions don't want you to know.

For *The Unofficial Guide™ to Managing Time,* we are proud to introduce the following panel of experts: **Keith Ellis** is a nationally known speaker, author, columnist, and management consultant whose unique insights about goal-setting and time management have made him a guest on talk shows across the country. A magna cum laude graduate of Georgetown University, Mr. Ellis is the President of Keith Ellis Seminars, a firm that specializes in training and consulting on state-of-the-art strategies for peak performance. He is the author of an exciting book called *The Magic Lamp: Goal Setting for People Who Hate Setting Goals.* He is also the author of BOOTSTRAPS, a monthly column on the World Wide Web devoted to self-help and self-improvement (www.selfhelp.com/bootstraps.html). For his pioneering writing, teaching, and leadership in the field of peak performance, Mr. Ellis has been listed in Who's Who In American Business, Who's Who In Media and Communica-tions, and the Dictionary of International Biography."

Jana M. Kemp is the founder of Meeting & Management Essentials. After a career in corporate training and development departments, Jana founded her company with the mission of helping organizations of all sizes to improve their day-to-day meeting and management skills.

Recognized as an international expert on meeting and time management, Jana provides a weekly feature about time-efficient meetings on the nationally syndicated Business News Network and hosts Momentum(TM), a weekly business-news-talk radio show. Jana's expertise in the field of time management began with her experience getting 4-H projects done for the annual county fair and has grown to include product development on the Time Mastery Profile(R) from Carlson Learning Company and monthly workshop delivery on the subjects of time and meeting management.

Jana's book *Moving Meetings* (McGraw Hill, 1994) has been released in Italian. Her published work also includes business columns for *Corporate University Review* magazine, her own Better Meetings for Everyone quarterly newsletter, The Idaho Press

Tribune, The *Idaho Business Review, Successful Meetings* magazine, TRAINING magazine and many more serial publications.

Sandra Pope is the owner of Project Completed, a consulting service focusing on professional organizing of information, space, and time for businesses, both stateside and internationally. Support Staff Training Workshops provide office efficiency tips and working with people of different cultures. She also does one-on-one training with supervisors and shorter training with management level personnel. Her professional speaking engagements include businesses as well as county and state seminars. Sandra is a Golden member of the National Association of Professional Organizers and the Prince William County Greater Manassas Chamber of Commerce. Her website is www.pwcweb.com/popeconsultants.

Introduction

In the last century, we've had more technological advances than in all of history combined. We can travel faster and farther, we can communicate with people in the most remote regions of the world—and even those traveling in outer space. We can connect to millions of pieces of information from one little computer in our home office, we can see television programs broadcast from different countries. And we all complain of one thing: We don't have the time to enjoy it all.

When Alexander Graham Bell invented the telephone in 1876, the only person he could call was his assistant—in the next room. Now, going into the next millenium, with faxes and computer links and people talking to each other, there are over 12 billion calls per day going through the system. Add to that e-mail, voice mail, answering machines, cell phones, and regular mail and it's amazing that we're still unable to reach someone at the exact moment we want them.

The trip that Lindbergh made across the ocean once created awe in the minds of people who wanted the freedom to travel more quickly. Now one can go around the world on a Lear jet, visiting many countries and seeing everything a person in the beginning of the century would take a lifetime to see—and we need give only a couple of weeks of our own time to do so.

Even our food is ready in less than five minutes. We've all watched people in restaurants squirm and squiggle if their dinners aren't coming out of the kitchen only moments after being ordered. Surveys say that non-employed people take more time to eat than those of us who have jobs and that men are now spending more than two hours a week *less* on meal times than they were in 1975. In addition, families are meeting for only one mealtime a day—if, in fact, they meet for meals at all!

We're even sleeping less than we used to. In 1965, for example, the average employed female slept approximately 55 hours a week; now she sleeps approximately 53 hours a week. Is she getting up early to do more housework before heading off to her job or to feed the kids before they go to school? Or is she staying up later to catch up on work that she's brought home from the office?

And we all know about the rash of road rage incidents during the past decade. They have become such a problem that the American Institute for Public Safety now has a Web site that attempts to help people deal with the problem through the use of humor. This epidemic has been largely proven to be caused by the stress placed upon all of us by the idea that we need to arrive someplace on time. Because we don't leave ourselves enough time, we get frustrated, and thus road rage—or the act of taking out our anger on those cars/people on the road around us—has become far too common. Yes, we have too much traffic on the road these days, but traffic would travel smoothly if people who were driving knew how to handle the anxiety caused by not arriving on time. Though there are other factors that cause people to drive aggressively, the lack of time is certainly one of them.

Have we lost our patience or is it that time is traveling so fast, we have to sprint to keep up?

Statisticians have proven that we actually have more leisure time now than we ever had in the past. But what exactly is leisure time? Are we spending more time with our families? Going on vacation more often and for longer periods? Using that free time to pursue hobbies or socialize or learn a new language? Most of us would have to admit that we don't know exactly what we're doing with that time, but if we're Americans, one thing is for sure: We're watching a lot more television than we did when the invention was first used for BBC broadcasts in 1936.

Today, it's estimated that 40 hours of our time each week is spent watching the television and that nearly every home in America owns one or more sets. In 1965, 35 hours a week were spent watching television. Perhaps the busier we get, the more we need that mindless recreation?

And what about the advent of the personal computer? There are many arguments about who invented the computer and when it was actually created, but the first use of the "mother" of all computers was back in the 1930s and 40s when people used them to do calculations. Since that time, we have seen the birth of digital and analog computers—and we don't intend to explain the difference here. The point is that the personal computers that most people own today have been around for only approximately thirty years—yet we now use it not only as a calculator (of sorts), but as a word processor, a communicator, a research tool, and an entertainment device.

The recent movie *The Net*, starring Sandra Bullock, was the first fiction to analyze the possibility that computers cause people to become less social. It also highlighted the dangers of losing your privacy to cyberspace. A little nerve-wracking, to say the least, but it makes one wonder just exactly how much time we're saving and what we're losing by spending hours in front of that little computer screen.

Doctors have been noticing the effect of poor time management on their patients' health for many years. Stress (translation: the anxiety felt when someone doesn't have enough time to meet life's demands) is the number-one cause of more than 75% of the illnesses killing people all over the world. Ask any cardiologist. Heart attacks are caused, in large part, by stress. And the other contributing factors may also be a result of stress. For example, someone might be overweight because they simply don't have time to cook, and subsequently eat too much junk food. Result? A high cholesterol and fat content, which in turn causes arteries to become clogged—and boom! It's heart attack time.

Don't have time to exercise? Your heart rate slows down, metabolism doesn't perform correctly, blood doesn't get to the places that need it, and chances are, you'll eventually become ill.

Running in place all the time trying to accomplish Wonder Woman or Superman–type tasks? You're in the fight-or-flight syndrome and blood pressure is skyrocketing. Result? Sleeplessness, at the very least, and many more terrifying results if it keeps up on a regular basis.

Even shopping isn't the relaxing and social activity it once was. Superstores have taken the place of Mom-and-Pop specialty shops. Malls that sprawl over miles offer everything you could possibly want under one roof. Stores that stand alone and downtown shopping areas have become quaint and many Americans are fighting to keep them preserved. But, in the meantime, more and more people are shopping online to save time and using catalogs as a means of accumulating gifts for special occasions. Instead of spending the time and meeting a friend for a day of shopping, people are ordering on the run—and impulse buying, as a result, is way up.

Why do you think New Age tapes, natural food stores, and yoga classes are making a comeback? It's because people are realizing they need to slow down, take care of themselves, and manage their time more effectively.

If you're one of the many millions of people who claim to have even less time these days than you did five or ten years ago, you are not alone. Books, programs, CDs, and seminars on time management abound and are incredibly popular with not only the American public but in almost every "advanced" country. Articles on "how to save time cooking" or "how to save time cleaning" or "how to spend more quality time with your children" or "how to cut the time moving up the ladder of success" are de rigeur in today's magazines. Look up the word "time" on any Internet search engine and the result is millions of hits. We are obsessed with grabbing more time for ourselves and finding out how to save as much time as possible.

So, if this is your problem, how are we going to help you solve it or at least get control over it? First, we're going to show you how to recognize it.

Not all time management problems manifest themselves in the same way with everyone. What you need to have time to do might not be what your neighbor needs, even though you both are complaining you're too busy for words. You might just be overloaded with work and have to deal with priorities, while your neighbor might be a procrastinator who has to learn to deal with that problem.

In Part I, we'll talk about the problems you're having and will then see if we can identify exactly where the problem areas are. You'll need to answer some questions and consider what you want out of life. Only you can analyze the areas where you'd like to focus and improve. Whether you simply need to make time to exercise, to spend more time with your family, or to organize your life so that you can get more work done in less time, it's important to evaluate where you stand now in order to figure out what kinds of time management skills you need to learn.

Perhaps your expectations of yourself are far too high, or maybe someone else is pushing you in a direction that you really don't want to go. The effects family, friends, and employers have on our lives are often detrimental instead of supportive. By being honest with yourself and figuring out what is most important to you, you might be able to adjust your life to meet some of the expectations placed on you by others.

Realistically, we cannot all accomplish superhuman feats when we're working within a certain parameter. What we hear most often is that people would like 48 hours in a day. That's impossible. We have 24 hours in a day and only 7 days in a week. That's something that we can't change, no matter how hard we try. The trick is to schedule your tasks/plans to fit within those parameters.

Part II will help you see where you need to build in more time and what kinds of priorities you consider most important. We'll also discuss the different types of people you are (and no, you're not schizophrenic) and how you can satisfy the goals of each of these "people."

One of the most important things that people need to remember when working on time management is that their time is worth money. Even if you don't come home with a regular paycheck, never consider that you're working for free. When you evaluate what you're worth in actual dollars, you'll be less likely to squander five or six hours on a project that makes no contribution toward the goals you want to reach in your lifetime.

Goals are extremely valuable to the person who wants to manage their time more effectively. Without knowing what direction your life is going in, how can you plan on what to do and when to do it? We all know plenty of people who are happy just letting each day come and they deal with problems when they crop up, but you can often head those catastrophes off before they happen if you plan for interruptions and traumas. Let's face it, no one makes it through life without a problem or two, a scrape on the knee, a bump on the head, or an illness or death. If we know they're going to happen, why not prepare ourselves for them?

In Part III, we'll talk about the various types of goals, how you perceive yourself, and how to go from one goal to the next. When we think about goals, we think about them in a pyramid shape. The goals you have today will bring you into shape for meeting your weekly goals, which will then build into your monthly goals, then your yearly, and finally, the basis of them all, your lifetime goals. If you don't meet your daily goals, you won't meet your weekly goals, and so on. Everything works together, and that's an integral part of making the time machine work.

By the time you get to Part IV, you'll have to face that wicked devil: procrastination. The truth of the matter is that we all procrastinate in one way or another. As a child, we probably wanted to procrastinate going to bed—and now that we're adults, that big, fluffy pillow is the most comforting place to lay our heads. Though we often procrastinate because we simply don't want to do a job, there are many other reasons for putting off till tomorrow what we should be doing today. By following the steps in Chapter 8, you can get past this big stumbling block and on to dealing with the curse of interruptions in Chapter 9.

Though some of us welcome the little interruptions that happen throughout the day because it forces us to pause and take a breather, often they can steal the time you should be spending on the work itself. When our cats steal across the keyboard, it's usually a signal for a "kitty hug," which means a warm, purring body against our shoulder and a well-deserved moment of peace. But all interruptions aren't as pleasant or as easily dealt with as a simple, "Shoo!" If you're unable to say no or to communicate your needs to those around you, then this is definitely the chapter for you to consider seriously.

Interruptions can come in many forms—like unnecessary phone calls, well-meaning social butterflies, and bored children—and can be dealt with in a number of ways. You don't have to be rude to let someone know you're working and would rather not be disturbed, but you do have to be a little assertive in the way you deal with people and things that steal those moments you should be spending putting the next brick into place.

What about if you're simply overwhelmed and no amount of to-do lists are going to take care of the pile of work that just arrived in your life? Do you know it's okay to ask for help from the troops? It doesn't mean that you're imperfect if you solicit someone to clean your house for a day, that you're a bad mother if you hire a babysitter to take over while you're finishing the last of the cleaning before the big holiday festivities, or that the boss will fire you if she knows you've delegated some of that big project to your underlings. Chapter 10 will tell you when and how to get the help you need and might just offer you the freedom to ask for it more often!

We also define the 80/20 Rule and Parkinson's Law in that chapter. Anytime you think people who succeed must work 20 of the 24 hours we're given every day, think again. Those people know that you should concentrate on the most important work, the work that will garner the biggest results. What it all boils down to is that 20% of your work results in 80% production. What does this mean? It means that 80% of your time is spent either spinning your wheels or doing meaningless tasks that bring you no closer to your goal. And what about Parkinson's Law? Basically, that rule relates directly to the amount of time you give yourself to accomplish something. If you give yourself three days, it'll take you three days. If you give yourself a month, it'll take a month. (That's why procrastinators usually end up getting the work done at the last minute.)

We haven't forgotten that everyone who reads this book won't be sitting in a high-rise office. We know that you all have different lifestyles and need different types of time, which is why we've created Part V. In the chapters included in this section, we talk about parents and how children can demand so much time (and how it's so difficult to balance all their needs while trying to earn the money to raise them), about creative people who often have to explain to everyone why their passion drives them to write or paint or make music when everyone else is at the neighborhood picnic, and about students whose time is so valuable that many burn the midnight oil trying to complete projects and papers by the end of the semester.

Then it's time to organize that paper blizzard that arrives every day in the form of mail and projects—whether it's across your kitchen counter at home or your desktop at the office. So many thousands of pieces of paper are created every year that it's amazing there are still trees alive in our forests, yet we waste more time sorting through that junk mail than we should. Why open it at all if you know it's junk mail? Tossing it saves invaluable time. Getting the junk mailers to take you off their lists saves even more—and think of all those trees…

In Part VI, we help you organize your personal and business workspace, learn how to take advantage of your computer's ability to save things you shouldn't have cluttering up your desk, and how to use the tools that really do help you beat the clock. We talk about handling a piece of paper only once—and meaning it! If you waste time passing the paper from one stack to the next, you're not only wasting time, but you're not getting anything done to boot.

And we're not only going to talk about paper either; we'll also talk about saving time in the kitchen, while you're traveling, and about hiring people to help you through the "crunch" periods of the year when you might benefit from a local accountant who can get you a little more from your tax return. We've shared all the tricks we have come up with during the many hours of research done for this book, as well as some well-worn techniques we've polished ourselves over the years. It's often difficult to make it through the day without wishing for more time, but all you really need to do is make the best use of the time you have. With an honest look at yourself and a revamping of some of your old habits, you, too, can create some time to go fishing, enjoy a day at the beach, or an afternoon with your family instead of sweating out the final deadline for a project you should have finished long ago.

Throughout the book, there are questions you should answer frankly and sincerely, suggestions you should adapt, schedules which will help shape the way you look at the way you use your time, and numerous resources to help you stop wasting time and start spending it the way *you* want to.

So, what's stopping you? Put that pencil in your hand and start reading. Time's a'wastin'!

So You're Having Problems Managing Your Time

PART I

Why Don't You Have Enough Hours in the Day?

Chapter 1

I s the world going faster or is it just our imagination? And if the world is indeed demanding more of us, then why can't we accomplish everything we need to do—especially since we have the most up-to-date technology imaginable?

One hundred years ago, people still made their own clothes, churned their own butter, walked to school, wrote letters, shared family dinners, visited with friends, worked full days, built furniture, read books, told stories, and never once asked for help. At least that's what we believe they did. Was it all better then? Perhaps, but what we don't remember is that they worked hard. Very hard.

❝

Half our life is
spent trying to
find something
to do with the
time we have
rushed through
life trying to
save.—Will
Rogers

❞

There was a time when an average housewife might do three loads of laundry (by hand—with lye soap) before the sun came up, then dip a few dozen candles, get the children and her husband breakfast, send them off to work and school, then feed the chickens, milk the cows, start the bread for supper, take in and fold the laundry, sweep the kitchen floor, weed the garden, then welcome the kids home from school, get them started on cleaning out the animal stalls, welcome her husband home from his work, get supper, read a bit or do some sewing, then fall into her bed.

Do you think she ever asked herself where the time went? She probably didn't have time to! Did she get a lot done during the day? You bet! How? She knew exactly what she needed to do and made time to do it. Again, how? She planned and kept to her routine and didn't waste time.

I imagine there was no such term as "time management" in those days before computers and cars, but people got more done during those 24-hour spans than we expect to today, and they complained less.

Yes, you might say, but they died earlier than we do today. Is it any wonder? No. But it's no wonder that they were able to get more done. They were probably in better shape than we are. They had no distractions like televisions and computers and telephones. They knew what they had to do and they got up earlier to do it, if they needed to. And their socializing was kept to Sundays and special occasions.

Today, we must consider all the interruptions in our lives. We also travel farther to go to work than those people did a hundred years ago. Our families are scattered far apart. We expect more luxuries;

thus we need to make more money in order to pro-
cure them. And all of the above take precious hours
out of our day.

The reason we all complain about not having
enough time is because we feel we have little control
over it. The truth of the matter is that we are in *complete* control. We just have to motivate ourselves to
exercise that control.

Chances are you are only half as productive as
you could possibly be—and down deep, we all know
that and we all continue to strive toward the goal of
100% perfection/control. You probably will never
get there, but you can learn to manage your time
more practically than you do now. And once you do
it, you'll feel much better about yourself, more satisfied with your life, more relaxed on a regular basis,
and more in control of your priorities.

So, back to our original question: Why don't you
have enough hours in the day? The answer: You
probably have plenty of time during the day. You're
just not operating efficiently.

Individual considerations

The beauty of human beings is that each of us is an
individual, thus any suggestions on time management are not going to work for everyone. Here is
the point where you decide what your individual
needs are.

Each of us will work within a certain framework
in our own individual way. That's just the makeup of
the human personality. It's like one person seeing
the glass half empty, while the next person sees it
half full. In and of itself, our individuality is beauti-
ful. It's what makes us all different and interesting
to each other. It's what causes people to choose to
follow different religions, makes us follow different

Watch Out!
Don't try to exer-
cise complete
control over your
life. Those who
do are A Type
personalities and
prime candidates
for heart attacks,
strokes, and
ulcers.

paths in our lives, and gives us all something to talk about.

It's also why one person's recipe for happiness does not necessarily equal your own—and why some people can manage to do a million things during one 24-hour-day and others can manage to accomplish only one.

The first question you need to honestly answer before attempting to manage your time is: Am I ready to make some changes in what I already do? If the answer is no, there is no need to read any further.

Timesaver
Instead of counting up all the pros and cons, just count up all the positives in your life. You save time—and make yourself happier.

If the answer is yes (and it probably is since you have this book in your hand), then you have to be willing to make some concessions, to change some things about your life and the way you deal with work, home, family and friends in order to be more prudent with your time, as well as more productive.

If you can't consider the most minute change in your daily habits, then you will go on wondering where all the hours went at the end of your day. And if you continue doing what you've always done, then you'll always have exactly what you have now.

Questions to ask yourself

If you're willing to take a close, hard look at some of the qualities of your life and begin to consider how you can change or rearrange some old habits in order to expand your time, then ask yourself the following questions:

- What kind of time do I need to manage?

- What am I willing to give up in order to build more hours in my day?

- Am I best in the morning or at night? When are my most productive hours?

- What do I stand to gain from learning to manage time?
- Will I lose anything by getting more done in less time?
- How much is sliding through the cracks in my life simply because I can't "get to it"?
- What do I really want to be doing with my life?
- What is the ideal way to spend my life?
- Where are the hours and days of my life going now?
- How do I define success?
- Do I believe I can't change things?
- Am I trying to be all things to all people?
- Do I waste valuable time trying to keep up?
- Do I find myself searching for lost items on a regular basis?
- Do I put off doing tasks until the last minute?
- Am I using lack of time as an excuse to get out of doing the things I don't want to do?

These are not easy questions to answer and may take some soul-searching on your part. It might even be a good idea to write down some of the answers, then look back at them again later. The more you think about the uses of your time, the more you'll realize that you have a lot more time than you thought!

Criteria to discuss with your spouse/family

It's likely that your family and mate/significant other will be very honest with you about the way you spend your time. A suggestion: Answer the questions in the preceding section, then sit down with your mate and family and ask them how they'd answer them for you. It's interesting to see whether they have the same view of how you handle time that you do.

When you start changing things in your life, you really need to let your immediate family know what's going to happen. Though they might have been nagging you all along to stop procrastinating or to spend more time with them, they need to be prepared that you'll be making some adjustments to how you spend your time.

Tempers flare when rhythms don't mesh. But when rhythms start moving together, you can better understand the other person and his/her needs. Dr. Stephan Rechtschaffen of the Omega Institute for Holistic Studies calls this phenomenon "timeshifting." In his book on the subject, Rechtschaffen says: "Looking at a relationship as long-term and cyclical means knowing that problems will inevitably occur and you will be able to navigate (*not* circumnavigate) the pitfalls. It means accepting differences, recognizing discordant rhythms, and attempting always to get back into sync with each other—even when entraining seems impossible."

People enter relationships with certain expectations. Then we settle into rhythms that become very comfortable. Those patterns are not always positive patterns, as I'm sure you're aware. Sometimes our patterns include arguments we continue to have over and over and over. If those arguments in your life center on how you spend your time, they might not be easily solved simply by you changing your own habits. That's why it's so important to keep the lines of communication open while you're learning how to manage your time. And it's also great if you

Bright Idea
Consider the Dalai Lama's philosophy of being happy. He says he simply expects nothing, then everything he gets is a gift.

can pass on what you've learned to your family so that they can learn to plan and prioritize with you— as well as understand the new "language" you'll be using.

Feedback from friends

Friends are the people we turn to for solace and feedback when we're at odds with our families and mates. Friends are also the people who are less likely to be affected by certain expectations of how they want you to act. Your mother, brother, husband, children, will all expect certain things from you in order to make their world complete. To your friends, you are a gift, an added surprise, a refuge, and a pleasure.

Are friends more likely to be honest with you about the way they see you spending your time? Maybe. It depends on whether you have truthful friends. Some pals will be just as selfish about what they want from you as your family/mate. Some will allow you to simply be who you are and will accept you with no expectations whatsoever.

Ask yourself into which category your friends fall before you ask them to honestly evaluate your strengths and weaknesses. Then make your own decisions about whether they are right or wrong. But remember that before you ask, you need to be prepared for their answers.

Now that you've prepared yourself, ask them for their honest opinion of how you use your time. You may be surprised by their answers. Then ask them if they have any suggestions for how you might be more efficient. Write the answers down and consider them as you read the rest of this book.

Moneysaver
When asking your co-workers for advice, you might want to bring them all to your house for a potluck powwow. Everyone brings something to eat, you exchange ideas for timesaving, and you don't need to worry about tipping any waitresses.

Suggestions from fellow employees/colleagues

If you've visited any restaurants in your lifetime, you've experienced the value of a good waiter/ waitress and the irritation of someone who keeps running by without stopping to see if there's anything they can offer you.

The "running around like a chicken with its head cut off" personality is not an attribute germane only to service personnel. We might do it ourselves or see it in the personalities of the people with whom we work. Those are not the people you ask for suggestions about how you might improve your own personal system for controlling time. They are the ones you learn *not* to emulate.

Pick the people around you who you know handle their own jobs but also manage a family and some kind of social life. Ask them the following questions:

- What does your normal day consist of?
- Are there any timesaver tricks you use on a regular basis? (*Note:* Most people who regularly handle extra work and make it look easy might be a little stumped by this question. People who are good at managing time often don't realize they are, because they've simply gotten into good habits and those habits have become a way of life for them.)
- What do you consider time-wasters?
- Could you make some suggestions about what I could do about the way I handle my time?

You might not think the people you work with have any clue about the way you manage your own hours, but they have probably noticed a lot about you and how you work—simply by being around you on a regular basis. Since most people are very flattered when they're asked for advice, you might get more than you ask for, but that's okay. You're just fishing right now, just looking for possible answers, and since you are a unique individual, what someone else uses might not be right for you. But keep yourself open to any and all comments, and then use what feels right for you. Your particular situation will be different from another person's.

For instance: I am totally comfortable getting up at 6:30 a.m. and taking advantage of a quiet house to get in a couple of hours of writing before my husband rises. I answer my e-mail, have a leisurely cup of coffee, and often read the newspaper on the back porch where I can hear the birds sing. Once he's up, he goes into full swing, and I lose my train of thought. In order to write, I need to have quiet, so my best work is done when the house is empty. He, however, needs to have the noise and companionship of others. I am the organized one who can manage two or three projects at once. He needs to be focused or he'll go in ten different directions, often leaving his tools all over the place. He spends hours searching for lost items, while I put the tools I use back in the same place on a regular basis. What takes him three hours to accomplish, takes me half the time. *But* he can stay up long after I go to bed, arrange his work for the next day, and answer his e-mail.

Two different people with different styles of managing their time. Is one better than the other? Is one more efficient? In some ways, yes—to both questions. In others: My husband would never be able handle the myriad items I do. Why? His attention span is shorter—and that's a physical fact of life, not a psychological one.

Unofficially...
During an interview, Gloria Steinem confessed that she felt women waste a lot of time trying to live their lives to please men.

Bright Idea
Set a time to talk to your boss about time management—and make sure you tell him/her how long your discussion will take. Make sure you keep within the time limit. You'll get more accomplished that way.

Those differences are what you should become aware of within yourself. This perspective will help you understand why that woman with three kids in your office manages to take a couple of night classes, hold a full-time job, and act as a full-time mother—all the while smiling and enjoying life, while the boss, a single man in his forties whose major interest is watching football on television, has trouble making meetings on time.

Talk to your boss

Why should you talk to your boss about time management? Because your boss will be able to help you deal with the priorities of what you need to handle at work. Your boss is also very aware of what your strengths and weaknesses are—and how those strengths and weaknesses mesh with his/her own needs.

Since it is your boss who you need to satisfy in order to qualify for raises and promotions, it is a very wise move to have a heart-to-heart with him/her.

- Let him/her know you've decided to evaluate your own system of controlling time.

- Ask whether there's anything he/she can suggest you might do differently.

- Request some advice about how he/she manages his/her time.

You might be a bit fearful of having this discussion, but most experts will assure you that nothing but positive can come from asking your supervisor for suggestions and help. Employers want to know their employees are striving to do their best. If you're trying to improve your skills, you can only impress the people for whom you're working.

Deciding what you want from your life

If someone asked you five minutes from now what you wanted out of your life, what would you say? A home? A family? A better job? More time to do what you want?

It might seem like a rather simple question to ask, but in our day-to-day lives it's one we really don't think about too much. Ask someone who knows their life is coming to an end, and they have an immediate answer: more time.

Because "time is money" is such a recognizable American maxim, most of us think that if we had more time, we could make more money. That's not the case. According to the 80/20 principle, which will be discussed at more length later in the book, we spend 80% of our time producing 20% of the desired results of what we want to get. Wouldn't you like to utilize that 80% more effectively? If you did, you'd produce better results.

Consider these:

- If you want a family, you need time to spend with them.

- If you want a nice home, you would also like to have the time to enjoy it.

- If you desire a good job, you need time to get to the top in that position.

- If you must have a new car, you want to have the time to drive it.

- If your passion is to fall in love, you must have the time to spend with the person of your dreams.

What are your priorities?

When asked what the most important thing in their life is, everyone's answer will be different. In order

Timesaver
Depending on your priorities, you'll notice where you need to adjust how you spend your time—as well as how much time you'll need.

Watch Out!
The bottom line is this: No matter what you want out of life, you need time to get it, enjoy it, live it.

to figure out your priorities, it might be best to make a list of the ten things that are most important to you, then number each item from 1-10, with 1 being top priority and 10 being lowest

How do you determine your priorities? Something you can't live without would be given first priority. Something that's important and means a great deal to how you live your life would definitely be in the upper 5. Something you're very interested in but could live without if you had to would fall in the 5-10 range. Don't be surprised if you have several priorities competing for the same spot in your list. For example: Your children, if there's more than one, are probably all equally important. Don't try to number them. Same thing with friends.

Your list might look like this:

1. Family

2. Friends

3. Writing time

4. Good job

5. New house

6. Pets

7. Vacation time

8. New car

9. Better furniture

10. Gardening time

Be honest with yourself. If your friends are more important than your family, then make friends number 1. You are the only person who's going to see this list. You don't have to impress others by stating that a new car is #8 if it's truly the #1 priority in your life right now. The point of this exercise is to see where you need to focus the emphasis on how you're spending your time so that you can meet your own personal priorities. You are the only one you need to satisfy! Once you satisfy yourself, you'll be happy and able to satisfy the others around you.

What do others expect of you?

Unless you're surrounded by people who are totally selfless and don't expect anything at all of you, you will be affected by others. There are very few people in the world who don't expect something from their family, friends, employees, employers, and co-workers.

Again, if you answer a few questions in writing, you'll be in a better position to evaluate where you stand with everyone else.

Family:

- What does my family expect of my time?
- Do they want me to attend meetings, games, recitals, and other school-related activities?
- Do they expect me to take part in housekeeping and other chores?
- How many hours a week do these activities take?

Friends:

- What do my friends expect of me?
- Do they want to meet me for lunch or coffee?
- How often and for how long?
- Are they e-mail people or must all contact be done by phone or in person?
- How long does an average amount of socializing with them take?

Co-Workers/Employees/Employers:

- What do my co-workers expect of me?
- Do they want me to show up for just the regularly scheduled work hours or do they expect

Unofficially...
Actress Michelle Pfeiffer recently confessed that she reads the gossip magazines while waiting in line at the supermarket or at her doctor's office. It's the only time she has a chance to keep up on industry news.

me to attend meetings, deal with clients, or
socialize outside the workweek?

- Are there phone calls I need to make after I get
  home from work?

- Do I need to travel?

- Are there hidden pockets of duties which take
  up bits and pieces of time that, when added
  together, create additional hours?

- How many hours a week do these work hours
  average?

Creating your own valid expectations of yourself

Our own expectations of ourselves are often much
higher than those around us. Since the advent of
computers, voice mail, paging systems, speech
recognition systems, cell phones, fax machines, and
e-mail, we have been primed to do far more than we
ever have before. Surprisingly, that creates more
leisure time for us, but that leisure time has been
taken up by the ever-present television, leaving us
with the impression that we need far more time than
ever—rather than less.

It also makes us realize how much more one person is capable of doing than ever before—and that
makes us feel like super people.

The conundrum in all of this is that we expect
more from ourselves and those expectations cause
us to have more stress, which causes us to want more
time to relieve it. It's a vicious cycle that we can easily escape if we clearly understand exactly what we
need to do to get to the place we want to be in our
daily lives.

Yes, I said daily. One day at a time. The
Alcoholics Anonymous founders knew what they
were talking about when they coined that phrase. If

> "
> For, he that
> expects nothing
> shall not be dis-
> appointed, but
> he that expects
> much—if he
> lives and uses
> that in hand day
> by day—shall be
> full to running
> over.
> —Edgar Cayce
> "

we chart our expectations and goals one day at a time, they are a lot less overwhelming than if we look only at the big picture. And it's true that with each step, we come closer to our goals.

So, that said, sit back and realistically evaluate your expectations of yourself on a regular basis. You can take a peek at the yearly or lifetime goals too, but don't expect more from yourself than you are capable of doing as a living, breathing human being—who wants to *stay* alive and breathing!

Bright Idea
Just say no.

The balancing act between *your* needs vs. *their* wants

One of the reasons people sometimes get into conflict is because one person's needs aren't the same as the other person's wants. For example: Your son, who's fifteen, wants to attend a local rock concert. He really *wants* to see his favorite group perform, but the concert is on a school night and won't be over until 2 a.m. You need to make sure he gets to school and know that he has a hard time waking up in the morning. The rules in your household have always been that curfew on school nights is 11 p.m. You *need* to make sure the rules are consistent for all your children, so you say no. An argument ensues.

It's a fine line to balance what you need to do during the day with what someone else wants. The best piece of advice anyone can give—whether he or she is a time management consultant, a psychiatrist, or a friend/family member—is that the lines of communication must be kept open.

Everyone around you must be clear about what your needs are—and the only way that's going to happen is if you voice them often. You also must be aware of what the people around you want, so you must ask about them often.

Make it a habit to voice what you need to do on a regular basis. Even though I've been a writer for my whole life and my husband knows my habits, I still have to tell him I need peace and quiet in order to write. I still have to occasionally put a sign on my door that says "leave me alone, I'm working" so that I can have the time I need to meet my deadlines. He, on the other hand, has to remind me that he wants to spend time with me occasionally and that there are times when my need to meet a deadline tends to cut him out of my life a little. It is only because we have been aware that we need to communicate that we've made the marriage last, through thick and thin and our fair share of problems, for almost 25 years.

Communication is not only the secret of a good marriage, but the secret of all good relationships. And the only way to balance your needs with their wants—and vice versa.

What you *must* do vs. what you'd *like* to do

One of the main reasons people procrastinate is because they're not doing what they'd like to do. Anytime you're afraid of a new project or haven't broken down a large project into smaller steps, it becomes a bit overwhelming, and the tendency is to put off the work. If you get a call from a creditor, you're not likely to return it right away unless you believe they're wrong. If there's a problem with a friend, most people will try not to be the first to make a phone call because the unpleasantness of dealing with the situation is not something they want to face.

When the things you must do are the ones that you really don't want to do, you might choose to turn to the things you want to do first. That's why kids would rather eat dessert first than finish their peas. If you find yourself tackling the laundry before you empty the kitty litter box, you're just putting off the least attractive task until last. Chances are, the cats won't be particularly pleased, but if you leave the box for too long, you'll discover the cats have found someplace else to leave their "droppings." Then you'll have to deal with the time-consuming task of cleaning up after them.

That's a pretty obnoxious example, but it's the clearest way of explaining that you need to pay attention to the things you must do and save the things you like to do as rewards.

Setting your goals

Goal-setting is an extremely important step in determining how you handle the minutes, hours, days, weeks, months, and years of your life. Without goals, you have no way of knowing what the end result of all this work will be. It's a bit like heading out for a trip and having no idea where you're going. How will you know how much money you need? Or clothes? Or gas?

In Part III of this book, we discuss different kinds of goals and how you can map them out for yourself. For now, start thinking about where your life is headed and how you'd like to get to your lifetime goal. Then consider how that ultimate goal will be broken down by working in a backward manner. How many years will it take for you to get to where you want to be? We'll go into a lot more detail later.

Realizing your limitations

Just because the worker in the cubicle next to you sells forty-two widgets a day doesn't mean you can too. Perhaps you're able to sell twelve today, then

Unofficially...
Florence Griffith
Joyner, Olympic
champion runner,
never let the
limitations of
growing up in
the Los Angeles
neighborhood of
Watts stop her.
She started run-
ning at the age
of 7, broke many
world records,
and still held
some at her
death from an
apparent heart
seizure at the
age of 38 in
1998.

twenty tomorrow and thirty-five a week from today.
Or what if your best friend is a basketball player, just
like you, but she's 6'2" tall and you're only 5'7" tall?
Naturally, you are not as likely to reach the basket as
often as she is.

Realizing your limitations doesn't mean you
need to feel sorry for yourself about what you *can't*
do. It means that you need to be more honest about
what you *can* do and stop expecting that you'll be
able to run the same game as someone else with a
different physical makeup.

We all have strengths and weaknesses. No one is
perfect. But if you expect yourself to be, then you'll
never be satisfied.

If you know that you can't type all day because
your back ends up in knots, then you're recognizing
a limitation. Once you realize that, you can deal with
it. You can do your typing first thing in the morning
or break your work into hour-long chunks and make
sure you get some stretching exercises in on a regular basis.

By recognizing and dealing with your limitations,
you're building in time to work within that framework. When someone is wise enough to do that, they
can adjust their work schedule and duties in such a
way that everything will get done more efficiently
and effectively.

Determining what is reasonable

Do you tend to bite off more than you can chew,
then find yourself staying up late to meet your deadlines? What are you accomplishing by doing that?
You're adding more unnecessary stress to your life.

Because there are so many adjustable factors, figuring out what are reasonable demands on your
time is often difficult. Doing what you want versus

what you need, while simultaneously pleasing others, can be extraordinarily difficult. But you *can* manage!

What's reasonable for you? How long does it take you to get your daily chores accomplished? Are you a slow, thoughtful person? Or are you a quick and decisive soul?

Don't try to take on more than you can reasonably finish. The best time managers in the world know that the strongest word in the English language is 'no.' Better start practicing it.

What can you do in an average day?

There are only twenty-four hours in a day. There's no use wishing for more because there will never be more. So you need to deal with what you have. How much can you fit into those 24 hours? Since most people sleep at least 1/3 of their lives away, you will probably need at least 8 hours of shuteye. That leaves you 16 hours. Unless you're into self-flagellation, you won't want to work the whole 16 hours, so let's figure you're going to work 8, then use the other 8 for travel, time with family/friends, eating, and doing other activities.

Is it reasonable to work an eight-hour day, then come home to another 4 hours of work? For some people it is. But for others, an eight-hour workday is all they can handle.

Let's be realistic

If you expect to totally change your life, become incredibly successful, wealthy, and loved, you're being unrealistic. If you think that utilizing some of the tools set forth in this book will teach you how to make the most of your time, you're right. But none of this comes without practice and without changing some old habits.

> 66
>
> The unfortunate thing about this world is that the good habits are much easier to give up than the bad ones.
> —W. Somerset Maugham
>
> 99

Be prepared to change the way you think and to find the change a bit difficult to master at first. But you can do it! And if you really want to help yourself get a better handle on how you deal with priorities, then you're in the right place.

Anticipating the overall life change: ready, set...

Time management is a skill that will allow you to accomplish more tasks in less time. Parkinson's Law states that work expands to accommodate the time you have to do it in, so anticipating all kinds of free time is probably unrealistic. What you can anticipate is a better-organized life, the ability to prioritize and plan, a better sense of what deadlines mean and how you can meet them, and new skills to help you manage your already heavy workload.

How long should it take to organize my time?

Depending on how anxious you are to make your new time-management skills work for you, it'll probably take a week to a month for you to read, digest, and put into action the suggestions made here. Some people will find it takes a little longer to get into the habits suggested, but remember the old saying that you need to do something three times to make it stick.

And be patient with yourself! Your time didn't get out of control overnight, so you probably won't get it under control overnight either.

What am I going to need?

You'll need the commitment to make this work, a reasonable set of goals, some simple tools (most times, a pencil and a piece of paper are all you'll need), and the cooperation of your loved ones, friends, and co-workers.

Moneysaver
Don't buy any fancy items to save yourself time if you don't have the money. Changing your habits is the most effective— and least expensive—way to save time.

Just the facts

- We actually have more leisure time today than we did a hundred years ago. We just waste it.

- Rearranging old habits and asking help from others will give you a better handle on the time you have.

- Keeping the lines of communication open not only saves time, but energy and irritation.

- Setting goals for ten years from now won't help you today.

- Buying expensive "timesaving" equipment doesn't teach you the habits that make for good time management especially given your own personal style.

Watch Out!
People who seem to be doing a lot might not be actually finishing everything they begin. Ask how many times they complete a project.

Getting to the Perfect Schedule

W hen determining how to better manage your time, you must first evaluate what you need the time for. Is it time to do more work? To play? To spend social time with family or friends?

And what are you going to do with the time when you clear it? Hopefully, you won't fill it with other work or things to do. A lot of people think they're managing their time well, when all they're doing is actually shifting around tasks so that their time ends up being spent different ways.

Parkinson's Law states that the job or task that we're trying to perform expands to fill the available time. In other words, when we have a deadline, most of us tend to wait until the deadline is right on top of us to take the action necessary to get the job done. If you were truly managing your time, you'd be taking little steps along the way instead of waiting until the night before to study for that test or pack that suitcase for that trip.

Watch Out!
If you have a
deadline, the
best way to meet
it is to break the
job down into
steps and do one
or more of the
steps each day
until you finish
the project.

Evaluating your needs

So, what are those reasons for needing more time?
Let's see if you can honestly evaluate your reasons
for wanting to get more hours out of your day. Ask
yourself the following questions, then we'll talk
about what your priorities are:

- Do I need the time in order to do more work?
- Does my family complain about not seeing me
  often enough?
- Do my friends make plans without me—and
  does that make me want to clear some time to
  spend with them?
- Do I find myself trying to fit 24-hours' work into
  an 8-hour day?
- Am I heading in the direction I want to with my
  life?
- Would learning how to manage my time cure
  my procrastination?
- Do I think that the longer I work, the more I get
  done, even though the opposite is true?
- Do I want to be better organized?
- Is it important to me to learn how to do several
  things at once?
- Am I tired of always chasing deadlines and
  being so busy that I don't have time to relax?
- Is my stress getting in the way of my enjoyment
  of life?
- Am I trying to learn time management because
  I think it'll make me a better human being?

When you're answering these questions, think
about all the different roles you play in your life:
husband, father, daughter, sister, friend, co-worker,
boss, etc. What does each of those roles demand of

you and how do you respond? Which ones do you *want* to respond to? Which ones are most important to the quality of your life?

What it all boils down to is that you have a choice of what to do and what *not* to do. If you can't find time within the 24 hours each day allots you, then you better give up, because 24 hours is *all* each day allots. What you *can* do is to make a choice about what you really *need* the time for.

Why do you need more time?

We all have reasons for wanting and needing things. What I need from my life is totally different from what you need.

We all have basic needs: food, clothing, and shelter. Beyond that, each human being is an individual.

I might say that a nice house is very important to me. I need the luxury of being able to heat and cool that house within a certain temperature range. The furnishings have to be Southwestern style and I need plenty of books to line my walls. The house should be close to work and large enough to accommodate some guests occasionally. It should also be built so that I can have a nice view of trees or open land—and being able to hear the birds in the morning is a must.

Someone else might think that living in an apartment is ideal. Hearing the traffic in the morning energizes them and being able to walk to work a few blocks away is wonderful. They delight in a tiny kitchen, love sharing the hallway with assorted characters, and especially like not having a lot of furniture cluttering the place up.

Two living situations. Both completely satisfying for the people who are living there. Both give the individuals the basic needs of a roof over their heads

Bright Idea
Instead of seeing people's differences as something that separates you, try thinking of them as a reason for you to learn from them. They might save you some time by teaching you something you wouldn't normally learn!

and also meet other needs as well. But one person wouldn't be happy in the other person's space, which is the reason why I've used this example.

Be as specific as possible when you answer the question: "Why do I need more time?" Consider the following parameters when deciding exactly the reasons why you want to have more time in your schedule.

- What kind of work will you do?
- What people will you share your time with?
- What essentials do you need?
- Do you need down time?
- What about exercise time?
- Do you need time for things you don't do now or more time for the things you already do?
- Are you clearing time for other people or for yourself?
- What would you like to spend less time doing?
- What would you like to have happening that isn't happening now?
- Is your quality of life at a satisfactory level right now?
- Are you overloaded with work but don't have time to catch up?
- Is your health going to pot because you're stressed all the time?
- Is it impossible to find time to exercise or play?
- Do you eat on the fly or do you make time for a sit-down, sociable meal?
- Is the house a mess because you're always flying in and out but don't have time to clean?

- Does your office look like someone should come in with a dump truck and haul away the pile of papers you've accumulated?

- Are you missing important messages/meetings because you don't have time to return phone calls?

- Are you beginning to feel like this is never going to end?

If you're beginning to feel overwhelmed, think of life this way: You can't possibly read every book that comes out, listen to every piece of music, go to every vacation location, or satisfy every person you meet throughout your life. Chances are you'll read some of those books, listen to the types of music you really adore, go on a vacation occasionally, and satisfy the people closest to you (sometimes!), but you won't do it all.

The trick to figuring out why you need more time is to take a real soul-searching look at what's most important to you. Sort those important items into categories:

- Those you can't live without

- Those that are important

- Those that you wouldn't miss

Then make some important choices. Decide which ones you really want to integrate into your life.

Now you know the *why* of needing more time. The world isn't going to end if you don't do the rest. In fact, you might even live a little longer. And in spite of all those high-tech devices urging you to go faster and faster, you won't be able to go at the speed of light unless you're some kind of alien.

Unofficially...
Paul Reiser, star of "Mad About You," told a reporter he'd discovered his original list of goals in his desk right before the show ended—and he'd met them all.

Expectations are important, which is why we've suggested you look closely at yours. Spend the time necessary to think about your values.

Yes, we'll teach you about how to manage your time better, but we can't give you more than you already have. So, the first step to getting to the perfect schedule is to figure out why you need it. And to remember that you're not alone. Ninety-percent of people in America feel the same way you do!

How to determine why you don't have the time you need

Some of us don't seem to have the time we need because other people are demanding pieces of our time that we simply can't give. Others of us don't have the skills necessary to determine which tasks are important and which can be left for later. Still others are being interrupted so often that to complete one simple five-minute task might take half an hour or more. And, finally, there are those of us who don't know how to say no, and thus are overloaded with work we didn't have time to complete in the first place.

Any one of these problems can be solved by simply learning how to control the time you have. You can learn how to schedule. You can ask people to stop interrupting. You can even learn how to say no. These are all skills that people who have good time-management skills have cultivated and polished. They are skills that you can learn as well, as long as you have the determination to change the course of the way things have been going in your life.

When you're stressed, it's often because you've bitten off more than you can chew. Learn that you are in control only when you can say no. Map out your time so you can pace yourself rather than leaving the whole kit and kaboodle until the last minute.

I still find myself sending e-mails when I should be paying attention to my writing and surfing the Web when I could be making phone calls, but I've learned that I can give myself a break every once in a while. I know that I'll get the jobs done as long as I plunk my butt in my office chair, face the computer and type. If I have lunch with a friend, I keep it to an hour. If I go out at night, I'll come home and do a little editing or correct some papers afterward. When I'm waiting for someone, I always have a book or paperwork with me. In other words, I'm organized now.

So, why don't *you* have the time *you* need?

Let's categorize the areas most likely to cause people to lose time, evaluate where you stand, and figure out where your problem areas are. If you fill out this chart, you'll be able to see exactly how much time you're losing and why.

Timesaver
Always keep your current work as close to you as possible—even if that means putting it in your bag and taking it everywhere with you. When you have a minute, work on it.

EVALUATION OF TIME LOSS

Interruptions	Who Interrupts	For How Long
Daydreaming		
Phone calls		
Television		
Visits		
Distractions		

In this section, consider interruptions at work and at home. Think about the people in your life and whether they consider what you're doing important and whether their interruptions are intentional or simply thoughtless. Remember all the times someone walks in on you while you're working, or while you're having a conversation with someone else. And think about those people who simply don't get the hint that you're busy and who want to talk on the phone for hours.

EVALUATING TIME SPENT DURING THE WORK DAY

Work	Time Spent
Planning the day	
Chatting w/co-workers	
Trying to get started	
Reading mail	
Straightening desk/tools	
Preparing projects for action	
Juggling tasks	
Business trips	
Appointments	
Meetings	
Routine work	
Explaining tasks to others	
Finding lost items	
Reading material already read	
Inability to say no	
Not finishing a project	
Handling incomplete/late information	
Taking notes	
Procrastination	
Telephone calls	
E-mail/voice mail	
Running errands	
Preparing to leave for day	
Planning for next work day	

EVALUATING TIME SPENT AT HOME

Home	Time Spent
Planning the day	
Getting ready to leave house	

Home	Time Spent
Helping other family members leave for school/work	
Preparing meals	
Household chores	
Handling budget	
Finding lost items	
Telephone/e-mail/voice mail	
Visitors	
Daydreaming	
Not finishing tasks	
Procrastination	
Organizing other family members' schedules	
Doctor/dentist appointments	
Errands	
Time for self	
Socializing	
Inability to say no	
Repeating explanations or instructions	

Watch Out!
Remember the Law of the Slight Edge: Small changes, over time, make a big difference.

By the time you evaluate how much time you spend on these activities, you'll begin to see what time managers have known for years.

The top ten time-wasters are:

▪ Procrastination

▪ Interruptions

▪ Poor planning

▪ Poor communication

▪ Lack of self-discipline

▪ Inability to say no

▪ Haste

▪ Insufficient delegation

▪ Unclear objectives

▪ Disorganization

But don't let this list or the evaluation of how you waste your time defeat you. By discovering what it is that you spend/waste your time doing, you have taken a step toward approaching the problems you are having. That is the most important step you will take. The next one will be actually taking the reins and solving the problems. Remember: You are the one in control of your life and your time. It is up to you to make the changes for yourself.

The steps to mastering time management

Although evaluating your day and how you spend time with people at work, at home, and in your social life will help you see exactly where the hours are going, you also need to have a game plan for yourself.

Time functions in a series of sequences and events. If you are in control of those events—or at least in partial control—you can foresee the steps to mastering how you manage your time.

The steps are listed as follows, but we'll be going into them in more detail throughout the book:

1. Determining goals/objectives

2. Planning

3. Making decisions

4. Implementing those decisions

5. Controlling the results

6. Informing and communicating with others

There are various ways to meet each one of these steps and we will offer you suggestions. You might even come up with your own along the way or adapt our suggestions to meet your specific needs.

Setting priorities

How often do you check your priorities? How often do you set them?

Most of us have priorities. We want to reach work on time, which takes priority over having that extra slice of toast. We want to make sure we remember someone's birthday, and that takes priority over buying the new CD for ourselves. We want to get married before we're 30 and that takes priority over planning the trip to Europe.

Some of us consider our families our top priority, while others believe their first priority is to serve their country. Many believe religion to be their top priority, yet there are many others who choose money as their number one priority.

Whatever the case, the priorities are yours and yours alone. And the choice of what comes first is also yours and yours alone.

The one thing we all have in common is that we can only do one thing at a time. Yes, there are going to be moments in your life when you're working on multiple tasks, but no human being can do that constantly. So, you need to figure out what comes first, do that, then take on the next priority.

Here's an easy way to figure out how to gauge your priorities. I'm going to give you a list of things I had to accomplish this morning, then show you how I numbered them according to priorities. I suggest you use a similar list whenever you find yourself with a number of things to accomplish that all seem to rank the same in importance.

Original To-do list for 5/22/99

- Write Chapter 2 of time-management book.
- Answer e-mail.

> 66
>
> Most of the important things in the world have been accomplished by people who have kept on trying when there seemed to be no hope at all.
> —Dale Carnegie
>
> 99

- Fill out a few forms for mortgage company.

- Pack a few boxes for moving.

- Feed the cats.

- Check on eBay auction.

- Enter a few more items on auction.

- Copy rebate slips and send them.

- Make copies of forms to renew passport and send.

- Contact people to help move.

- Call termite inspector.

- Call antiques dealer for appraisal of furniture.

- Refigure deadlines for move.

- Contact a few friends re: coffee before move.

As you can see by this original list, I have a few too many things to do today. Moving and being on deadline for a book at the same time aren't easy tasks, but I know what I need to get done, and here's how it worked out. I renumbered the events according to priorities, then figured out how to delegate some of the tasks to my husband, and I'll check off the items as I accomplish them today. Whatever's left over, I'll do this evening or tomorrow. The most important thing is that I stay on task.

Prioritized To-do List for 5/22/99

1. First hour of morning:

    - Feed the cats.

    - Answer e-mail

    - Check on eBay auction.

    - Enter a few more items on auction.

2. Once first cup of coffee has kicked in:

    - Write Chapter 2 of time-management book.

Moneysaver
When figuring out your priorities, consider the ones that will cost you money if you don't finish them first.

3. When I'm finished with the chapter (probably by late afternoon):

   ▪ Fill out a few forms for mortgage company.

   ▪ Pack a few boxes for moving.

   ▪ Contact people to help move.

   ▪ Refigure deadlines for move.

   ▪ Contact friends re: coffee before move.

4. Delegate to my husband:

   ▪ Call termite inspector.

   ▪ Call antiques dealer for furniture appraisal.

   ▪ Copy rebate slips and send them.

   ▪ Make copies of forms to renew passport and send.

5. Tonight:

   ▪ Prepare chapter reference material for tomorrow.

While I was writing this, I experienced one of those interruptions that you simply cannot control: My computer shut down. So, an hour was spent doing a virus scan and getting the computer all set up again. Thankfully, my word-processing program is set to save what I'm working on every two minutes, which means virtually nothing was lost. But the unplanned interruption was not a pleasant one and sent me scurrying for another cup of coffee—and a few deep breaths—before I could continue with this chapter.

Learn a lesson from what happened to me: When you prioritize, make sure you leave room for interruptions and little catastrophes!

The To-Do list with Priority Numbers

   ▪ #1   Write Chapter 2 of time-management book.

Timesaver
Lesson learned:
priorities don't
determine when
you're going to
do something,
just how impor-
tant it is for you
to do it.

- #6 Answer e-mail
- #4 Fill out a few forms for mortgage company.
- #3 Pack a few boxes for moving.
- #1A Feed the cats.
- #2 Check on eBay auction.
- #5 Enter a few more items on auction.
- #7 Copy rebate slips and send them.
- #11 Make copies of forms to renew passport and send.
- #8 Contact people to help move.
- #9 Call termite inspector.
- #10 Call antiques dealer for appraisal of furniture.
- #13 Refigure deadlines for move.
- #14 Contact a few friends re: coffee before move.

Okay, here's the list with priority numbers. Compare this to the preceding version and you'll notice that what I marked first priority (this chapter) was not the first thing I did. Why? Because I need a cup of coffee and some brain exercise before I dive into writing in the morning. I know my work patterns, and getting little things out of the way first helps me to see my way clear to working on the most important task of the day.

What you need to ask yourself when prioritizing and organizing is, "What's the most important thing to do right at this moment?" Naturally, the cats had to be fed before I did anything else. Then I warmed up on the computer for a while and by the time I was ready for my second cup of coffee, I was also awake enough to write down a few words on this chapter.

Personal priorities

Your personal priorities are those that deal with just you as an individual, not you as a worker or you as part of another group, such as your family. These might include:

- What you want out of life
- What time you'd like to spend on hobbies
- What books you'd like to read
- Whether you'd like to enhance your intellectual skills
- What kind of person you'd like to fall in love with
- What kind of success you'd like to have in life

Personal priorities are purely emotional in nature. They are private promises we make to ourselves that we'd like to see fulfilled someday. Often, we don't share our personal priorities with anyone other than those extremely close family members and friends we trust implicitly. It's highly unlikely that someone would say to a stranger, "I'd really like to have the respect of everyone around me before I die." That's an intensely private wish that most of us have, but few of us would share that wish.

Sometimes your personal priorities will clash with your other priorities basically because we, as humans, all tend to be a little on the selfish side. Your personal goals for success might not mesh with the goals your corporation has set for itself. And your own goals might not be exactly what the rest of the members of your family are looking forward to.

But as long as you know that your personal priorities are individual matters, you should be able to separate them from the others in your life and

weigh their importance against the other objectives
you must meet.

Business/career priorities

Unofficially...
Many business
executives,
including Donald
Trump, Bill
Gates, and Ted
Turner, have cre-
ated priority lists
during their
careers—and
check back on
them frequently.

Clarifying what your business priorities are might
take a bit of rational thinking. You need to keep
emotions out of the list of objectives when you're
considering what will be best for your career.

Priorities might include attaining promotions,
accomplishing a certain task, or making a six-figure
income by the time you're 30. Whatever your priorities might be, it's wise to figure out the steps you
need to take in order to attain them.

You should consider that your business priorities
will have to be matched up against your boss's priorities or the company's priorities. You could be
causing major problems for yourself if your own
goals and objectives are totally different from those
of the people with whom you work. Remember your
customers, your co-workers, and your superiors
when you create a list of priorities for your business/
career.

Family/friend priorities

Why are your priorities for your family/friends different from your personal priorities? Because you
are dealing with other people whom you might want
to please, instead of just prioritizing your own immediate goals.

When you consider setting priorities for how you
deal with family and friends, for when you see them,
how often and for how long, and how you spend
that time with them, you are dealing not only with
your own goals, but with other people's. And those
people are, presumably, people about whom you
care a great deal.

Sometimes setting priorities in this arena means considering how much you're willing to give to those people you love. Do you consider your son's football game a major priority? How about him? What does *he* think? And if your friends are getting together for a barbecue and you are invited, is that occasion tops on your list for a weekend getaway or would you rather be working on your yard? What about *them?* What if your significant other's family is in town and she just has to have you there for dinner but you would rather be anywhere else? Do you change your priorities because you care about how she feels, or are you more likely to listen to yourself?

This is a sticky area and one in which priorities can get confused quite easily. Better to have a good idea of what's important in this case and what you're willing to give up in order to put these family and friends (and their activities) high on your list of priorities.

Academic priorities

People who are either in school now or want to be soon sometimes have to rearrange their lives in order to devote time to their studies. School is demanding and deadlines are frequent. In order to keep up with them, you need to constantly recheck your priorities.

Questions can often be difficult because not only are you weighing your personal life against your academic life, but you might also be handling a job, family, and friends. Goals may seem to be scattered and priorities often collide when people are devoting their time to receiving an education.

Even within the academic world itself, there are priorities. Do you finish the math assignment first or devote your time to doing research for the history

Moneysaver
Ask the admissions office at school if they have a school calendar. Get a free one. It'll save you money and will give you all the important dates you need to remember.

paper if both are due the same day? When finals come, do you have time to visit with Aunt Sally if she's in town for the first time in ten years?

Because academics and the time they demand cause so much stress, most schools offer time-management classes or at least some suggestions on how to juggle your various priorities.

What you need to do for yourself if heading for an academic career, or if you're already involved in one, is to reassess the rest of your life and realize there are some things that are going to have to be put on hold for a while—until you're finished with school.

Fitness priorities

In David Miller and T. Earl Allen's book *Fitness: A Lifetime Commitment*, the authors say that nutrition, weight management, and some type of exercise are some things that need to be top priority if people are interested in leading a healthy and long life. Where on your list of priorities does fitness fall? If your life is hectic and you are already having a hard time getting things done, will you make time for exercise?

Most people believe that feeling good is a major concern, but those who actually make it a priority are becoming fewer and fewer. Yet, the authors make a point of stating that with more of our work being done by machines or automation, fitness should be more important now than it ever has been before.

Especially in America, people spend less time outside on physical activity than ever before. We tend to be couch potatoes or spend hours in front of a computer, never moving more than several muscles at a time—yet there are hundreds of muscles in our bodies.

If stress is a big part of your life, becoming fit is one of the only ways to combat the negative effects stress has on your body.

Even if fitness isn't one of your major priorities, you should devote some time every day to walking or stretching. If fitness *is* a major objective, you might consider combining your exercise time with some of your socializing so that you can visit with friends while you're getting into shape—and save time as a result!

Travel priorities

If you love to travel and experience other cultures, then going places is one of your lifetime priorities. Some people have a list of countries and cities they really feel they must visit before they die (I'm one of them!).

If travel is a priority in your life, then there are things you will do without in order to put money away to go on your next trip. Maybe you might even combine some of your other priorities with vacationing. For example, you can arrange to meet friends you don't see often by planning a vacation with them. You can do the same with family. In fact, you can kill three birds with one stone by organizing a holiday trip to a place you want to see and inviting certain members of your family (or friends) to meet you there.

Some people who travel on a regular basis take their work with them—even arrange to have careers that will allow them the luxury of travelling while also giving them a paycheck. A friend of mine who writes and loves to travel plans a trip at least once or twice a year. She works with a travel evaluation service and visits the countries she wants while getting paid to incorporate side trips to certain hotels and

Moneysaver
If you set your lifetime goals the way you'd set goals for traveling, you will find yourself more likely to bank part of your paycheck every week.

restaurants. While at the hotels/restaurants, she evaluates their amenities and sends reports back to the travel evaluation service with her findings. She's saving time and living her life the way she wants simply by combining several of her priorities.

Holiday priorities

The majority of people we know want to spend holidays with friends and family. Unfortunately, not everyone who works a regular job has holidays off. If this is a priority for you, you might want to consider your career. For example: People who work in the restaurant business or any other service industry very rarely have holidays off. My daughter, who graduated from the Culinary Institute of America and immediately became an executive chef, soon found out that one of her main priorities was spending holidays with the people she loved. But her work prohibited it. For years, she spent weekends and holidays at work instead of where she wanted to be— with friends and family. Finally, she decided she just couldn't give up those special occasions anymore and she switched careers.

Not everyone will do something as dramatic as that, but depending on where holidays fall in your list of what's important to you, you might find yourself making compromises or adjustments so that you can create some happiness for yourself.

Holidays also present the double-edged sword effect—not only do you need to consider where they stand on *your* priority list, but you need to decide where they are on the lists of your closest family members and friends. There are plenty of people who really don't care one way or the other about holidays, and if you belong to a family like that, it's going to be difficult for you if you consider those occasions important. On the other hand, if you've been raised with no consideration for holidays, it might be easier for you to pursue careers in fields that would require you to work on those days.

Creative priorities

People whose lives revolve around the arts and creativity often find it difficult to balance their priorities because what they feel in their hearts doesn't always match the reality of putting food on the table and pleasing friends/family.

If you've chosen to make your creativity a top priority in your life, then learning to manage your time should also rank as a top priority. One of the reasons for learning to juggle your time when you're artistic is that most people will consider any time you spend on the arts to be "non-work" time or "wasted" time. It takes a lot of devotion to keep going in the arts when you have opposition.

Another thing you need to consider when placing priorities on creative time is that you should schedule it as you would work hours. Make time for your art and you'll be able to fit in time for everything else in your life as well. You'll be feeding your soul—and if your soul is happy, you'll be able to offer the best of yourself to anyone else who is important to you.

Financial priorities

Are making money and knowing how to spend it or invest it important to you? If so, you know it doesn't happen magically. Investing and earning money take time, and that time is something you need to make sure you have plenty of.

If money is a priority, then a set of goals broken down by week, month, year, and lifetime are extremely important. Winning the lottery isn't an

Watch Out!
One word of warning: if you put money ahead of people, you'll never achieve any satisfaction in your life.

option. You must give yourself a step-by-step process of how you will reach the financial goals and expect to have interruptions and snafus that will keep you from attaining some of those goals.

Important time-management checklist

Before you put any more time into checking out goals and starting to think about putting some behavior changes into action, go through the following time-management checklist and see if you're in the right mindset for putting the suggestions in this book to work.

- Have I forgotten any fantasies about being able to do ten times more than what I can fit into a 24-hour day?

- Have I considered that the only thing I can do with time is spend it?

- Am I ready to work more intelligently in order to be more productive?

- Do I realize I don't have to work longer hours in order to accomplish what I want?

- Am I ready to re-evaluate my goals and be realistic about them?

- Do I now know the difference between priorities and the things I can put on the back burner?

- Am I ready to cope with the interruptions you will invariably encounter?

- Do I want to get rid of the stress in my life?

- Do I realize that I can get a lot of little projects done while waiting for something else?

- Am I ready to learn more?

If you've answered yes to at least half of these questions, then it's time to take the next step.

Bright Idea
Post the time-management checklist and your answers somewhere where you'll be sure to see it on a regular basis. It'll keep you on track.

Just the facts

- What you need time for is the most important consideration in your life.

- Making the choices of what's vital, what's simply important, and what's not important at all is the first step to managing time.

- Stress is usually the result of unclear expectations of ourselves and what we're capable of accomplishing.

- Personal priorities and work priorities often conflict.

- People in the arts usually have to be even stricter with their time management because most family members and friends don't take them seriously.

Matching Your Time-Management Needs to Your Wants

Chapter 3

In the last chapter, you roughly estimated how much time you spend on what you do each day. Now it's time to break that down into percentages. Let's be a little more specific this time.

How will you lay out your time budget?

Here's your job: Using the form below, I want you to keep track of your time for a whole week. Make seven copies of this form, one for each day of the week, and keep the form with you all the time. Write down *religiously* every moment you spend on every task/project. Nothing is too small a detail to note—even brushing your teeth! (*Note:* You may have to adjust the hours according to your time schedule.)

Then, at the end of the week, figure out the types of time you spend on a regular basis and how much time each day you spend on those types. I'm going to offer you a sample of my average after this form, so you can see how it looks broken down.

Timesaver
Keeping track of your time is the first step in figuring out how to control it. Use a small pad that will fit into a pocket or pocketbook and attach a pen to it so you don't always have to look for one.

TIME SPENT

TIME	ACTIVITY	AMOUNT OF TIME SPENT
7:00 A.M.		
7:15		
7:30		
7:45		
8:00		
8:15		
8:30		
8:45		
9:00		
9:15		
9:30		
9:45		
10:00		
10:15		
10:30		
10:45		
11:00		
11:15		
11:30		
11:45		
Noon		
12:15 P.M.		
12:30		
12:45		
1:00		
1:15		
1:30		
1:45		
2:00		
2:15		
2:30		
2:45		
3:00		
3:15		
3:30		
3:45		

TIME	ACTIVITY	AMOUNT OF TIME SPENT
4:00		
4:15		
4:30		
4:45		
5:00		
5:15		
5:30		
5:45		
6:00		
6:15		
6:30		
6:45		
7:00		
7:15		
7:30		
7:45		
8:00		
8:15		
8:30		
8:45		
9:00		
9:15		
9:30		
9:45		
10:00		
10:15		
10:30		
10:45		
11:00		
11:15		
11:30		
11:45		
Midnight		
12:15 A.M.		
12:30		
12:45		

66

I recommend you to take care of the minutes: for hours will take care of themselves.
—Philip Dormer Stanhope, Earl of Chesterfield (1694-1773)

99

Okay, now here's an average of what I've spent this week and where the activities fall. This form looks a little different from the one above because I've classified my activities. This is how you can see what's valuable time and what time has been wasted. Remember this is an average of a whole week, so yours might look a little different.

Time Spent Form

TIME	ACTIVITY	AMOUNT OF TIME	TYPE OF TIME
7:00 A.M.	make coffee	10 mins.	housework
7:15	feed cats		
7:30			
7:45	e-mail	45 mins.	e-mail
8:00			
8:15			
8:30			
8:45			
9:00			
9:15	write	1 hr. 15 mins.	work
9:30			
9:45			
10:00	coffee break/		
10:15	chat w/ Bobby	30 mins.	socializing/interruption
10:30			
10:45	pack 2 boxes	15 mins.	housework
11:00	answer phone call	15 mins.	interruption
11:15	planning/research	30 mins.	planning
11:30			
11:45	break to exercise	15 mins.	exercise
Noon			
12:15	lunch	45 mins.	eating
12:30			
12:45			
1:00	check e-mail	15 mins.	e-mail
1:15			
1:30			
1:45	write	1 hr. 30 mins.	work
2:00			
2:15			
2:30			
2:45	pack boxes	15 mins.	housework
3:00			
3:15	phone calls	45 mins.	interruption
3:30			
3:45			

Moneysaver
When you remember that time is money, you can see the sense in keeping track of time much more clearly. And you save money by keeping track of time!

Once I figured out the types of time spent, I added them up and did an average. Remember, we have 24 hours a day to work with (that's all!), so you have to figure in all the hours in the day, not just the ones when you're awake.

TIME	ACTIVITY	AMOUNT OF TIME	TYPE OF TIME
4:00 4:15 4:30 4:45 5:00	watch Rosie O'Donnell	1 hr.	television
5:15 5:30 5:45	store/supper	45 mins.	errands
6:00	talk to husband	15 mins.	socializing
6:15	phone calls	15 mins.	socializing
6:30 6:45	filing	15 mins.	work
7:00 7:15 7:30	supper	30 mins.	eating
7:45 8:00 8:15 8:30	packing	45 mins.	housework
8:45 9:00 9:15 9:30 9:45	answer mail/ write bills	1 hr.	planning
10:00 10:15 10:30 10:45 11:00	television or out w/ friends	1 hr.	television or socializing
11:15 11:30 11:45	reading	30 mins.	reading
12:00 12:15 12:30 12:45			

Here's how the percentages broke down:

AVERAGES OF TIME SPENT

ACTIVITIES	AMOUNT OF TIME	PERCENTAGE
Work	3 hours	12.5%
Sleep	7 hours 30 mins.	31.25%
Eating	1 hour 15 mins.	5.21%
Errands	45 mins.	3.125%
Planning	1 hour 30 mins.	6.25%
Exercising	15 mins.	1%
Socializing	1 hour 45 mins.	7.29%
Television	2 hours	8.33%
Reading	30 mins.	2.1%
Housework	1 hour 15 mins.	5.21%
Telephone	15 mins.	1%
E-mail	1 hour	4.17%
Interruptions	1 hour	4.17%
SUB-TOTAL	22 hours	91.67%
Wasted time	2 hours	8.33%
TOTAL	24 hours	100%

After looking at this breakdown, I was surprised. I thought I'd worked longer hours, but what I actually did was to lose time—consistently. Why? Because I was walking from the office to the kitchen to get coffee, because I went to the bathroom, because I was looking for things—a million reasons, but there's two hours I cannot account for. Two hours I could have used in any number of ways. Two hours totally wasted.

A further analysis showed me that if I had been spending "normal" time, I would not have used 5.21% of my time doing what I've called "housework." That "housework" actually translates into packing to move. Consider that an interruption—

and that 5.21% actually becomes time that I would have spent working/writing.

The socializing time I've spent this week is higher than usual because my husband is home and we've been spending a lot of time talking to and visiting with friends that we know we won't see once we move. I figure I usually spend about half an hour socializing, and there's another hour and 15 minutes usually spent working.

Just a quick glance proves that I've had some important time stolen this week because of an unexpected event: moving. Remember that when you do your own schedule.

This little experiment proves something very valuable. Even though I figure I'm pretty good at managing my time, there's still time in my day to fit in more exercise and I'm wasting too much time on my e-mail. As a result, I'll reschedule my day so that I spend only 15 minutes in the morning and 15 minutes at night on e-mail, and I'll utilize some of that lost time exercising.

The good thing about keeping the log is that I've seen where I'm doing two or three things at once. Though it doesn't show on my schedule, when I was watching television, I was also on the telephone or talking to my husband. When I was eating, I was often at the computer working or in the car driving to errands. And when I visit with friends, I'm often doing some research for a book or talking about business. And at no time when I wait for anything am I *not* busy.

What does this have to do with a time budget? By analyzing the percentages of your time that you spend on specific tasks, you can get to the next step,

Watch Out!
Don't think that those little five minute segues into Instant Message or looking for something don't add up. If you spend five minutes every three hours wasting time, you're actually wasting almost five hours a week!

which is figuring out where you can slice some time to use it where you need more time.

Figuring out what you need

With what you already know about your priorities and how you spend your time, it should be easy to figure out what you need.

Say your boss has handed you a new project that's going to run your life for the next couple of months. First, you need to clear your desk and prepare. Then you need to find the time to do it. And finally, you need to explain to all your friends and family that your life won't be your own for a while and they're going to have to work with you if they want to see you at all.

Look at your schedule. How much time are you wasting? If you are surprised (as I was) by the time you can't account for, then you have the perfect opportunity to take that time and make it work time. If you see other pockets of time, you can also hand those over to this project.

But you might tell me that you also need to have time with your family and friends. You can't leave them out of the equation. Okay, then look at that television time you're spending and shut the thing off for a little while. Utilize that time (which experts have figured is approximately 15 hours a week) as socializing time with the people you love.

You could also use other pockets of time, such as meals and interruptions to get in ten minutes here, twenty minutes there on your project.

The trick is to break that life-stealing project down into smaller objectives and determine to do a certain amount each day. You'll be more satisfied with reaching your goals that way, you'll discover you have more time to work on it than you think, and you'll also have time to spend with your family. Yes, you'll be watching the clock, but you'll fit everything you *need* to fit into your schedule—and all without staying up later or getting up earlier.

Goals and objectives

When getting your time budget together, you need to project your goals and objectives, as well as your needs. What's the difference? Needs are what you should do; goals are projected times when you need to accomplish tasks; objectives are the dates when you'd like to meet those goals—or the end result of the projects/tasks.

Goals are what you'd like to achieve by a certain time/date. They are something you anticipate and wish to bring under your control. Rationally, you need to realize that by setting goals, you are doing some wishful thinking. If you meet your goals, wonderful. However, when we set our goals we often fail to realize that the art of time management means that we're actually able to control events. There are going to be events, however, that we *won't* be able to control. And that's where realistic goal-setting comes into play.

By setting goals, you can establish some sort of life plan for yourself that will give you an idea of where you're headed and how you're going to get there. It also gives you a realistic appraisal of your own values and priorities, and will help you create some balance and harmony in your life. Goals are how people set up the steps to reach their dreams— and we all need dreams. Without them, we have nothing to live for.

When you set goals, you can see what it is you need to do in order to keep your life moving harmoniously. We all have a past, a present, and a

Bright Idea
Get a copy of Ralph Waldo Emerson's essay "On Self-Reliance" and keep it in your bathroom to read whenever you have a moment. It's one of the best treatises on time management.

future. By drawing on the lessons we've learned in the past, we can make it through present events and plan future ones. By looking at how we've reacted to certain events, we can determine whether we need to bring them under control or whether our priorities are being met (or ignored). It always takes many different factors to move you toward your goals, but knowing the difference between goals and objectives is the first step.

We'll talk more about exactly how to set goals in Part III of this book.

Objectives are important in that they determine every factor of your work. By setting clear objectives, you spell out certain specifics about each job. Patrick Forsyth, author of *First Things First: How to Manage Your Time for Maximum Performance,* uses the acronym SMART to spell out objectives. It stands for: **S**pecific, **M**easurable, **A**chievable, **R**ealistic, and **T**imed.

To apply this acronym and its help in creating specific objectives, let me use this book as an example.

▪ **Specific**

To provide readers with some hints on how to better manage their time by writing a book on the subject that utilizes the best hints/suggestions already available on the market and combining them with what I already know. The book also must be complete by the first week of June, a six-month deadline.

▪ **Measurable**

How will I know I've met my readers' needs? The first indication will be if my editors are

happy with what we expected the book to be.
Then there will be reviews, and finally, feedback
from readers themselves.

▪ **Achievable**

Can I achieve this goal? Considering my deadline and the plethora of information available
on the topic, it is well within my reach. However,
there will be some considerable time management on my behalf in order to get the book
done by deadline.

▪ **Realistic**

Considering the timeline, I will have to be well-
prepared to spend a minimum of 24 hours a
week researching and writing the book in order
to offer the most complete explanation of the
subject with as many solid and concrete examples as possible. Will I be able to please everyone? Probably not, but helping a good portion
of people is my goal—and that, I believe,
is realistic.

▪ **Timed**

As long as no major interruptions occur, the
timing part of these objectives should be met.
I'll work in extra time for unexpected happen-
ings (like selling my house and moving!), and
I'll rearrange other on-going projects (such
as end-of-semester grading) to make room for
this book.

    By analyzing objectives in a SMART way, you can
easily foresee what might end up being a problem.
You're not necessarily scheduling at this moment,
just seeing whether you can meet your expectations
or objectives.

> **"**
> I was never more
> certain of how
> far away I was
> from my goal
> than when I was
> standing right
> beside it.
> —Vincent, a
> character in the
> movie *Gattaca*
> (1997)
> **"**

The unexpected

Charles R. Hobbs, author of *Time Power*, states that there are five categories of events that anyone who wishes to manage their time should know about:

- Events you think you cannot control, and you can't.

- Events you think you cannot control, but you can.

- Events you think you can control, but you can't.

- Events you think you can control, but you don't.

- Events you think you can control, and you can.

Some of these events fall into what I call the unexpected—otherwise defined as traumas, catastrophes, interruptions, and acts of nature.

When you set your goals, build in some time for the unexpected. Expect the roof to fall in or the storm of the century to happen and you'll have a secondary plan. I'm not saying you should be negative; I'm just warning you not to get your heart set on meeting your dream of making a million by the age of 30, only to be disappointed when a terrible hailstorm ruins every car on your used-car lot.

Realize that there are certain events and people over which you have no control whatsoever. And when you are faced with those situations, you must adapt. There are many people who have faced immense odds and still reached their goals because they were determined to. And there are many more who simply don't set goals at all because they've convinced themselves they'll never reach them anyway. That's sad. If there were no doers, inventors, strategists, explorers, and dreamers, we'd have no knowledge of the solar systems outside our own, no lightbulbs, no best-selling books, no peace treaties with foreign nations, no computers or cell phones.

Watch Out!
The old adage "expect the unexpected" should be firmly ingrained in your mind once you set your goals— and you should be prepared to reset them on a regular basis afterward.

Know your strengths and weaknesses

Some people work best in the morning, while others prefer late afternoon or nighttime hours. Some work best in quiet, and others prefer the buzz of a noisy office with phones ringing and people yelling. Some workers like having projects that are long-term and involved, yet there are many who like the simple repetition that doesn't require much brainpower.

If we were all the same, then there would be no stock market and no libraries, no fast-food and no gourmet restaurants, no urban and no rural areas. Everything would be a bland shade of gray, everyone would look and speak in the same manner, and everyone would be pretty bored.

Though this whole book is about time and how to manage it, underneath all the tricks of the trade is the truth of the matter: We're all different. We all work on different inner clocks and we all need to know how to manage *ourselves* in order to get control of that clock.

If you know your strengths and weaknesses, you can better plan on how to utilize what you have to work with and fit your styles into your own personal clock in order to work more effectively. No one works well if they're at the lowest ebb of their biorhythms and no one works well in an environment that is irritating to them.

Personally, I like the morning hours when everything is quiet. The phone doesn't ring, no one is talking to me or interrupting my train of thought, and I feel most alert at that time. I use the morning to do my toughest work, then I quit during the latter part of the afternoon. That's when my motor skills are at their best, so that's when I either go for a walk or do some housework, before settling in for an hour of down time. Because I've assessed myself so well, I know that I get absolutely nothing done in late afternoon/early evening, so I use that as rest time. After supper, I get another surge of energy, but I use it for different tasks because I've found that I can't get back on the computer again (my eyes are usually tired from being on all morning). So, during the evening, I answer mail, edit my work, read, or make phone calls.

It's all a matter of knowing yourself and your own personal rhythms, your work styles, and your strengths. Most people have not taken the time to even think about *how* they work and what skills are their strongest. They simply keep trying to do whatever is necessary, often wondering why they're feeling frustrated.

Perhaps if your assessment shows that you're more creative than mathematical, or more likely to work best in a group than alone, you can adjust your work style accordingly. Sometimes, a little adjustment actually adds what we believe to be more speed to our day. But all you're doing is taking advantage of your own work and learning style. Quite simple, right?

Are you type A or type B?

According to most professionals, there are two basic personality types in the world: Those who must do everything and do it perfectly, and those who are quite happy just to do, period.

Type A people are those who have to get everything done right away, are extremely competitive, hostile, and angry. They're the ones who honk at you when you're driving too slowly, find it hard to confide in others, believe that their work takes precedence over everything else, and that people who don't know what they're doing should stay out of the way.

This type of person tends to intimidate others and expresses general dissatisfaction with the world. They don't know how to relax and eventually all that stress ends up taking its toll on their bodies. Type A people are the ones most likely to have heart attacks, strokes, migraines, ulcers, and digestive problems.

The best advice if you're Type A? Slow down! Learn to relax, let go, and enjoy life. Get out and have some fun with your friends. Remind yourself on a regular basis that no one is going to remember how much you worked when you're lying in state at your funeral. They will remember that you weren't there for your family or your friends and that you hardly ever smiled.

Type B, on the other hand, is just the opposite. This type of person smells the roses all too often. They don't have any aggressiveness and sometimes miss out on opportunities because they're simply too calm and relaxed to chase after anything. Though Type B people are easy to be around and usually healthy, they could use a little spice in their life and can often irritate others simply because they can't get out of their own way.

Right in the middle is what we should label Type C (that's *my* label, not a psychological one). This type of person knows when and how to relax, but can also pick up the pace and do a challenging job. They get angry occasionally, but it's not an explosive type of anger, and they're generally easy to be around. Work gets accomplished, family and friends are part of their lives, and they have both good days

> 66
> You know there are two types of people in this world: Those who get stomped on and those who do the stomping.
> —Mitch, a character in the movie *Dirty Work* (1998)
> 99

and bad days. Type C is where you want to be—and this is the type of person you also want to have on your team.

What kind of learner are you?

Throughout the years, many theorists have developed tests and descriptions of different kinds of learning styles. Each person is said to learn in their own individualized manner, and the more we know about how we learn, the more we can understand why we "don't get it" sometimes.

Not only are learning styles different, but there is also what is called 'multiple intelligence.' This term means that some people learn by seeing, others learn by doing, still others by hearing music or painting, and others by incorporating a number of techniques. The result is that some of us are creative, some are mathematical, some are social, and some are a combination.

The Myers-Briggs test is one of the most common given to students to see what kind of learner they are. The Myers-Briggs Type Indicator is not a learning style inventory per se, but it attempts to measure and identify a person's "type." Originally, psychological theorist Carl Jung created what he called archetypes. He saw three, but Myers and Briggs have added a fourth, as follows:

- Introversion—Extroversion
- Thinking—Feeling
- Intuiting—Sensing
- Judging—Perceiving

What this means is that:

- An introvert is drawn to solitary activities and thinking while an extrovert relies on outside stimulation.

Unofficially...
Personality tests like the Myers-Briggs and others are used regularly by heads of corporations to evaluate incoming job candidates or to figure out whether people should be promoted.

- A thinker makes judgements based on impersonal data, while a feeler judges on personality and emotions, taking into account how someone else might feel.

- An intuitive learner is drawn to innovative and theoretical pursuits, while a sensor gathers information and processes it through the five senses.

- A person who learns by judging is apt to plan well, control, and organize, while one who learns by perceiving tends to be open, spontaneous, and autonomous.

Where you fall within these categories might tell you how you will learn in new situations and help you understand what qualities you need in order to attain new information.

What's your work style?

Did you ever notice that there's always someone who shows up on the job earlier than everyone else and stays later? You might think that person is brown-nosing or that they're purely an irritant, or perhaps that person is you and it's imperative that you work twice as hard and twice as long as everyone else.

There's also always that person who's running around like a chicken with its head cut off, trying to meet deadlines at the last minute, or trying to get someone else to pick up the loose ends that he or she dropped. The person is disorganized and scatterbrained, yet somehow manages to stay on the job.

Then there's the happy medium: the person who comes to work, does their job, then goes home and forgets about work so that they can spend quality time with family and friends. The person always seems relatively happy, rarely gets stressed, and manages to work with many personality types. Sounds perfect, right? But look around you—there's always someone like that in the company or on the team.

What kind of worker are you? Here are a few questions that might help you assess your strengths/weaknesses in the employment field. These are also questions you might be asked during a job interview by those who are interested in how you might fit into their company/group.

Bright Idea

For a more complete evaluation of your personality and skills, you might want to take some of the tests offered online. Within seconds, you can get a printed readout of where you fall within the ranges offered.

1. What are your strongest:

   Abilities:

   Skills:

   Interests:

2. What abilities, skills and interests do you want to stress?

3. Describe in two or three sentences who you are.

4. List your major accomplishments.

   At work:

   At school:

   In your personal life:

5. What challenges you the most?

6. Are you a creative person? or analytical? mechanical?

7. Do you prefer working alone or with others?

8. Do you need someone giving you instructions and deadlines, or would you rather set your own pace?

9. How important is variety to you?

10. How much stability do you need?

11. What qualities about you do people praise?

12. Which habits do they criticize?

13. How much of an individual are you?

14. How do you handle long hours? Heavy pressure? Deadlines?

15. How do you get along with others? Are you a natural leader? A team player?

16. Are you an overachiever? Do you not care about achievement at all?

17. Would you like to meet new people and have new experiences in the future? What kind?

18. What do you believe others think of you? What would you like them to think of you?

19. What are the 10 most important things you are looking for in a job (can include things like: travel, challenge, stability, 40-hour workweek, benefits, etc.)?

Evaluate your health

Often your family history can determine what happens to your health throughout your life. If anyone in your family has had a heart attack or died of one, your chances of heart problems are high. If you have a history of cancer in your family, it would be wise for you to take precautions, if you can. If high blood pressure plagued your mother and father, you'd better get yours checked on a regular basis.

Though you cannot avoid all kinds of illness in your life, you do have control over the ones caused by stress. A simple 10 question self-test will tell you whether you need to adjust some of your habits in order to maintain good health.

1. Do I regularly have an upset stomach or gas after I eat a meal?

2. Are headaches a regular part of my workday?

Timesaver
Schedule your annual physical at the same time as a friend's or family member's and you can use the time waiting in the office to catch up on what's happening in their lives.

3. Are my menstrual cycles regular and painless?

4. Do my shoulders and neck get tight when I'm working?

5. Am I able to walk up a flight of stairs without getting out of breath?

6. What's my cholesterol level?

7. When did my last have my blood pressure and heart rate checked? What were they?

8. Do I catch every cold and flu that comes around?

9. Am I getting a regular good night's sleep?

10. Do I have good eating habits and avoid the overuse of alcohol and tranquilizers?

If you have a history of family illnesses and are not taking care of yourself properly, now's the time to make the switch to a healthy lifestyle. Work some exercise time into your schedule, eat regularly and well, and get those checkups! Nothing will wreck your health more quickly than stress, and my bet is if you're trying to manage your time, it's because you're feeling stressed.

What about procrastination?

How often do you find yourself working overtime or longer hours because you've put off working on a project you knew about a couple of weeks or months ago?

When I meet a new class (I teach English/ Writing at the college level), one of the first things I do is give them a list of their assignments for the whole semester. Then I tell them that their last assignment is the most important one and they should start putting aside research material for it now, because if they don't, the end of the semester brings with it a lot of stress. Two weeks after the beginning of the semester, I then ask them for a commitment on which topic they want to research.

Again, I remind them that they need to start working on the project. When we're finished with the group project, well into the second half of the semester, I check in with them again and remind them not to wait until the last moment to do the research assignment.

But no matter how often I do this and how much I break the assignment down into segments for them, some of my students always end up doing the project the night before it's due. They come into class bleary-eyed and out of breath from running. They hand me a paper that's been printed at the last minute, or they beg my forgiveness and ask if they can get an extension because when they were printing their paper (five minutes ago), the printer ran out of ink.

By that time, it's too late, and I just shake my head and remind them that I warned them of this three months ago. They know I'm right, and I hope they learn a valuable lesson from the stress they've put themselves under by committing yet another act of procrastination.

If you tend to procrastinate, you're putting off doing something because you either don't like the job, don't feel you have time for it right at the moment, or can't manage your schedule in a way that provides adequate preparation and planning.

Is this healthy? No. Is it common? Yes. Can it be cured? Most definitely.

Through prioritizing and planning, even the worst procrastinator can learn new habits. Take a look at Chapter 8 if you want to overcome this bad habit.

> ❝
> Delay always breeds danger; and to protract a great design is often to ruin it.
> —Miguel de Cervantes
> ❞

How flexible are you?

If you're planning your day to within a millisecond, you're over-planning, and that can be just as bad as not having enough time at all. You need to build in time for interruptions, problems, jobs that take longer than expected, and relaxation time for yourself.

You might need to "rob Peter to pay Paul" occasionally, so it's wise to be as flexible as you can. Yes, I know sometimes it's impossible to move an inch, but if you can do it occasionally, you'll save yourself a lot of fretting and anxiety.

When you're working on setting up your schedule, always build in extra time for traveling, meetings, lunches, and big jobs. That way, if you finish early, you can take a break. Remember Parkinson's Law: Work expands to fill time.

Just the facts

- By religiously keeping track of how you spend every moment of your time for a week, you'll be able to see if and where you're wasting it.

- Goals are what you want to do, while objectives are how you're going to meet them.

- A Type A person is stressed, angry, and more likely to die of a heart attack than the laid-back and relaxed Type B person.

- Your health is largely determined by your family history and the way you take care of yourself—although stress plays a huge factor.

- People who don't build in extra time for large projects and relaxation often find their inflexibility leads them to poor time management.

The Real World: Time Management Pays

GET THE SCOOP ON...
How to figure out exactly what you're worth on
an hourly basis ▪ How to equate time with
money—and not feel guilty about it ▪
How to figure out where your time is going and
how to value that lost time ▪ How to evaluate
which stressors are affecting the way you
handle your time

How Much Is Your Time Worth?

Chapter 4

Y ou've all heard (and probably *said*) that time is money. But no matter how many times you hear it, you might not know exactly how much your time is worth. As far as what time is worth, I think it depends on what you're doing. If you're doing something you love to do, the compensation is more spiritual than financial, and you don't have to charge so much. If you're doing something that you can't stand to do, but you can do it well, your time is worth a lot more. In my humble opinion, anyway!

What we waste in time could probably fill Fort Knox if that time were converted into solid cash. We waste time waiting in lines at stores, banks, and in the doctor's office. That time could be spent more productively working on a favorite project or spending time with our families or making a few business calls.

Bright Idea
Don't ever go to
a doctor's or
dentist's office
empty-handed.
Take something
to do!

We waste time being disorganized and looking for things that we've lost. If those items were organized and we could put our hands immediately on whatever we need, we'd have time left over to attend to other needs.

We lose time when we're stressed and our bodies give in to their burdens and we become ill. If we maintained a low stress level, we would be less likely to get sick and wouldn't waste time in bed staring at the ceiling thinking about everything we should be doing.

Evaluate your worth in dollars and sense

Each of the moments we spend every day has a value—whether it be in dollars or in sense. No, that's not a misspelling. I mean sense—the sense it takes to figure out whether what you're doing is worth your time/money.

If we use our heads, we can figure out that every moment of our lives means something. Thinking that "something" translates into actual cash might turn off some of you, but it's the truth. None of us lives on air alone. We need money to put a roof over our heads and food in our mouths. We need money to support our children, put clothes on their backs, and send them to school. We need money to pay taxes and to buy a few luxuries so all those hours spent working feel worthwhile.

Unfortunately, in this crazy world of (h)ours, everyone has a different worth. For example, a parent of five will be eligible for a much larger slice of life insurance than a single person with no living relatives. The reason for this is that life insurance is meant to leave something to survivors. The more survivors, the more money to be left in order for the survivors to go on.

Why should you want to evaluate what your time is worth? Perhaps because it will spur you to be a little more prudent with your time if you see it as money. Or maybe because it will cause those of you who own companies to realize that when you don't train your employees to manage their time efficiently, you stand to lose time—and by losing time, you lose productivity, and if you lose productivity, you don't make the same amount of products/ transactions, and if you lose those products, you lose money, and money is the bottom line.

For example, take people who work at home. One writer I know says people are always surprised that she doesn't have time to do the socializing everyone else does, and they believe that because she's published, she makes millions. Not only is that definitely not the case, but when people ask her to do "a little writing" for them, they're amazed when she brings out her rate chart. She then asks, "What does your mechanic charge?"

Self-employed people often have a difficult time proving their worth to customers, as well as family and friends. Why? They work more hours and often have more responsibilities than many company executives—largely because they're the head honcho, the jack/jill of all trades, the person who does it all—then have to cook the dinner, clean the house, and take care of the laundry as well.

If we all knew what we were worth, it'd make our lives much easier. And perhaps serve as a solid reminder of what we are throwing away when we fritter away the days of our lives.

Every person in the world will have a different answer to the question of what their time is worth. Sometimes they're right; other times, they're wishing upon a star. Some millionaires might want to

Watch Out!
If you're self-employed, remember that each moment you spend is worth twice as much as it would be if you were working for someone else!

break their time down into minutes (because they do so much in an hour, it'd be impossible to calculate), while others would ask whether they're worth anything at all. But everyone has a value.

A friend of mine starts her day when the stock market opens and ends it at 4, when it closes. But after that time, she's doing research on new stocks to see where she should shift her money the next day. As a day trader, she can stand to make or lose thousands with one bid, so it's difficult to put a value on that.

Another friend is a writer who has spent many years producing book after book, but has not sold a single one. Though she has worked nonstop for years, she believes her work doesn't have any value specifically because it hasn't sold yet.

Still another friend has three children and has spent their formative years at home taking care of them while her husband shouldered the responsibility of bringing money into the house. Hers is perhaps the hardest value to figure because she has not made a salary or contributed to social security at all, yet hers is one of the most important of these three jobs because she was responsible for raising an entire family.

Very few employees would ever have input into their own salaries unless they're self-employed. And most of us don't have that luxury. The way the corporate world figures out how much to pay people is this: they hire consultants to determine salary, and it's a long drawn-out process. They collect statistics from other businesses, do comparison studies, and look at the community and its cost of living, then arrive at salaries for various types of jobs. If your job doesn't fit into the norm, they have a certain amount of wiggle room that you can negotiate—but it's not infinite. If you figure out your yearly salary based on percentages of what you do with each day, it'd come somewhat close on average.

When evaluating how much your time is worth, you're thinking of the value for a reason: To see why wasting precious moments of your time will eventually cost you in dollars and cents. You have reasons for wanting to save as much time as possible or to manage the time you are spending well. Whether you want to cut down on your workday or buy a few extra hours with the kids or earn some free time to go fishing, time is important to our lives. And that's why we should all know exactly what we're worth.

As I was searching for answers to these questions, I happened to come upon several Web sites (no, that's not where I do *all* my research!) that actually evaluated a person's worth in gold or silver. That's relatively easy: you calculate your weight in kilograms and multiply it by the going price for silver or gold. Makes you want to become the gold figure in the James Bond movie *Goldfinger*. But that won't help you much when figuring out how to price your time, so let's move onward and upward.

Who gets the benefit of your hard work?

Hopefully, the answer is you. But most of the time, the larger share of your time is going to help someone else, whether it be your boss, the company itself, your family, or others.

Depending on your job or your talents, different people will benefit from what you're doing. If you think about it for a moment, you're affecting an awful lot of people. It's like dropping a pebble in a pond and watching the concentric ripples spread farther and farther until the water is smooth again.

Moneysaver
It's a good idea to invest in a ledger book or program that will calculate your net worth. If you keep it up-to-date, you'll save money and time when applying for a loan or evaluating your financial situation.

As a teacher, I usually have approximately four classes of approximately 25 students each semester. Each day that I teach a lesson, all of those students are affected in some way (even if they fall asleep!). If each of those students uses even part of the information I teach them in a semester, they'll be passing on what I've done to a minimum of two other people, who'll pass it on to two more. And so on. Before I die, I will have affected over a million people. If I were to get $1 for each person I've directly affected, I would be a very happy woman. Unfortunately, that's not the way it works.

What you need to do to make time management work for you is to make sure that the bulk of your time works for *you* rather than for someone else. The 80/20 principle comes into play here and needs to be a major consideration for you. Though this "rule" is explained more completely in Chapter 10, let's just say here that what this means is that it's been proven that 80% of your output will garner you 20% of the results you desire. Wouldn't you rather put more of your time into things that make *you* happy and that pay off for *you* rather than someone else?

If the answer is yes, continue reading and learn how to practice good time management.

Is time money?

If you consider all your time leisure time and you don't have to worry about making a living, then time isn't money. But if you're like the rest of us and you have to eat and find cash to pay bills, then yes, of course time is money. Even the wealthiest people in the world know that the way they spend their time directly affects how much money they'll have—or how the money is spent or invested.

If you're a worker, you need to know that to your employer, you are an expense—and they need to know that they're spending their money well by employing you. If you happen to know what other workers who are doing the same job as you are making, then you have a yardstick by which you can measure yourself.

If you're a small-business owner, you usually have to do more than time permits. You probably wear many hats and have to accomplish jobs that larger companies farm out. Maybe you're chief baker, accountant, human resources director, purchasing agent, and president all rolled into one. In this case, your time is highly valuable because every single moment counts.

If you waste time on insignificant tasks instead of focusing on the work at hand, you'll find you have fewer hours to spend on something you really enjoy. Or, something that will move you along more quickly in your career.

And if you want to know where the saying "time is money" came from, here's the story: In the Jewish religion, the Torah expressly prohibits anyone from cutting in front of someone in line. It is believed that to do so constitutes stealing and is a major transgression. Whether the line you're waiting in is in a bank or store or whether the line consists of business vehicles, the line is considered time and your place in it is money. According to the Torah, if someone is ahead of someone else on line, they "own" a "time advantage," and that time advantage is worth money!

The Torah states that the way to estimate the monetary value of time is to take the average salary for the common laborer on the market and halve it.

Unofficially...
Stanley Marcus, the Chief Executive Officer of the upscale department store Neiman-Marcus, felt that none of his time was ever free and commented that he was often miserly with his time on some matters so that he could spend lots more on others.

For example, say the minimum wage is $5.15 an hour, half would be $2.58. So, the time you spend waiting is worth $2.58 per hour (minimum).

Due to this belief that every person's time is worth a minimum of the average salary, the Torah says that each person is obligated to gauge his own actions with honesty and fairness.

How to calculate your worth on paper

What your time is worth is different from your net worth. Your time is what you'd get paid to do what you do during the hours in your day. Your net worth is the value of your assets, (i.e. your estate, investments, retirement, possessions, etc.).

To figure out what your personal time is worth, take the annual amount you earn and divide it by your working days per year. Then divide that daily figure by the hours, and the hours by the minutes. Let's say the average person works 244 days a year, 8 hours per day (your days and hours worked might be different). For example: You earn $20,000 a year and we'll say you work 244 days, so your daily wage is $81.97. If you work eight hours a day, then you make $10.25 per hour and $.17 per minute. If by rearranging your time, you are able to save an hour a day, you will save $2,501. That's quite a savings, isn't it? Naturally, if you figure out what you believe you're worth when you're not actually working, these figures will differ. And you can use the chart following to decide whether you want to save twenty minutes a day or four hours. You calculate whatever your goal is—and you'll be amazed at how much you're worth!

Here's a chart based on these projections:

66
No, when the fight begins within himself,/ A man's worth something.
—Robert Browning
99

WAGES AVERAGED BY HOURS AND MINUTES

Annual income	Hourly wage	Per-minute wage
$20,000	$10.25	$.l7
$30,000	$17.93	$.30
$40,000	$20.49	$.34
$50,000	$25.61	$.43
$60,000	$30.73	$.51
$70,000	$35.86	$.60
$80,000	$40.98	$.68
$90,000	$46.10	$.77
$100,000	$51.23	$.85

Of course, some people who make $100,000 a year are actually making more per hour. Lawyers, for example, charge on an hourly basis. They don't always, however, get their full hourly rate. Say that a case they're working on doesn't go to trial, then they make a percentage of what they win. If they don't win, they don't make any money. If, however, they are getting paid on a contingency basis, they might make more than their actual hourly rate. And there are many times when they don't get paid at all because their clients are either indigent or simply don't pay.

Thus, this chart is good if you're on a fixed salary, but someone who is paid on an hourly basis should consider how many hours a week they work for the number of weeks a year that they're actually employed. Teachers would not include their summer hours unless they actually work during that period of time.

Naturally, there are all kinds of factors to consider when working out how much your time is worth, but the chart above will give you a basis to go by. Now it's up to you to do the math.

Bright Idea
If you're wondering where all the time goes, why not carry a small pocket notebook with you for the next 7 days and jot down exactly how long it takes you to do everything you do in each day?

After you're done figuring out how much your time is worth, it's time to figure out how much time in your day goes to certain activities. Below is a chart that will help you break down the actual hours in a day and determine what percentage of each you spend on basic human activities. My suggestion is that you keep this chart for several weeks running, then take an average of time spent before you start figuring out where you're losing time, and how much that lost time is costing you.

DAILY TIME SPENT

		Hours	Percentages
1.	Work		%
2.	Food		%
3.	Sleep		%
4.	Entertainment		%
5.	Personal Grooming		%
6.	Physical Activities		%
	Total:	24	100%

The most important thing to remember about this chart is that the total hours must add up to 24 and the percentages must equal 100 or your figures will be off.

Once you've figured out what percentage of your day is spent on work, then you can proceed to evaluate what that portion of your time is worth. How do you do that if you're self-employed or manage a home? You can figure the average yearly salary for someone who does what you do, then figure your hourly wage (this might be off a bit, especially if your actual yearly wage comes nowhere near the average across the nation, but this is your *value*, not your IRS statement!).

An at-home mother/father should be a little more specific in breaking down the percentages of what they do each day. Instead of just figuring "work" as a percentage, how about a breakdown of how much actual time is spent cooking, cleaning, chauffeuring, doctoring, teaching, coaching, and all the other duties? Those percentages would then directly relate to what the going wage is for that particular job. For example: If you cook 2 hours a day, then that is 8% of your day. If a cook makes $6.50 an hour, then two hours of your day, you'll be worth $6.50 an hour. And so on.

Here are some average salaries for a variety of jobs that you might be able to use as the basis for figuring out what you're worth if you're self-employed or an at-home parent.

AVERAGE SALARIES BY JOB

Line of work	Annual average	Hourly average
Accountant	$40–65K	$21–33
Architect	$70–100K	$36–50
Artist	22–40	12–21
Assistant coach	15–25	8–13
Attorney	70–150	36–78
Aviator	20–185	10–95
Buyer	45–55	23–28
Chauffeur	18–50	9–26
Computer industry	35–75	18–50
Day care professional	20–30	10–15
Dentist	71–125	36–64
Engineer	65–125	33–64
Entertainer	40–700	21–359
Executive chef	32–62	16–32
Fast-food worker	11–16	6–8
Full professor	40–75	21–50
Hospital executive	100–160	51–82
Hotel/restaurant mgr.	21–75	11–38
Housekeeper	15–25	8–13

Timesaver
When trying to figure out what your time is worth, ask some co-workers or friends what price they'd put on your hours. It's cheaper than getting a full evaluation done by a professional.

Line of work	Annual average	Hourly average
Human resource specialist	38–68	19–35
Internet professional	50–100	26–51
Librarian	31–58	16–30
Licensed Practical Nurse	23–35	12–18
Life insurance agent	115–250	59–128
Manufacturing professional	65–125	33–64
Nonprofit organization executive	25–65	13–40
Office staff	14–25	7–13
Psychologist	36–100	19–51
Public relations executive	53–85	27–44
Real estate broker	75–150	38–77
Sales professional	55–125	28–64
Small-bus. executive	63–110	32–56
Stock broker	110–210	56–108
Supermarket mgr.	35–65	18–40
Teacher	27–32	14–17
Telemarketing professional	24–50	12–24
Writer (full time)	15–35	8–19

(*Note:* Remember these are averages taken from many sources and that salaries change depending on your geographical location, number of years experience, education, and many other factors. These are not written in stone! All hourly averages are figured on a 244-day/8-hour-day work year.)

The bottom line: Mo' Time = Mo' Money!

Now that you've figured out what your time is worth, you need to seriously sit down and think about it. If you spend an hour arguing with the people at the telephone company, it's going to cost you $xxx. If you wait in the dentist's office for half an hour, you'll be spending $xxx of your own money. If you spend two hours cooking a special meal and that certain friend of yours shows up half an hour late, it'll cost $xxx.

Sounds a tad cold, doesn't it? Well, perhaps you're not giving yourself enough credit. Your time is valuable. Everything you think about that time and about yourself is going to affect all the events for the rest of your life.

Now, it's important. Isn't it?

Once you start seeing yourself and your time as valuable, others will too. It's amazing how quickly it works. Gail Radley, a well-known children's writer, once told me that she was afraid to charge speaking fees, but when she talked to her editor about it and found out what everyone else was charging, she thought she might be short changing herself. The next time an organization asked her to speak, she held her breath and plunged in, asking for about half of what her editor said to charge. Without missing a beat, the organization not only agreed to her fee, but paid her expenses as well. Gail was simply not realizing what her time was worth. After that awakening, she became a bit more choosy when thinking of how to spend her time. Though she's not a wealthy woman, she now gets more done during the time she has and isn't as stressed as she used to be by trying to be all things to all people.

Dr. B. Eugene Griessman, author of *Time Tactics for Very Successful People* says you should give yourself a raise once you figure out what your time is worth. "Whatever your present value per hour, double it or triple it. Then, invest your high-priced hours deliberately. Don't give them away unless you choose to. And don't consider that everybody else's time is more valuable than your own."

That advice is definitely worthwhile, and I'm going to add my two cents. By remembering what you're worth and giving yourself that raise, you'll be less likely to waste time. And if you're not wasting time, then the time you spend is actually more valuable than at this very moment!

Stress on your time equals stress on your body and mind

Since you now know time is money, here's something else to remember. Time spent without earning anything equals stress. And too little time to do all you need to equals a *lot* of stress.

Stress can also be caused by a number of other things, such as environment, relationships, job design, socioeconomic factors, and illnesses.

In your environment, the following factors are proven stress inducers:

- Not enough space
- Inadequate lighting
- Noise pollution
- Poor ventilation
- Uncomfortable furniture

Relationship stress-causers can include:

- Inadequate respect
- Lack of support
- Poor communication
- Ineffective co-worker/spouse/friend
- Uneven distribution of work
- Misunderstandings
- Lack of relaxation time
- Unreal expectations

The job reasons which might cause you stress are:

- Uneven work pace
- Overload of work

66

If at first you don't succeed, try again. Then quit. No use being a damn fool about it.
—W.C. Fields

99

- Long hours
- Inadequate breaks
- Repetitive tasks
- Constant sitting
- Working too quickly
- No control
- Working beneath skill levels

Socioeconomic factors that induce stress include:

- Inadequate pay for work performed
- Childcare problems
- Transportation problems
- Discrimination
- No future benefits
- Dissatisfaction with job
- Balancing work and home
- Bills higher than wages

The results of all these stress factors on your life can cause many different outcomes such as headaches, fatigue, tension, depression, irritability, frustration, cynicism, loss of direction, forgetfulness, negative attitude, poor concentration, lack of control, isolation, resentment, loneliness, and an antisocial attitude.

Those emotional, spiritual, and mental outcomes directly affect your health, and it's been proven time and again that heart attacks, cancer, and other illnesses are the direct result of stress.

Time to take control of your time, right?

How do you know when enough's enough?

When do you walk away? When do you quit? Or, say it's time for me? In Kenny Rogers' words, when do

Bright Idea
Schedule a physical at the same time every year. Not only will you save time, but you might also ward off a debilitating illness by catching it early. Prevention is the best cure!

you know "when to fold 'em...know when to walk away...know when to run"?

If you've tried everything you know, invested an incredible amount of time, and communicated every which way but Martian, then maybe it's time to consider letting go and getting on to another project/job/relationship.

The smartest time managers are the ones who know when it's time to cut their losses. How do you tell? Ask yourself the following questions:

- Have I investigated all avenues of information?
- Are there any other ways I can work on the situation?
- Is my time invested mattering at all?
- Is there a payoff here or am I losing money?
- What's the cost to keep the job/relationship going?
- Is it my habit to keep beating a dead horse?
- Why am I continuing in this route?
- Do I have enough strength/money to continue?
- Am I willing to compromise to get what I want?

- What's my firm deadline to quit?

If you're totally honest with yourself, you'll see whether it's worth it to try to figure out another way to adjust your time/money/feelings, or to walk away and try something new. Be honest!

Is your productivity waning?

If you discover that you're not finishing everything you start, there's got to be a reason. Is it because you're not interested in the work/relationship? Is it because there's so much on your plate that you just don't have time? Are you depressed because you can't handle everything that you thought you could?

Once you discover the reason why you're not working as hard as you used to, then it's time to sit down and refigure your goals and priorities.

Some questions to ask yourself might include:

- If I'm not happy, what would make me happy?

- Is there a way I can arrange my work/personal schedule to make me more productive?

- Can I hand some of my work to someone else for the time being so that I can regroup?

- Am I expecting more of myself than I'm physically able to handle?

- Am I ready to make the changes necessary in my lifestyle so that I can start producing again?

Once you've taken a truthful, hard look at the reasons why your productivity is waning, then you'll be ready to address the issues.

Take the stress test

In order to evaluate where your stress is coming from and whether time management will alleviate some or all of it, you need to sit down for a few moments and make a couple of lists. When you finish these lists, give yourself a break to recuperate from the stress of thinking about all that stress.

On one side of the page, list the stressors themselves. On the other side of the page, list the ways you can deal with the stressors—ideas for how to handle them and activities in which you can engage to either take your mind off the stress or remove it from your life.

Bright Idea
If you're trying to evaluate where your stress is coming from, sit down for coffee with a trusted friend while you go over the ingredients. They might be more honest than you will be with yourself.

Unofficially...
Psychologist B.F.
Skinner advised
people to wait
until they caught
someone doing
exactly what
they wanted,
then compliment
them with posi-
tive reinforce-
ment so that
action would
continue.

STRESS MANAGEMENT LIST

	Stressors	Ideas
A. Job-related stress		
1.		
2.		
3.		
4.		
5.		
B. Relationship stress		
1.		
2.		
3.		
4.		
5.		
C. Environment stress		
1.		
2.		
3.		
4.		
5.		
D. Socioeconomic stress		
1.		
2.		
3.		
4.		
5.		

Now, take that break I told you about. When you come back, make sure it's with a resolve to do whatever it takes to control the time you spend.

Just the facts

- Your hourly worth can be calculated by figuring what you earn per year divided by 244 working days divided by the number of hours you work each day.

- The average salaries of people in your profession should be considered when you're figuring out your worth.

- There are at least five different types of stress that affect how we handle our time—and five times as many ways to deal with that stress.

- Listing the causes of all your stress on a piece of paper often helps you think about ways to deal with them one at a time.

GET THE SCOOP ON...
How to accomplish the things that are necessary ▪ Determining how to prioritize your tasks
▪ How to achieve control over the items on
your to-do list ▪ How to become more
organized and get rid of old habits

Trying to Handle Everything at Once

Chapter 5

What do you really *have* to do? You really have to live, eat, and breathe. That's it. Everything else is optional.

Do you have to make a million by the time you're thirty in order to stay alive? No, you really don't— even though you think you might. Do you have to marry someone who loves you "until death do you part" in order to maintain a healthy lifestyle? No, though it might be nice if you did. Do you really have to work 24 hours a day, 7 days a week in order to reach your goals? Definitely not. In fact, it's been proven that you probably have to work far less than you do now, as long as you get rid of what my psychology professor called "fidi coco."

Fidi coco is a Polynesian word that basically means all the extra, the crap, the pieces of "stuff" that are unnecessary. It's the white noise in our existence, the words that don't mean anything, the hours that go by that we can't account for. It's the stuff you can get rid of and never miss.

Separating the wheat from the fidi coco

So, let's dispense with the fidi coco and get down to brass tacks. What do you absolutely, positively, desperately need to do during each day of your life?

Each of us will have a different answer to that question, but here are some possibilities:

- You need to do the work assigned to you by your boss—or the work you assign yourself.

- You need to keep yourself happy and give to others around you.

- You need to schedule yourself so that you don't waste time doing things haphazardly.

Pretty simple, right?

The truth is, you are forced to make decisions about what you need to do on a momentary basis. How do you do this?

- You focus on what really matters by constantly checking with yourself and asking: "Am I wasting time?"

- You don't stress out when the schedule you planned that morning is being disrupted by other more important tasks.

- You remember that the day doesn't have to be crammed with work for you to be productive.

- You expect interruptions and distractions, and you go with the flow.

- You learn to distinguish the urgent tasks from the important tasks.

Is it urgent, or is it just important?

Our lives are defined by how fast we can go. Packages are delivered overnight. Instant messages reach someone's computer almost immediately.

> **"**
> Fantasy is a necessary ingredient in living. It's a way of looking at life through the wrong end of a telescope...and that enables you to laugh at all of life's realities.
> —Theodor S. Geisel, a.k.a. "Dr. Seuss"
> **"**

Processes like credit applications and mortgage procedures are accomplished online in seconds when they used to take days. We are going so fast that everything has gone from "do it when you can" to "I need it yesterday."

Is everything really that urgent? No. Getting someone who's having a heart attack to a hospital is urgent. Saving a drowning child is urgent. Taking care of your own health or salvaging a relationship is urgent. The rest can wait.

Let's take the urge out of urgent and recognize that the work you do and the tasks you need to accomplish during the day are not a matter of life and death (unless you're in the medical profession or at the controls of a nuclear weapon). Let your heartbeat slow down a little, look at things more practically, and maybe you'll actually get something done within the time frame you need to do it.

One of the main reasons why people procrastinate is that they're frozen by the decision process. If you think everything is urgent, then there's absolutely no way you can make a decision whether to do Project A or Project B first. As a result, neither gets accomplished and you have an anxiety attack while going back and forth between them.

Part of this indecision is blamed on the fast pace we expect ourselves to keep. But part of the reason why we can't manage our time is because we don't know how to distinguish between the urgent and the simply important jobs we need to accomplish or problems we need to attend to.

If you attach the word "vital" or "urgent" to each trivial thing you have on your plate, then nothing takes greater importance over something else. It's self-defeating for you to try to manage time when

Watch Out!
Stress and all it
entails is largely
caused by unreal
expectations of
what we can
accomplish
during a given
amount of time.

you think that everything needs to be done now. So let's try to separate your tasks into three categories: vital, important, and trivial.

First things first, let's define each of these categories:

- Vital/Urgent: Something that calls for haste, immediate action; necessary to life; indispensable.

- Important: Something that means a great deal, that has some significance and value or influence and power.

- Trivial: Something unimportant, commonplace, insignificant or trifling.

Examples of tasks that would fall into these categories might include:

Vital:

- Anything the IRS asks you to do within a certain time frame.

- Demands from a lawyer/court to appear before them.

- A job you must do for your boss immediately or else you'll be fired.

- A spouse's threats to divorce if you don't...

- A child's threat to commit suicide.

- Handling an upset person/client/family member.

- Repairing a necessary piece of equipment.

- Paying the IRS what they demand or they will take your paycheck/house/car.

Important:

- Jobs with an upcoming deadline.

- Meetings you must attend, or preparation for important work.

- Keeping relationships intact.

- Preventing any kind of problem.

- Answering mail.

- Paying bills.

- Things that need to be done before the end of the day/week.

Trivial:

- Dealing with unimportant tasks or busywork.

- Handling junk mail.

- Fending off interruptions.

- Answering some phone calls (surveys, contest come-ons).

- Communicating with certain people (salespeople who solicit on the phone or door-to-door).

- Watching television.

- Some cleaning tasks (those that can easily be done whenever you have five minutes to spare).

The most ironic thing about determining what's important and what's urgent is that if important things are put off, they soon become urgent. And if you keep up with important tasks, your list of urgent jobs is going to be smaller.

Back to the example I gave you earlier: If my students had done that important paper little by little, they would have accomplished it on deadline or before, with little stress and more success. However, by putting off that important paper until a week before it was due, it became urgent.

Unofficially...
Marilyn Monroe was consistently late to her final movie, *Something's Got to Give*, and as a result, was fired from the production. Her problem? Fear and a very large dose of procrastination. Some of that stress could have been the result of the sinus problems she suffered from during the shooting of that film.

You have control over whether some of your projects are important or urgent. Scheduling your time is the way to control your own reaction to those urgencies, as well.

How to evaluate what needs to be done first

Think about these five questions:

- What is the most important thing in your life?
- What defines your life and gives it meaning?
- What do you want to do with your life?
- What do you want to accomplish?
- What would be the thing you would want to do most if you knew this was your last day?

If you use these questions as guidelines, evaluating what you need to do first every day is simple. However, when you have more than one item that ends up first on your list, you might need to come up with more specific evaluation questions.

What you do first reflects directly on your priorities. If your priority is to play sports, then making sure you clean out your closets is definitely not the first thing you're going to do today. However, if your mother has just informed you that if you don't, she's going to do it herself—and if she does it herself, she'll find the stash of adult entertainment magazines you have hidden in the back of the closet—then that task has just risen dramatically on your list of things to do today.

Whatever your decisions are means that you are deciding *against* doing something else. To further determine what's important, we have to ask ourselves another series of questions. Although I'm going to list them here, most of us can provide answers to these questions very quickly. It's only when several items end up being equally important to you that the decision becomes harder to make.

I strongly suggest you ask yourself these five questions for each day's decisions about what to do first. This is the best way to determine what's urgent, what's important, and what's trivial.

- What's my goal for the day?
- Which goal will bring me the greatest sense of accomplishment?
- Which completed task will affect the most people?
- Does the goal of completing one task rely upon or affect another?
- What will be the result if I neglect one of the tasks?

These questions should help you make decisions about what to do first, but remember that if you ignore making a decision, you are in effect still making a decision. And that non-decision could be the one that causes your important tasks to suddenly all become urgent at the same time, throwing you into a major tizzy.

Plan before you jump

With a bit of long-range planning, we can anticipate problems that might crop up with larger projects. We can also increase our skills in handling time if we prioritize and get used to doing it on a daily basis, checking on the long-range projects every week or month (depending on how far ahead you're planning). Once you get into the habit of planning, you won't have so many fires to put out along the way, and you'll reach the deadline intact, relaxed, and with a better product.

Quite a few writers face very tight deadlines on a regular basis. Writing is an art that is best produced with time and care, but some of us simply don't have

Timesaver
When planning a large project that will be spread over a long period of time, it'll save time if you create some sort of plan from the beginning, rather than waiting until you're well into the project.

that luxury. When an editor wants a book, it's in our best interests to meet that editor's deadline. However, writers are like everyone else and some tend to procrastinate. When that happens, they're burning the midnight oil trying to finish a book that could very easily have been done by producing 2 or 3 pages a day.

One good friend spent several weeks closeted in her home, working until all hours of the night, and literally pushing herself into a physical breakdown trying to finish a book. Instead of creating a weekly schedule for herself, she'd simply looked far into the future and went on with her daily life, writing a little as she went along, but not keeping to any specified page limit per day. The deadline came up too quickly for her, and as a result, she didn't meet it, lost her contract and her position within the editor's stable of writers.

One way writers meet deadlines is to figure out the page count they need to produce (whether the book is fiction, nonfiction, or a children's book), then divide that page number by the number of days between the time they agree to do the book and the date it's due.

When the figuring is done, it is time for the writer to figure out what is urgent, important, and trivial in his/her life. The important matters are deadlines for the first 25%, 50% and 100% of the book, but they don't need to be attended to right away if the editor wants a sample chapter before the contract is finalized. The way to accomplish the task at hand? Shove aside some other work, some appointments with friends, and another novel, and produce the sample chapter within a week—as agreed.

During the time set aside for working on the book, writers remind themselves of certain dates in the other parts of their lives: other appointments and matters to attend to by certain deadlines. "Trivial" matters, such as watching television and cleaning the house, are left for moments when the writer needs a break from writing. Potluck dinner parties for groups of friends are planned so the writer can see those he/she cares about all at once, instead of scheduling individual lunches. And some of the household chores are delegated to other members of the family—or hired out.

The writer figures out what he or she needs to accomplish each day, and by doing so, keeps the stress to a minimum, avoids interruptions and the occasional wrench that gets thrown into the works.

How do you evaluate what needs to be done first? With any kind of work, you need to take baby steps before the running begins. If you start running first, you're going to fall flat on your face. But, unlike babies, most of us have problems getting up and trying again and again and again—not to mention that picking yourself up and continuing is one of the greatest time-wasters. If you evaluate your tasks first, the likelihood of falling down is minimized.

Some of us do first what we hate to do, simply to get it out of the way, but I never met anyone who became successful by keeping up with their filing (my least favorite task). We also tend to follow habits. If you've always turned on the television first thing in the morning and watched the news, then it's hard to not reach for that knob and instead answer your phone messages first so that you can see how to plan your day.

Bright Idea
Keep track of *all* your time and how you spent it in a small notebook or in the day planner that you carry with you at all times. Also note your expenses so that you'll have them when it comes time to bill the client or pay yourself.

What are the urgent jobs? The tasks that you cannot put off. The ones you must accomplish before going on to anything else.

What's most important? The jobs that contribute to your goals in some way or another. That's the answer, pure and simple.

If a task doesn't get you anywhere, then it's not important and should be shoved farther down the list. You can do that type of job when you have time.

How do we decide what we're going to do and when we're going to do it? Here are some general guidelines:

- Scheduled items usually are accomplished before unscheduled items; thus, keep a to-do list of everything you need to do on a daily basis.

- The projects for which we have the tools or resources will be finished before the ones for which we're not prepared.

- People tend to do easier jobs before the more difficult ones.

- Whatever arrives first, gets done first.

- When a job can be completed in an hour/day, we'll do it because of the instant gratification.

- Jobs that will help our personal goals are the ones to which we'll attend most quickly.

- The squeakiest wheel will get greased quickest.

- Our habits dictate at what time of day certain jobs will be done.

- Deadlines are the best guarantee a job will be completed.

Creation and prioritization

Creation is the birth of an idea, project, or being. It is the actual moment of conception and the best time to set a schedule or to plan. Because this is the first step in a job or the result of a brainstorming session, few people look beyond creation until they start thinking about how they're going to reach the ultimate goal of what they've (up until now) only dreamed of in their minds.

For lawyers, the point of creation of a lawsuit is when they actually begin billable time. Advertising people start charging clients as soon as they come up with a feasible idea in a brainstorming session. An architect's initial drawings are charged to the clients, just as the finished products are. Even if you are self-employed, you should consider the birth of any new project as the time when you actually start paying yourself for work on that job.

The creation of a project gives you the perfect opportunity to see your work as something fresh and new. It's also the appropriate time to sketch out how many hours/days/weeks or months you believe the project will take to complete. I'm sure George Lucas had a vague idea that the two Star Wars trilogies would take a long time, but who knows whether he realized it would be almost two decades before he'd even be close to finishing? However, I've heard rumors that he was pretty aware of how much money he'd have to spend to produce the first film. His budget projections were pretty close, but his expectations of what the film would take in were way off—thankfully, he made tons more than he ever imagined. And we have more of his fantastic work to look forward to.

Once a project/job/relationship is begun and plans are tentatively made for how it will continue, it is time to consider priorities. It is important to consider when and how you will accomplish the

Unofficially...
The latest *Star Wars* release from George Lucas, *The Phantom Menace*, began, as all Lucas's films do, in a loose-leaf notebook and continued through almost four years of filming. The process was recorded by documentarian Lynne Hale.

various tasks or activities attached to any job or relationship, and as we've already stated, learning how to prioritize is an immensely integral component of time management.

Lynne Wenig, author of *The A to Z of Time Management*, suggests using a "triage" system for setting priorities. In medical terms, a "triage" system considers each case on an as-needed basis. On the battlefield, triage is commonly used to determine who is taken care of by quickly checking on their chances of survival. If a person has a chest wound and is unconscious with low blood pressure, triage would probably determine that that person would be one of the first to be taken to the operating room or worked on by doctors. By watching reruns of the television show "M*A*S*H," you can understand how this system operates. The instant decisions made during the triage process automatically prioritize the cases coming through the medic's station or in the hospital ward, and can be utilized by you to determine how to handle your own work.

On the battlefield, triage gives the person who needs immediate attention first priority, and the person who is injured but can wait for treatment gets second consideration. The last setting is for those victims who will most likely die anyway, so shouldn't be treated, the doctors' time being better spent on those whose chances for survival are much higher. It's a harsh way to look at your work, but if all activities were high priority, nothing would get done. In battle, if the doctors tried to treat everyone, but in no particular order, many more would end up dying. While seemingly harsh, triage has saved many lives—this same system, applied to your work, can save you precious time as well.

Wenig suggests index cards with different colors to indicate the priority of each task (green for critical, yellow for important, red for sometime in the future). Personally, I believe if you create more paper, you're going to waste time; I would suggest a simple numbering system, as mentioned earlier.

Think of priorities as you would the division of work between the CEO of a company and the receptionist. The CEO attends only the most important meetings; the rest he or she delegates to vice presidents, etc. The CEO deals with a select group of executives—probably fewer than six in number actually report to him/her. In a normal day, it is possible that the CEO never answers her/his own phone or writes his/her own letters. Golf time and vacation time is scheduled whenever he or she pleases and the rest of the company works within his time frame.

The vice presidents do the bulk of the supervisory work at the top management levels, work a solid week, but have vacation time and expense accounts built into their salaries. They often have 10-20 people reporting to them on certain projects, but they also have a supporting staff to take care of the less-important tasks.

Their secretaries/assistants usually work 40 hours a week and some overtime, answer their own phones and type their own letters, handle brushfires on a daily basis, fend off unwanted problems before they reach the vice president's desk, have a small support staff, and the usual amount of days off and vacation days.

Even farther down the totem pole are the people in the factories who work overtime on a regular basis, are paid far less, are responsible for produc-

Moneysaver
Pretend your time is worth twice what you've figured it to be, then calculate what you waste on trivial matters. The figure will amaze you and spur you into spending less time on unimportant tasks.

ing the very products that keep the CEO in golf shoes, and handle stress on a regular basis.

What's the point in this example? The number of priorities at the CEO level is less than the number of priorities at the bottom of the ladder. The decisions, believe it or not, are easier to make most of the time because there are people making secondary and lesser decisions all the way up the ladder. I'm not saying that CEO's have less stress; what I'm saying is that the unimportant jobs are usually done by others or can be delegated to others, thus the job actually becomes easier as the responsibility quotient gets higher. The CEO values his/her time, as do those around him/her. It is less likely to get wasted or squandered on insignificant tasks.

Perhaps you should believe you're a CEO—in charge of your own life—and that your time is just as valuable as that of the owner of a multimillion-dollar company. Then you will realize that making decisions about how to spend your day is extremely important and that you should be judicious in creating priorities for yourself.

Important questions to answer honestly

To be successful at keeping track of your tasks, prioritizing those that are important and those that can be left for a rainy day when you have nothing better to do, you really have to be honest with yourself about what's important.

You have to be aware of the psychological, physical, and mental implications of all your priorities, and keeping that in mind, here are some important questions you should answer honestly:

- What's my mission in life?
- How are these particular jobs or my roles in these situations going to affect my mission?

- For whom am I prioritizing—myself or others?
- How important are those other people to my ultimate goal/mission in life?
- How does my role in what happens today affect my life and the lives of the others around me?
- Who's making the suggestions for how I spend my time—and how important are those people to me?

This is what it's all about: people. When we realize that, everything else seems to fall into its proper place.

Searching for the proper balance

Your reactions to your circumstances determine how you handle priorities and the stress that goes along with misdiagnosed changes in your time. In order to keep everything in balance and to make the best use of the time you have, you need to keep a tight rein on your concentration and energy levels.

Each time you prioritize, you review and analyze your list with the past in mind, the present in planning view, and the future in consideration.

Be confident in your choices and know that even though you have written down what you want to do on a particular day, that list can change if the balance is thrown off.

Keeping your balance when managing your time is a bit like trying to walk a tightrope while juggling some balls. Better to let the balls fall than to lose your footing on that rope.

The best way to keep the balance is to keep your list in plain sight, make the decision to do the work, then do it, finish it, and move on to the next task on the list. The faster you move through the list, the

"

You and I periodically need to reprioritize and to sort out that which is extraneous in our lives.
—The Reverend Bartlett W. Gage, Associate Rector, St. John's Episcopal Church, Stamford, Connecticut (© 1997)

"

more quickly your goals will be realized, and the more productive you will be. Surprisingly, when you're done, you might glance up at the clock and realize you still have some time left. And how will you spend that time? Perhaps doing a hard-earned bit of relaxation? Or getting a jump on the next project?

How to reprioritize

Reprioritizing is the next step in managing your schedule. Often a project is begun, priorities are set, the job starts and someone realizes that Part A needs to be done before Part B, and that requires more materials or more help. That often happens in the movie business, and to use George Lucas as an example again, that was what he learned when studying how to write screenplays.

It's a fact of life in the writing business that stories often change and have to be adjusted because of those changes. Sometimes it's the characters themselves who tell the writer that a certain scene won't work (don't laugh—once a playwright or novelist or screenwriter takes the time to make a character come alive, that character often lets us in on secrets that we hadn't planned—and those secrets lead the story in a different direction than the writer had originally envisioned). If that happens, it's back to the drawing board to do a rewrite.

No story worth its salt was ever written and completed on the first run-through. A work is always edited and rewritten, sometimes pulled completely apart and started all over again.

The same is true with any business proposition. If everything went smoothly and perfectly, people would have no challenge, there'd be no jobs for those who are good at putting out brushfires, and there'd be no such word as reprioritizing.

When reprioritizing, it's always good to be able to give those involved in the job some notice, but it's not always possible to do so.

When you're the only one involved, it's a good idea to check on the progress you're making and reprioritize when:

- You see that one job has moved up in priority.

- Your deadlines have changed.

- You've finished something sooner than you expected.

- Someone has asked you to do something immediately.

- An urgent matter has popped up unexpectedly.

- You're sick and everything takes a backward slide.

Recognize disorganization and eliminate it

Disorganization is largely a result of not recognizing the importance of the things you are doing or the events in your life. Although it is sometimes caused by disorders such as Attention Deficit Disorder, disorganization plagues most of us—and steals time.

By being disorganized, you are failing to realize how much time you're losing by simply trying to find things. This is a major disruption. If you use a time log to figure out exactly how many minutes per day you're spending looking for that document you're sure is underneath that pile of other documents on your desk, you'll realize that by being organized, you could probably add at least another hour to your day.

Though it's often said that a messy desk is the sign of genius, that's not true. A messy desk or house or room is the sign of someone who's simply not taking the time to put something away in a place

Timesaver
Take a moment at the beginning and end of every day to check and see whether you've met your priorities. And give yourself extra time between jobs, just in case.

where they'll be able to instantly find it the next time they need it. A messy person is a disorganized person and a disorganized person is someone who has no control over their life and without that control, is losing valuable time.

How do you cure disorganization?

Timesaver
Handle each piece of paper that comes across your desk or into your mail only once. The more you throw away, the less you'll have to muddle through on your desk or countertop.

1. Clear off your desk. Use only what's necessary.

2. Create a system so that you'll know where important documents are filed.

3. Get rid of the idea that messiness = genius.

4. Screen out all the junk mail and everyday jobs and either dump them in the trash or let someone else handle them. Don't put them aside for "just in case" or "later" if you can pass them on. If it's something only you can deal with, transfer the information to your "to-do" list rather than keeping the extra piece of paper.

5. Stop procrastinating. Get rid of those tough jobs first.

6. Use a calendar or pocket planner to keep track of meetings and other important dates so you don't forget. Don't keep sticky notes or small pieces of paper to help you remember. Keep your calendar all in one place.

7. Create a plan and keep to that plan—every day.

8. Stop the interruptions. Put a sign on the door or let someone else know that you're not to be disturbed.

9. Focus! Don't let your attention be diverted by something else you'd rather do. Stick to the job until it's done.

10. Create priorities and if necessary, reprioritize.

Increase personal time

The number of hours we Americans spend on work has actually decreased with the advent of technology, yet the cry I hear from so many is that they don't have personal time. If you don't have personal time, it's not because you're working too hard. It's because you're not working efficiently enough to give yourself a break.

Get the fidi coco out of your life and leave some room for contemplation, relaxation, and communication. Check yourself every time someone asks, "What are you doing this weekend?" If you answer, "Well, I have a full weekend ahead of me. I'm so busy. I have to do XYZ," then you're not giving yourself a shot at true happiness.

When you ask a financial advisor where to put your money, they tell you to pay yourself first. Start a bank account and put the money into that account right away, before you get a chance to touch it. Get the company you work for to direct deposit that money into that account and get used to living without it. Then don't touch that money. Let it grow and don't count it unless you absolutely have to. That way, if you need it for an emergency, it's there.

You need to think of your time as your money and put some of that time away for yourself. First. And before you start spending your time on something else. Consider your personal time the most important time in your life—and schedule it before you schedule anything else.

You'll be happy you did—and you'll probably be healthier and have great relationships with family and friends, too. Isn't that the most important aspect of your life?

Moneysaver
Buy organizers
for your desk
(mini files, pen
and office-supply
holders, and a
small bookshelf)
when they're on
sale at the
beginning of the
school year, and
you'll save both
time and money
looking for items
you need on a
regular basis.

Eliminate time-wasting interruptions

Interruptions come in all shapes and sizes to rob us of the time necessary to complete the jobs and duties we need to during our everyday lives. By eliminating interruptions, we'll build an enormous amount of time back into our days.

Sometimes stopping interruptions is as easy as communicating with others about your work time vs. off time. Other times, more drastic measures need to be taken.

Some suggestions:

- Determine a certain period of the day when you'll answer all the interruptions. Don't do it at any other time except the time you designate.

- Create a set meeting time for those people who constantly have questions and remind everyone to write questions down and present them at that time.

- Turn off phones and computers when you truly need to work. Let technology work for you.

- Learn how to communicate your needs to those you work with and are close to so they'll understand when you say no.

- Keep a time log to see if you're being interrupted by the same things on a regular basis and analyze for patterns.

- Read Chapter 9.

Just the facts

- By dispensing with the fidi coco or unnecessary elements of your day, you can get the important tasks accomplished.

- Attaching the words vital or urgent to everything you have to do only serves to make prioritizing more difficult.

- By dividing jobs/tasks into three categories (vital, important, and trivial), you can more easily distinguish which jobs need to be done first.

- Once a job or relationship is created, the plan for how your time is used to fulfill its obligations begins.

- A disorganized desk/workspace is *not* the sign of genius—it's the sign of someone who's going to waste time looking for things.

- Schedule your personal time *first* and use it!

Goals and How to Meet Them On Time

Meeting today's goals in order to satisfy your lifetime goals ▪ Creating workable lists of goals and dealing with the need for changes ▪ Balancing deadlines without losing time ▪ Differentiating your perception of the future from the view of the people around you

Hourly, Daily, Weekly, Monthly, Yearly, Lifetime Goals

When I think of goals, the first person who comes to mind is Abraham Lincoln. I don't think Honest Abe ever kept a daily to-do list, because paper was too valuable to him when he was growing up, but I do sense that he had some goals that he worked toward from the first time he stepped foot in a school.

I fantasize that Abe sat in that one-room cabin reading his books by candlelight, dreaming of what he would become one day. Each moment that he spent reading and studying was a moment he stockpiled toward his lifetime goal. He took firm and positive steps in the right direction, learning all he could, making connections with people who could teach him, and taking the steps that would eventually bring him to the presidency.

Chapter 6

Timesaver
If you need
to share your
daily goals with
family, friends, or
office personnel,
make a copy of
them as you're
writing your
original to save
time. Carbon
paper is still
around!

Lincoln's journey was not an easy one. He lost all his money when a store he was working for went bankrupt, he lost his love (Ann Rutledge) when she died at the young age of 22 from a fever, he battled depression while studying for his law license, he ran unsuccessfully for the Whig nomination for U.S. Congress in 1843, and he had numerous other problems that plagued him throughout his rocky life. But he met his goals of leading the country and became one of the best presidents ever.

Many of his sayings have been extensively quoted, but I am most drawn to the ones that relate directly to work and time; thus, I'll give you my two favorites here. Regarding goals/planning, he said, "We must ask where we are and whither we are tending." And he also stated: "Nothing valuable can be lost by taking time."

No one could have defined goals and how to manage them better than that great gentleman.

Keep his steps to the White House in mind when you are separating your own immediate goals from your long-term ones.

Separating the immediate goals from the long-term goals

The idea of daily goals is one that we've already established and what most everyone thinks of immediately upon entering work or getting ready for the day. We can even think in advance to what we're going to do for the week or what plans we're making for the weekend. But how often do you think about the month? Or the year? Or your entire life?

Yes, we do a bit of dreaming now and again. We think of where we'd like to go and what we'd like to do, what we conceive of as our dream job or dream house, how we'd like to spend our retirement. But do we write down those goals and check on them on a regular basis? If not, we should!

One problem people have is realizing that our daily goals fold into our weekly goals and our weekly goals affect our monthly goals which, in turn, affect our yearly and lifetime goals. All are connected, all depend on one another, and we can't concentrate on the short-term while forgetting the long-term.

A basic way of determining which goals are immediate and which are long term is to think of the immediate goals as those you need to reach before you can get to the long-term goals. Immediate goals need to be accomplished today. For example, Lincoln had to learn how to read before he could finish a book. He had to practice his oratory skills before competing in a political campaign. He had to serve as a member of the Illinois General Assembly before moving on to becoming the Whig floor leader.

You get the point.

How to schedule yourself

One of the steps to planning the goals you'll meet throughout your life and career is to remember to set the goals. I know, that seems stupid to say, but so many people just go through life taking each moment as it comes, that they forget there's a reason for goals to begin with. And while I don't advocate expecting yourself to be able to meet all those goals, I do believe in using a roadmap to plan out where you're going and how you're going to get there. No one ever made it to Iceland from South America simply by driving North and hoping they'd hit it sooner or later. You have to plan. You have to have a map. And you need to realize that, at some point, you're going to have to take a boat!

> **"**
> It's better to have a bad plan than no plan at all.
> —Charles De Gaulle
> **"**

Scheduling yourself means that you must have a thorough understanding of the amount of time you have and the number of tasks you have to do within that amount of time. In that respect, deadlines are wonderful tools because most of us wouldn't accomplish a darn thing without them.

One good idea in beginning the scheduling process is to watch the connections between your short-term and long-term goals by writing them down.

- **Create a master list.** By instituting a master to-do list that details the steps you'll take toward each long-term goal, you'll be able to see the road in front of you and anticipate any turns and dead-ends along the way. You might not always see them until you almost run off the road, but anticipating them means you'll have a Plan B in case you get derailed.

  This master list is not written in stone. It'll change on a regular basis. For instance, if you change your mind about where your life is taking you, if you fall out of love with the person with whom you were going to spend the rest of your life, or if you decide that nuclear medicine just isn't for you, your master list will change as a result. Be flexible. Let those changes occur and remember that change will be the only constant in your life.

- **Make your goals as specific as possible.** Don't say, "I'm going to make enough money to build a house," say, "I'm going to save $15,000 within ten years, so that I can start building a three-bedroom, two-bath house."

  When you create a specific goal, your path to that goal becomes clearer. You can then work on the steps you'll take to finish the job/task or reach the goal. Without specific details, it's almost impossible for you to map out a time schedule.

▪ **Assign yourself deadlines.** Give yourself a certain time frame within which you want to get specific jobs accomplished. Some of those tasks will already have deadlines attached to them when you start them, but if they don't, it's up to you to build a due date into them.

By giving yourself a deadline, you're implanting a timely device into your mind that will urge you to finish the project or meet the goal by that date. Without a date, we will have a tendency to put off the job until the pressure starts to build. Procrastination builds stress—and who needs that?

▪ **Set reasonable goals for yourself.** By really thinking about what you need to do and when it should be done, you are able to be rational. Giving yourself a challenge is fine, but be realistic. Don't think that because one person built a company and made a million dollars the first year, that you'll be able to do the same. Figure the average amount of time it takes to complete the goal you're trying to reach, then figure out what your work schedule and patterns are, before you set the goal.

If you set too many goals for yourself within a short span of time, how many of them will you actually be able to reach? Remember that for time management to work, it needs to be based in reality, and the reality is that not all goals are going to be attainable. Don't make it difficult for yourself from the get-go. Give

Moneysaver
Keep a copy of your master list of goals inside your checking account/savings book. Every time you write out a check or make a withdrawal, you'll be reminded of saving money for what you *really* want to do.

yourself sensible time limits to see your dreams realized—and don't put yourself so high in the clouds that you can't still place your feet on the ground.

▪ **Create balanced goals.** If you have several things you want to do, make sure they are compatible with each other. A desire to dance on the Broadway stage isn't going to be realized if you have no intention of spending lots of hours in a dance studio learning the steps. It's also probably not going to be possible to have five children while you're trying to attain the goal of dancing on Broadway—literally because being pregnant and kicking your legs up as high as a Rockette simply hasn't been done before.

If you find that one of your goals is keeping you from reaching another, perhaps you need to make a choice between the two. People often find that this is a problem when they're weighing certain relationship goals against career goals. It's difficult to make the choice between the two, but often it simply has to be done. Weigh which one is more important for you and choose the one that will bring you closer to the lifetime goals you've set up for yourself. Sometimes it's necessary to find a middle ground—some point at which you'll be comfortable. Compromise is often a very good thing. It eases stress when you let go. And saves the time you'd waste worrying about making an otherwise impossible decision.

▪ **Write your goals down.** Whenever you do a checklist of what you want to do and when you want to do it, you need to put it on paper. Don't just do a checklist in your head. When you write down your goals/deadlines/objectives, you're doing more than giving yourself something to cross off a list. You're clarifying what's really important to you. By writing down your goals, you're showing yourself how invested you are in seeing those things happen.

When your goals change, you need to rewrite that list. Keep your list of lifetime goals somewhere you can see it or get to it often. Putting it in a safety deposit box may seem a little over-the-top, but at least you know where the list is when you need it. Some people post their goals above their workspace so they'll be reminded on a daily basis; others do not want people to see their list, so they prefer keeping it in a small notebook or their daily planner. Wherever you keep yours, keep it! Your goals give you the direction and purpose you need to move forward in your life.

Quick ways to create lists of goals

The best way to work out your goals is to list them in four columns: lifetime, annual, monthly/weekly, immediate. I strongly suggest doing this on an erasable board, so that each time you finish a project/task or reach your desired goal, you can erase it and start over again. Other people suggest you write your lifetime goals down on paper and put them away so you can check on them later, but if you want to have your goals recorded where you can see them, a little message board right by your desk, on the refrigerator, or next to the phone is easiest.

List only fifteen events, then check the "time" column where the event belongs. As the event moves closer to your immediate time frame, all you

Bright Idea
Make an appointment with a friend or loved one to go over your goals at least once a year—perhaps as a New Year's resolution—to see whether you're both still on track.

then have to do is erase the checkmark in the weekly/monthly, annual, or lifetime column and move the check up.

Here's what the original will look like when complete. I've inserted my goals from a month ago. I'll also show a rewrite with today's version, so you can see the difference.

Watch Out!
Don't forget to cross off the tasks you've finished or the goals you've reached—and to celebrate by taking a deep cleansing breath before plunging into the next task.

Activity/Goal	Life-Time	This Year	This Month	This Week	Imme-diately
Trip to Bahamas					X
Finish 9 chapters of book				X	
Move to Lake City			X		
Find Mortgage					X
Pack					X
Get paperwork for mortgage					X
Raise money for down payment		X			
Contact group to see movie					X
Send out copies of short story		X			
Birthday cards for May			X		
Publish novels	X	X			
Accumulate retirement	X				
Trip to Africa	X				
Condo in New Smyrna	X				
Prepare for tenure		X			

Once the master list is done, you can see what's ahead of you and those tasks that need to be broken down into smaller tasks so you can reach your ultimate goal. For instance, in order to finish nine chapters of my book, I had to reach a daily goal of a certain number of pages, edit them, e-mail them to my editor, then wait for his reply and editing suggestions. That one goal turned out to be multilayered because there were a few tasks that needed to be accomplished in order for that goal to be met.

Look at how that list has changed in the past month.

Activity/Goal	Life-Time	This Year	This Month	This Week	Imme-diately
Finish 9 chapters of book					X
Move to Lake City				X	
Find Mortgage			X		
Pack					X
Get paperwork for mortgage					X
Raise money for down payment					X
Send out copies of shortstory		X			
Birthday cards for June					X
Publish novels	X	X			
Accumulate retirement	X				
Trip to Africa	X				
Condo in New Smyrna	X				
Prepare for tenure		X			

Several of the items have disappeared from the list (i.e. Trip to Bahamas, Contact Group for Movie) or been changed (i.e. Birthday cards for May has changed to June and become an immediate task) and others have moved into another column (i.e. the moving tasks have become things I need to attend to today). In addition, I could add more tasks to that list, but I wanted you to simply see how it changes.

Naturally, this is a quick and easy overall goal list. In order to take the steps to complete each of these tasks/goals, you must create a to-do list on a daily basis, and that list needs to enumerate the specific steps you'll take on that particular day.

What's on your to-do list today?

As we get older, our lives become more complicated. We also don't produce as many dendrites as we used to, so sometimes things get forgotten. And I'm not just speaking to septuagenarians out there. When you have a number of projects or tasks to attend to, it's very easy for you to forget one of the steps or one of the things you were supposed to pick up at the store. It's not necessarily a sign of aging or Alzheimer's—it's simply a sign that we have too much going on and need to take control over it. I call it intellectual overload, a nice way of saying I'm trying to fit too many things into my already full brain.

To believe that you can keep track of all your appointments, errands, jobs, tasks, relationship commitments, promises, needs, and wants without writing at least some of them down is absurd. Even those with the best memories tend to forget something occasionally. And it's nothing to be ashamed of. Powerful people like Hillary Clinton, Bill Gates, Madeleine Albright, and many others rely on lists to get them through the day. One of the bestselling devices of all times has been the day planner and its computerized version, the palm planner. Why? Because busy people make lists of what they need to do that day, prioritize the tasks on the list, then check them off as they finish them.

By taking a moment or two in the morning, you can jot down what you believe you need to do during the day. Take a quick look at the list and figure

> **"**
> It would be interesting to impress your memory engrams on a computer, doctor. The resulting flood of illogic would be most entertaining.
> —The character Spock in "Star Trek" (1966)
> **"**

out what can be delegated to others, then divide the tasks up according to when you want to accomplish those tasks.

Some simple hints for your daily to-do list:

■ Keep it on one piece of paper.

■ Keep it with you at all times.

■ Check off the tasks as you finish.

■ Write down phone numbers/e-mail addresses of people you need to contact right on that list (saves time looking for them later).

■ Do the things you like least when you have the most energy.

■ When you feel yourself getting tired, do one of the high payoff/most satisfying of your tasks and you'll be recharged.

■ Group similar tasks, errands, or appointments so they can be done simultaneously (like phone calls or picking up items from the store).

■ Estimate the time it will take to complete each task.

■ Schedule time for yourself to take a breather.

■ At the end of the day, push all unfinished tasks to the next day or delegate them to others.

Managing deadlines

When you have several converging deadlines and you're trying to figure out how to keep all those juggling balls in the air, the best thing to do is take a deep breath and figure out how to do a bit on each project during the same day. I've often had to balance end-of-the-semester finals with book deadlines, or as I am doing now, a book deadline with moving and mortgages and all that goes along with them. People often ask how I do it and I honestly don't know sometimes. There are days I feel like the top of my head is ready to blow off and that I'll get nothing accomplished; then I buckle down, make a list, and take care of first things first.

Bright Idea
It's best to remember what meteorologists were saying when Hurricane Floyd whipped up the East Coast of the United States in 1999: Take care of your lives first. You can replace belongings.

Through the research for this book, I see that most people who are good at managing time commonly do the same thing: They realize that it's impossible to get everything done, so they take care of the most important aspects first. If a house is burning down, you don't worry about the furniture, you worry about the human beings, then the animals, then perhaps some treasured, irreplaceable items, but the material things come last. Life comes first.

One of the most effective ways of handling deadlines is to recognize them ahead of time and prepare. For each item on your to-do list, you assign a date and time when it needs to be done. If you keep on top of all the chores you need to do on a daily basis and you've successfully broken down the larger assignments into smaller chunks, then when your deadlines loom, most of your work will already be done.

If your deadlines are not reliant just on the work you produce but the work produced by others as well, then encourage your co-workers or family members to utilize to-do lists as well. When you have a moment, get together and compare lists to make sure the people with whom you're working are moving along at the same pace (or at least close to the same pace) on the project as you are.

What happens if you miss a deadline? If you've known the deadline beforehand and still miss it because you had some urgent matters come up or the car didn't start or the pipes under the bathroom sink exploded, then you'll pay the piper. And you pick yourself up and continue. However, if you miss a deadline simply because you procrastinated or let trivial matters get in the way of important ones, then you'll lose valuable time and money (ask anyone who's not paid a parking ticket, missed the April 15 tax deadline, or lost a license because they forgot to renew it).

Sometimes the deadline comes up and hits us in the forehead, demanding we pay attention to it. If we do, we're able to close those doors and binge— spend all our time on the project—and come out blinking and yawning, but done. However, doing that on a regular basis is not only poor time management, but will do a job on you physically. Simply planning ahead for your deadlines and meeting them in a rational, sane manner will remove the anxiety-ridden feeling and replace it with a smile.

Working smart/smart work

If wasting time on irrelevant projects or disorganized thinking is leading you astray from what you need to do, you then need to get tough on yourself. If you've figured out all your priorities and your deadlines and you're still not meeting them, you need to sit yourself down and ask yourself why.

Are you afraid of succeeding? Is there something in your life that keeps telling you that you need to be punished by yourself and those around you? What's the real reason all this is happening if you have the skills necessary to manage your time and work smart?

Working smart simply means you do what you need when you need to do it in order to get where you want to be. You don't waste time on interruptions, you don't shuffle papers on your desk that you've looked through a million times before, you

Watch Out!
Plan a few moments occasionally to recharge your batteries. Some gazing-at-the-clouds time will help you keep your energy level up so that you can meet deadlines with relatively little anxiety.

don't run to someone else and complain for an hour about not being able to meet the deadline when you can utilize that time to do something about it!

This is tough love, folks. You are responsible for making sure that you work in an organized, professional, timesaving manner. In your hands, you have the tool that will take you from losing time, money, and energy by spinning your wheels, to making time for yourself, meeting your monetary needs, and conserving your energy for things you really want to do.

You make the choice to work smart and do smart work, work that needs to be done at that moment so that you can reach your goals. Only you can make that decision.

So, what are you waiting for?

The future and how to meet it

Change is one thing that is an absolute constant in every person's life, yet it is the thing we resist the most. You can see change in the world around you every day. Trees grow, flowers blossom and die, the sand shifts around the seashore, mountains change shape, volcanoes erupt, animals either adapt to new surroundings or become extinct.

In relationships, we tend to interpret change as something bad. We think about people whose marriages have fallen apart and about their reasons for divorcing—"He's not the same anymore. The passion has died down." Relationships change, because we all change on a daily basis. But is that change necessarily bad and should we give up on those relationships or the world around us because of change?

If change is such a constant, then why do we resist it so strongly?

Over the relatively short course of time that this world has been in existence, it has gone through so many changes that some specialists have spent their lifetimes studying them and wondering about them. We have gone through an Ice Age, an Industrial Age, an Atomic Age, and we're still going. People have predicted the world would end thousands of times, yet it's still here. Different, maybe, but we're still around.

Perhaps I'm getting a little philosophical here, but I can't help wonder why time and the changes it brings with it aren't accepted more readily. Why do we resist the thought that as the moments go by, the world evolves? It's a fact, and there's nothing we can do to change it. Life begins, and it ends. The cycle continues, whether we like it or not.

And why do we think that if people around us change their habits, they are more difficult to deal with? And, the most important question, why do we, ourselves, balk at the idea of adjusting our own habits to make life a little easier?

The only way to deal with our future is to realize that change will come. It's the one constant we have in our lives—and how ironic that the constant we have is that everything will continue to change on a regular basis. There is absolutely nothing that remains the same throughout its whole existence. Why should we?

To face a future in which you wish to manage time more sensibly, you must first realize that there will be moments when you will have to shift gears in order to maintain some semblance of control. You'll have to adjust, in some respects, in order to get the desired result. You'll have to reprioritize, check your goals once again, change your mind, adjust your thinking, reevaluate your beliefs.

Unofficially...
When President Clinton was going through the Monica Lewinsky scandal, the one positive thing the media and people in the know could say about him was that he always rolled with the punches and adapted well to change. That was his strength.

Your perception of the future

We always expect the future to be brighter than the past. We look forward to it with the same kind of anticipation that a child does Christmas or birthdays. We expect everything to be better, bigger, more complete. What we don't realize is that there will be no changes in our future without some positive changes today.

What we do now affects how our life is going to be ten years from now. If you waste time now, it will affect you later somehow. If you don't take care of a problem now, it won't go away. If you don't pay that IRS bill today, they'll catch you a couple of years from now.

The future is twofold: You do have some control over it, but you don't have any control over some of the aspects. It's the acceptance of those two converging realities that most of us have problems balancing.

If you use your goals as steps toward building your future and realize that you'll have to adjust to changes along the way, you'll be in the best position to utilize time to your advantage as you move toward those goals.

We need goals to stay alive, to reach that precious future. Having something to shoot for is reason enough to take that next breath and build toward the next day. Perhaps that's one of the reasons that retired people who have had dynamic careers are dead within 18 months after reaching that "goal" of being retired. Those who keep working have a better chance for a longer life—whether that work is different from what they've done during the better portion of their career or whether it's the same job they have had since they were seventeen.

Recently, a television movie starring Sidney Poitier titled "The Simple Life of Noah Dearborn" eloquently established that truth. Dearborn, a man devoted to his work, has somehow evaded age, and when a psychologist starts investigating, she is amazed that one of the reasons this man appears to have stayed young is that he spends each moment active and working. It's a philosophy that affects everyone else in the movie and ultimately changes their lives. What I got from the story is that Noah was devoting his life to something he loved (the creation of fine cabinetry and wood furniture) and by keeping his talents alive, he kept his brain and body active, thus lengthening his life span.

At one point in the story, he states that his beliefs came from what his uncle taught him: "When a man loves his work, truly loves it, sickness and death will get tired of chasing you. And just finally give up and leave you alone." Though that theory might not work for everyone, it defines Noah's view of the future. He believed he had a future and that life would continue.

Another example of that positive work ethic is the Delaney sisters. When they wrote *Having Our Say*, both sisters were over 100 years old. They attributed their long life to having a healthy diet, doing yoga, and looking forward to the future. Born at the end of the 1800s, both women were quite familiar with the hardships of slavery since their father had been a slave, and the sisters themselves endured the prejudice of growing up in the South, and the hardships of trying to get a college education when it was simply not acceptable. Yet their whole family (all ten siblings) were graduated from college and went on to become successful.

Unofficially...
Mary Kay, the owner of Mary Kay Cosmetics, prints up little pink note pads for her employees on which she urges them to list "The Six Most Important Things I Must Do Tomorrow." She got the idea from Jay Schwab, president of one of the nation's largest steel companies.

Did the sisters look back on their pasts and feel sorry for themselves? Did they let their pasts stop them from being hopeful for the future? Did they let their experiences color their thoughts? Yes and no. They learned from their pasts and adjusted themselves accordingly. Instead of being defeated, they grew stronger. They gathered wisdom and used it to honestly look at the road ahead of them and figure the best way to traverse it.

In a nutshell, that's what you should be doing as you learn how to manage the moments you have today. Focus on what you are learning, don't wallow in failures, and keep revising those lifetime goals so you won't wander aimlessly.

Always ask yourself: Am I doing the best I can with my time right at this moment? And if you do, the future will take care of itself.

Others' perception of your future

Maybe your mother wanted you to be a doctor or your father expected you to follow in his footsteps and take over the car sales business, but you had different ideas. Others see our future as fitting in with theirs and they have their own agendas for how they need you to be there—and their agendas, more often that not, do not mesh with yours.

How do you overcome the conundrum of someone else's expectations of your life, your responsibilities, duties, and dreams being different from your own? Perhaps showing them your list of goals would be a positive step in helping them see where you are headed in your life. Or, a sit-down talk where both of you spell out exactly what you want from each other might be in order.

When you try to be what everyone else wants you to be, you lose a piece of yourself. In order to

maintain your individuality and keep your goals/
dreams intact, you need to be able to communicate
to others that what you want, need, or desire can
dovetail with their wants, needs, and desires...but
only if you talk it out. You might need to make some
compromises (i.e. spending weekends with your
family in exchange for extra meeting time during
the weeknights or giving up your book collection in
order to make room for your roommate's computer
desk), but you can find some balance if you both
write down your goals/needs and compare them at
a time when you're not angry.

Be reasonable and compassionate when trying
to balance the time you need with someone else's
time considerations. You might not get everything
you want, but you both will end up with some satisfaction if you figure you'll both come out on top in
the end if you work together.

Call it compromise

Compromise is the healthiest solution when you're
expecting to do one thing and the people you're
working with, living with, or in love with expect you
to do another. Don't think of compromise as failure
or as losing something you want. Think of it as getting at least half of what you want.

If you need to compromise on something that
affects your time schedule or a deadline you have
set, first see if there's a way that you can rearrange
your time to accommodate both. If there's not, then
a sit-down, intelligent, rational, and reasonable discussion is necessary.

As Mr. Spock of "Star Trek" says, being illogical
doesn't work. You must use logic and weigh the pros
and cons of the different types of compromise on
the table in front of you. Your first inclination will

be to choose the one that benefits you the greatest, but what you really need to do is decide what your priorities are. If the most important priority is your relationship with the person, then you need to be a bit more flexible. If the first priority is the job at hand and the person is not someone who's important to your life, your career, or your future, then figure what's going to best benefit your ultimate goal.

Whatever the case, compromise and move on. You've got a lot of work to do and wasting time being frustrated by this compromise is just that: a waste of time.

Interpreting how your world works

There are several facts about the world that are simply not negotiable: We are born, we suffer a little (or a lot) and we die. As Jim Morrison of "The Doors" said, none of us gets out of this place alive. We're not going to live forever, no matter how well we take care of ourselves, how organized we are about our time, and how nice we are to everyone around us. Yet some of us live as though that were the case, and we all grieve when those we love pass on.

The basic parameters for human life are the same for everyone, yet the way your particular world works largely hinges on how you react to people, how you manage your life and time, and what your attitude is.

Understanding the patterns of your life takes little more than listing the important events you've experienced and your reactions to them.

We are creatures of habit and we tend to repeat the same patterns over and over again. That's why it's so difficult for people to make changes in their lives—like eating the right foods, getting rid of bad habits, learning to incorporate exercise into each day, or managing the time spent. If you examine the patterns you've followed and understand them, it's the first step toward making any big changes you need to incorporate in order to enjoy a better, more fulfilling life.

Just the facts

- Immediate or daily goals should blend easily into your weekly, monthly, yearly, and lifetime goals in order for everything to be accomplished in a timely manner.

- Scheduling yourself is a necessary habit to have if you want to save time. Without a schedule, it's like getting into a car and just heading straight—you won't get anywhere but into an accident.

- A master to-do list will show you everything you need to accomplish and give you some idea of what needs to be done first.

- Taking a moment every morning to create that day's to-do list saves you hours later on.

- An honest evaluation of what you see in your future and a conversation with those close to you about it will help everyone understand your needs.

- Compromise is not failure. It's simply a different way of meeting your goals and good practice in working with others as a team.

GET THE SCOOP ON...
Planning for your different life goals ▪ Setting
up your personal, professional, creative, and
academic goals ▪ How to differentiate between
family and personal goals ▪ How to meet someone else's deadlines without sacrificing your
own goals ▪ How to be proactive

Goals

Chapter 7

Those of you who think that people who talk about their goals are just voicing pipe dreams don't have the respect that you should for that type of planning. Goal-setting is a basic ingredient of good time-planning and those who are able to speak about what their goals are for today, next week, and the future are actually setting some of their plans into motion just by talking about them.

Without dreams, people give up the zest for living and fade away. Even those with the most horrible of lives have goals—sometimes it might be simply to get through the day alive or to make it to the next meal or through another night without freezing to death, but those are vital goals, goals that are based in reality and serve to provide life for the people who plan them.

Then there are those who have what we need and want and still need and want more. Their goals might be loftier and monetarily based, more materialistic than that person on the street who wants a warm place to spend the night, but to them, their goals are equally as important.

> **"**
>
> Our song is the
> voice of desire,
> that haunts our
> dreams.
>
> —Robert Bridges
>
> **"**

In order to differentiate between the various types of goals that might fuel your existence, you need to break them down into categories, then break those categories down into importance and deadline factors.

Differentiating between your many goals

Every one of us believes we have a future. And every one of us has heard that our future is what we make of it. If you feel that you are spinning out of control, that you are lost, confused, overwhelmed, regretful, guilty, or frustrated, then you need to align your goals in a way that will enlighten you to what you really need—and the realistic ways for attaining those needs.

We don't get a second chance at this life. This is it. The now is what you get, and as Tony Robbins says, "Positive changes can't happen without goals."

So, start somewhere. Concentrate on putting your life into focus. Create some steps to reach the goals that are important to you, then set your goals again and work toward them once more. Continue in that process until you see that by setting goals you're giving yourself a chance to live the way you really want to and to take control over that downward spiral of time that has you unhappy enough to pick up this book.

Setting goals is a powerful process. It:

■ Keeps people in dire situations alive.

■ Helps creative people continue to send out their work for public critique.

■ Gives a sense of meaning and importance to our lives.

■ Allows a person with a terminal illness to miraculously spring back to life.

Don't deny your goals. Take them in hand and let them rule the way you use your time.

Personal goals

When we look from the point where we now stand toward the future, we sometimes think the future will never come; but time has a way of catching up with us and overtaking us before we have a moment to plan. Take that moment now and think about what your ideal life would be like.

Ask yourself the following questions:

■ If I had my choice of the ideal life, where would I live?

■ What would I do for a career?

■ What kind of family would I have?

■ Who would be my friends?

■ How much money would be enough for me?

■ What would people think of me?

■ What strengths would I have?

■ What would be the ideal career for me?

■ How would I deal with people?

■ How old would I be when I died?

Now think of these questions and draw a lifeline for yourself. Place each of the answers to your questions on the line and determine when you want certain things to happen. It might look like the following personal-goals timeline.

By analyzing this timeline, you can see that some goals will take a short portion of the 90+ years I'd like to live, while others will be worked on throughout my lifetime.

In addition to looking at the timeline positively, you might also consider creating one by asking yourself questions like:

Bright Idea
Set goals for broadening your horizons! Think about travel and cultural activities in your future.

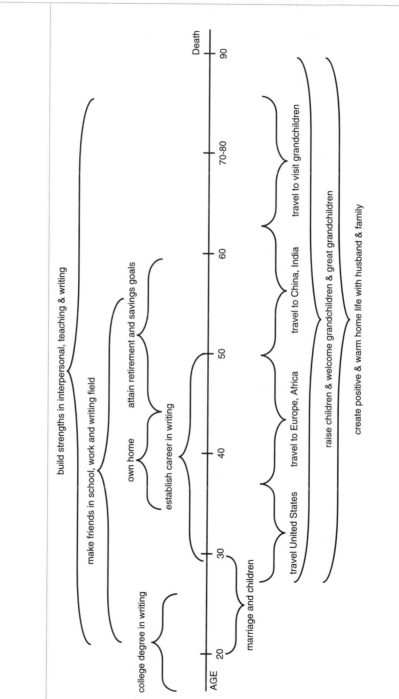

- What have been my greatest disappointments?
- What have been my greatest joys?
- What are my greatest successes?
- What are my most devastating defeats?
- Where do my weaknesses lie?
- What about my strengths?
- What do I still want to do?
- What are the goals I've already achieved?
- What other trials and tribulations might I face?
- What do I want to see in my future?

Do the timeline the same way as the example. Put your failures on one side of the line and your successes on the other. Make sure you create the timeline to cover just the age you already are.

Now, list your personal goals in a chronological fashion. Consider your age, then look forward 1 year, then 5, then 10, then 20, 30, 50 years, and be specific. Remember that you should include information about the relationships in your life (or those you might like to have) and how they will affect you personally. Keep these goals as personal as you can—we'll deal with career goals later in the chapter, but you might want to include career goals if they will affect you personally.

For example:

- One year from now I'd like to be:

1.

2.

3.

4.

5.

Watch Out!
Be careful not to bite off more than you can chew. Remember that an unwieldy task is more likely left undone.

■ Five years from now, I'd like to meet the following personal goals:

1.

2.

3.

4.

5.

■ In ten years, I want to be doing the following:

1.

2.

3.

4.

5.

■ In twenty years, I hope to have reached these goals:

1.

2.

3.

4.

5.

■ By the time I'm ____ years old, I hope to have attained all of the following goals:

1.

2.

3.

4.

5.

Keep this list for yourself and check it on a regular basis. Give yourself a check (or star, or heart) each time you reach a goal—extra credit if you reach it early! Then periodically make the list again and see how your goals have changed or rearranged themselves according to how your needs have changed as you age.

Business goals

Your career goals are likely to be the ones about which you have the clearest definition. You probably know what you'd like to be professionally and where that particular career will take you in 5, 10, or 20 years. By taking a close look at your professional goals, you can define the specifics of how you will meet those long-term goals by working on steps on a daily basis.

Your goals should work like a pyramid, with your immediate goals at the top and the overall reasons for having those goals supporting base of the structure. In a typical daily planner, to-do lists are broken down in the following manner: hourly, daily, weekly, monthly, yearly. That's the basic pyramid structure into which you need to also break your career goals. Your hourly tasks will fit into your daily goals, which will join together to meet your weekly, monthly, annual, and ultimately, your lifetime goals. Without taking your objectives step by step, you will not be able to create the whole package and meet the ultimate goal of success: where you want to be professionally by the time you retire.

By setting your career goals down on paper, you can then work backwards and figure out exactly what it's going to take to make those goals a reality. Sometimes this backwards-time approach is the only way you can see whether you're being realistic in believing that you'll be the CEO of John Smith Company within the next ten years or whether dropping out of society to spend time discovering the

Bright Idea
Set specific short-term goals that will be definitive steps toward your long-term, more complex, goals.

wilds of Africa for three years will be beneficial to your ultimate career as a primatologist. At thirty, your goal of being CEO might be reachable if you're already in a management position. At forty, it might make more sense—especially if you're a high-powered vice president of that company. But at twenty, you have a few more details to consider—and the time to do that type of planning. Remember, however, that what you decide to do at twenty will affect the rest of your life…. Make careful decisions and remember your future depends on how you plan where you are in your life and where you want to be.

Remember when creating a list of goals for your professional life that you break those goals down into small steps. If we give ourselves specific increments to achieve, we can celebrate that triumph and take a deep breath to get ready for the next one.

Don't do this:

- Weekly goal: Ask boss for raise and promotion.

- Monthly goal: Start own business.

- Yearly goal: Maintain high sales and increase financial security.

- Lifetime goal: Retire on the income of the stocks from my company.

These goals are vague and, as such, you're not going to be able to take the steps you need to reach them. You should be a lot more explicit when defining your goals and how you'll reach them. If your lifetime goal is to retire on income from your stocks, then your initial goal should be to buy several stocks out of each week's paycheck. Then pray the Dow does its thing and your stocks don't bottom out during the next decade. The point is to make specific plans, not vague pipe dreams.

Instead, be reasonable. Remember how long it takes to get certain things done. For example:

- Weekly goal: Apply for positions in local engineering firms.

- Monthly goal: Begin a job.

- Yearly goal: Learn what your company has to offer and start planning for promotion.

- Five-year goal: Attain lower-level managerial or executive position. Obtain an MBA.

- Ten-year goal: Branch out and start own consulting firm.

- Twenty-five-year goal: Maintain successful firm with several employees. Earn at least six figures a year and start preparing to retire on IRAs and pension plan set up fifteen years earlier.

This plan is much more specific and can be achieved by simple work ethics that are practiced on a daily basis.

Remember when setting your professional goals that you need to analyze your own strengths and weaknesses, as well as your reasons for choosing the career you are focusing on. If your choice of a legal career has been made because your girlfriend thinks John Grisham is really cool, but you absolutely love aeronautics, then you're being unfair to yourself. Sometimes it's wiser to listen to your own heart and follow the talents you have than to believe in what others tell you. Don't try to be a mathematics professor if you have trouble balancing your checkbook and don't follow the sun on your surfboard if you wipe out every five minutes.

If you can't quite figure out which career would be best for you, take some of the aptitude tests offered on the Web or go to your local employment

Watch Out!
When planning goals many years in advance, make sure you consider *all* the steps you need to take to reach those long-term objectives. By considering them now, you'll save time and energy later.

center and speak with a counselor. Life is too short to waste time going from job to job because you can't find one that suits your talents and desires. Better to decide now that you want to be a photographer and work toward that goal than to realize when you're 60 that you wasted most of your life as a telephone operator.

Here are some things to consider about yourself if you're lost as to where your professional life will lead you:

Timesaver
Read the periodicals specific to the market you want to enter long before you get into a responsible position. By studying them, you'll be ahead of your constituents.

- In what areas do you think you have the greatest knowledge?

- What's your personality like? Do you work well with others or alone?

- How about physical fitness? Are you a couch potato or a rock climber?

- Do you tend to lead others or are you a follower?

- Is your mental acuity a strength? Are you quick to make decisions?

- Can you act quickly on the spur of the moment or do you always have a plan? Do you tend to do things before thinking them through?

- What are your greatest successes and how did you achieve them?

- What are your greatest failures and did you overcome them? If so, how? If not, why?

- How do you work? Are you consistent and systematic or do you accomplish more when "flying by the seat of your pants"?

- Are your personal skills honed? Do you like to talk to others or would you rather listen?

By evaluating your honest answers to these questions, you should be able to divide your strengths and weaknesses, according to five general areas: knowledge, communication skills, leadership qualities, mental abilities, and personal skills.

Then match the goals you have with the skills you have. If you want to sail the South Pacific, but get chronically seasick, then you might as well strike that goal off your list.

To reach your career objectives, you must be honest with yourself. If you find you're heading for a goal but you don't have the necessary means to get there (like the right degree or connections), then you need to pause and build the required experience or gain the necessary abilities you need to reach the goals you've set out for yourself.

Creative goals

Creative people are often discouraged from setting goals by disparaging friends and family who believe that you can never make a living from your art. I don't think that Michaelangelo, Meryl Streep, Stephen King, John Updike, Georgia O'Keefe, the Beatles, Maria Callas, Bob Hope, Rosie O'Donnell, Mikhail Barishnikov, Judith Jameson, Bill Cosby, Ernest Hemingway, Virginia Woolf, Bob Fosse, Walt Disney, Stephen Spielberg, Sidney Poitier, Igor Stravinsky, Beethoven, Mozart, Frank McCourt, Frank Sinatra, Louis Comfort Tiffany, Mariah Carey, Cher, and countless others would agree.

Though it's often difficult for creative people to withstand the challenges of working artistically and trying to make a living, it can, has, and will be done by those who aren't afraid to follow their dreams.

The questions a creative person needs to ask in order to set their goals are a little different from others. Even those people who simply want creativity to be a part of their lives—not their

Moneysaver
Investigate those companies that will train you or pay for education, then hire on with them and save yourself money on new degrees or classes by taking advantage of that benefit.

career—have to be prepared to make the extra effort to allow time for following their passions.

One of the ways I've used to get people in touch with their creativity is to have them create a collage of what they would like to have and who they believe they are. Here's a way to put together one for yourself (or people close to you). In an artistic manner, it shows you where your passions lie and can help you construct a way to meet those goals.

You'll need:

- ten magazines
- large piece of construction paper (8 1/2" x 11" is fine for a quick collage but a larger piece is better)
- glue (a glue stick is easiest)
- scissors
- pen
- 1 piece of lined paper
- approximately an hour's time

1. Collect at least ten magazines—all different types. Try to choose some that you might read and others that you might not normally look at.

2. Flip through the magazines quickly and cut out all pictures or words that appeal to you. Pile them at your side.

3. As you go through the magazines, think of what you love, what you'd like to be, where your creativity might lie, or what about your creativity you'd like to arouse.

4. When you have a fairly substantial pile, start pasting the pictures/words on the construction paper. Start from the middle and work your way outward. Don't be neat—just fit the pictures in where you can. It's okay if they overlap.

5. If you've filled the page but still have pictures left over, look to see where you can fit them in or glue them atop something else. Search for meaningful, or even unexpected, connections.

6. Once you're done with the collage, get the pen and piece of paper and write down a list of images/phrases that directly connect to your creative goals. You'll be able to see them clearly and make connections from what you've just created through your collage.

7. Analyze the list you've made and prioritize the goals you see on your lined paper.

8. Check to see which of those goals are "today" goals and which are "tomorrow"—which ones are lifetime goals and which are goals you might meet within a year.

9. By lettering the items on the list, 'F' for family/friends and 'P' for personal, see which of the creative goals you can meet alone and which you'll need support for.

10. Hang your goals collage in your office or on your refrigerator to remind yourself that there are creative dreams in your future—and the written list is your roadmap to seeing them come true.

Watch Out!
Remind yourself of the goals you've already achieved. Creative people are often too discouraged by the goals they haven't yet reached!

If it's difficult to maintain a positive outlook on your creative goals, remember that you are not alone. Everyone who ever made it as an artist had to deal with the heartbreak of rejection and the struggle to remain seriously connected with their goals. John White's book, *Rejection,* has helped me deal with many a rough period in my creative career. Just knowing that Decca Recording Studio was wrong in 1962 when it turned down an unknown group because it believed guitars were on the way out—and that group ended up going on to fame and fortune as the Beatles, makes me feel there's still hope. When I see that Charles Goodyear lost everything and spent time in debtor's prison before he invented vulcanized rubber, I think I'm not the only one who has been rejected. And when I remember that *Gone with the Wind* was rejected 38 times, I can write another sentence.

Some suggestions for keeping your eye on the future:

- Frame those diplomas and hang them on the wall!

- Make a print of that photo of you at 8 years old dancing in the Christmas play, frame it and put it where you'll always see it. Remember to relive that moment often.

- Buy a calendar of inspirational quotes and read one every day.

- Read a biography of someone in your field who struggled to overcome adversity and eventually reached his/her goals.

- Get together with a friend in the same field and talk about your goals on a regular basis.

- Think about your definition of success and how your creativity fits into it.

- Above all, remember that those who threw their typewriters off the cliff (or their guitars out the train window, or their ballet slippers from the Empire State Building) never made it. You have to keep on going to meet your goals.

Academic goals

Setting goals for an academic career can mean the difference between completing all your classes and

Unofficially...
Actor Bill Cosby graduated from college long after he'd been fully accepted as a superstar in the entertainment industry. And he believes his doctorate in education is his greatest achievement.

degrees within the specified period of time and having to delay finishing because you don't have enough money or simply have not planned your time well. Most people who begin college right out of high school have not taken the time to consider exactly what's expected of them. The first semester acts as a wake-up call, a shocker that brings them into the reality that is the university world. They realize they haven't budgeted their time well, that there are certain classes in which they're falling behind, that college studies require dedication, competence, persistence, and quite simply, a lot of hours. Even those who are happy just to get by with average grades have to put some time and effort into going to class, producing papers, taking tests, and studying to do so.

It's better to think about what's expected of you and to map out what your goals are before you step foot into the admissions office than to be bitterly disappointed when you flunk out because you took on five classes and also tried to work a full-time job or because you hadn't taken the time to investigate all of the possible financial-aid programs. Think before you go to school! This is an important chunk of time out of your life and it can be much easier if you've mapped out your goals and made your plans ahead of time.

Things to consider:

■ What degree is most applicable to the field you want to enter?

■ Do you have the talents, skills, and passionate desire to pursue your chosen career?

■ Have you done some research, and spoken to some people in your field, so that you have a thorough knowledge of what's expected?

- Do you have the finances or scholarships to make it through the minimum years of schooling to reach your goal?

- If things do not go as you expect, what else will you do?

A four-year degree is typically what most people shoot for, but if your ultimate goal is to be an engineer, lawyer, doctor, psychiatrist, professor, or business executive, you should be thinking further ahead and shooting for at least a Master's. That means a minimum of six years in school. Do you want to do it all at once or do you plan to get your Bachelor's and then find a job, work for a few years, maybe get married, then go back to school? Or will you ask your future employer to fund the rest of your education?

The financing for an education is critical. In today's colleges, it's not uncommon for a graduate to have to think about a minimum of $5-10,000 a year for tuition, books, and housing. That doesn't even include other supplies, fees, food, and the occasional party. A good percentage of people who take out school loans are amazed when they finally finish, start a job and think they have the world by the tail—only to discover that their school loans now have to be paid and will mean at least a $200-300 per month minimum out of their pockets. It's better to think of that now rather than later.

If you build your academic goals a step at a time, you can break them down into categories that will help you think more specifically. Let's consider these three now, just to save you a little time.

- **Finances.** By thinking of setting up your finances now, then resetting them every year

> **"**
> O! This learning, what a thing it is.
> —William Shakespeare
> **"**

and remembering that you'll still probably have something to pay when you get *out,* you'll be ahead of the game. Remember to always add at least a thousand or two more than what you think you'll need for each semester. Then you'll be able to eat!

■ **Studies.** Classes that will help you reach your ultimate goal are the ones you need to concentrate on. All those extracurricular classes might be enticing, but if you want to save time and reach your goal, you'll want to focus on those courses that are required for you to reach the requirements of your major. Check out your school's student handbook to see what you need, then figure what you'll take for the next couple of semesters to get the requirements out of the way.

■ **Relationships.** Some personal relationships might have to be put on hold for a while if you're going to a school that's away from home. This is the time to consider having a conversation with those closest to you. Talk about your goals and how important they are. Ask them questions about whether they realize what you're up against and how much time it'll take away from your relationship with them. Set the standards and make your needs/wants clear so that they can share your goals.

By setting your goals down on paper by year, you can clearly see what will be expected throughout your college career. Here's a suggested form you can use to plan the goals you hope to meet:

ACADEMIC PLAN

Goals	Year	Specific steps necessary	Result
Financial:			
Scholarships	1999	Guidance forms	Pell Grant Sallie Mae school
Loans	1999 2000 2001 2002 2003	Apply	
Studies:	1999	Freshman Eng, Math, History, Biology	Dean's list
	2000 2001 2002 2003		
Relationships:	1999 2000 2001	Girlfriend, family, friends	Time for vacations, e-mail & phone
	2002 2003	Marriage after graduation?	

Though this form is not completely filled out, I have started it and you can see where it's going. Now it's your turn.

Family goals

You might have included some of your family goals in the personal section, but your family goals should include the specifics about what you'd like to see for your family members and yourself in the future.

Plans for a child's education, your goals for family trips, a new home, a boat, the way you'd like to teach your children, or the way you'd like to deal with your parents and siblings are all goals that can be clarified and set down in this section.

Consider your relationships with those to whom you're related.

- How do you affect their lives?
- How they do affect yours?

Timesaver
If you talk about dreams and goals every night at supper, you'll not only save time, you'll know your family better and they'll understand your goals as well.

- What changes would you like to make?

- What goals would you like to achieve that would also affect them directly?

- What would you like to do together?

- How will you take the steps necessary to meet those goals together?

When creating your goals list for family-related aspects of your life, it's a good idea to divide your list up with respect to who will be making the decisions with you and sit down with them to coordinate your goals. If there are any compromises to be made or discussions to be had, better to do it before anyone starts dreaming of what they're going to do because your vision of the future is never going to be exactly the same as your loved ones'—no matter how much you agree!

Financial goals

Depending on your needs and how important finances are to you, your financial goals can be either at the top of your list or at the very bottom. Wherever they are, it's best to set them early in your life so that you'll have something set aside for when you are no longer producing a regular income. With the way things are going, we can be pretty sure the social security system as we know it will not be as stable and reliable as it has been in the past—and with that knowledge, we need to prepare for the future.

Planning for your financial future doesn't necessarily mean just putting a few dollars in a savings account every week. One of the reasons I put this set of goals last is because everything else in your life will depend on whether you're financially set to meet your other goals. Your personal, business,

Moneysaver
Most of the new computers come complete with a financial program. By learning how to use that program right away, you can begin managing your finances immediately.

FINANCIAL BREAKDOWN

Goals (be specific!)	Deadline (year or exact amount of time)	Amount (come as close to the dollar amount as you can)	How much per week? (how much will you need to meet this goal
Personal			
1.			
2.			
3.			
4.			
5.			
Academic			
1.			
2.			
3.			
4.			
5.			

Goals (be specific!)	Deadline (year or exact amount of time)	Amount (come as close to the dollar amount as you can)	How much per week? (how much will you need to meet this goal
Professional			
1.			
2.			
3.			
4.			
5.			
Creative			
1.			
2.			
3.			
4.			
5.			

family, academic, and creative goals will all dovetail into your financial goals. If you plan on taking a trip to Fiji within the next five years, you should start putting away some money toward it now. Figure out what you'll need to fly there and stay there, add something to that (because the prices won't be the same five years from now) and earmark part of your finances for that goal.

If you divvy up your finances this way and figure in what you expect to be making, you should be able to meet your goals. (Remember: When listing your goals, be specific. I've been very general here, but you'd best put down "brand new Mercedes-Benz" instead of just "new car" if you're going to plan on having the right amount of money to meet that goal!)

You might be thinking that some of the goals you already listed won't cost you anything. Think again. Nothing comes without a price. If you want to pursue a career in art and you're happy to be a starving artist, that's fine, but don't forget you'll have to buy paint and put a roof over your head— and you'll have to eat something! If your needs are meager, you'll still have to pay for the essentials. The more you need, the more you're probably going to have to pay, so set your goals now.

Are your goals truly yours?

Now that you've finished breaking down your goals into specific categories, you need to look deeply and think about whether the goals you've outlined are *truly* yours or whether you're trying to do what someone else wants for you. Why? Because it's not going to make any difference how good you are at setting up goals and priorities if your heart isn't in the ultimate end product. If you really don't want

66

One must beat with his own rhythm—at any price.
—Henry Miller

99

that boat or that career in banking, if you're not sure you want 4.3 kids and a house in the suburbs of Chicago, if you would rather be a musician than a professor of music, you'd better go back over your goals and think about your life one more time.

We are all affected by others in our lifetimes and often we go off track simply because someone has said, "You know, you're really good at talking to people. You ought to be a psychiatrist." That kind of compliment puffs us up a bit and we think, "Wow, that's nice. I could make a good yearly income doing that and since she thinks I'm good at it, I must be, so I'll go for it." We go to school for the required 6-8 years, struggle through every Jungian and Freudian lecture, all the while longing to be on the basketball court. Then we get into an office, start seeing patients, and realize we are horribly miserable. Everything we did to get to where we are was for naught.

A waste of almost ten years? More than likely. That's a lot of time and it's gone simply because you didn't search your heart and think about what you really and truly wanted out of your own life. Not what someone else wanted or thought you should have in your life, but what your own desires and goals were.

This is the time to go back and recheck all your lists. See if the goals are yours or if they come from voices in your head—voices belonging to other people who have influenced you or coerced you into believing you want something you don't. Before you start managing your time to meet goals that aren't yours, think once more. And if the goals change, that's perfectly fine. Then it'll be ten times easier to manage your time because it'll be *your* choice!

Unofficially...
Franz Kafka's father had different plans for Franz. He ridiculed him for writing and told him he'd never be anything unless he studied law. Kafka proved him wrong.

Achieving your goals in the time allotted by someone else

When someone else gives you deadlines to meet, you often have to scurry to shuffle your own goals around in order to meet those deadlines within the timeframe given. What they've chosen for a deadline might seem impossible to you, but if you don't have a choice and your goal will be affected if you don't get the work done by that date, then you need to go back to step one and work on reprioritizing your goals.

Sometimes some goals have to be shifted or temporarily moved aside in order to meet others, especially when you don't have control of the timeline. If that's the case, then you need to take a deep breath, figure out your priorities, and adjust your goals.

One of the reasons we write our goals in different categories is so they will be easily adjustable in case of changes in our lifestyles or matters that are out of our control.

When you are working with deadlines that are created by someone other than yourself, you need to just let go and be flexible. Build in time for yourself and always remember your first commitment is to yourself, then to others.

Begin to initiate rather than to react

In order to be in control of anything, you have to be the one to act rather than to react. Though there will be many times in your life when reacting is the only recourse, you want to be able to take the reins as much as possible in order to be able to efficiently manage your time.

Here's how to be proactive and meet your time constraints and manage your goals:

- Anticipate problems and meet them head on.

- Create solutions for existing problems and put them into effect immediately.

- Make a phone call to head off an argument before the other person makes one to you.

- Try to be one step ahead of the competition.

- If you can meet deadlines early, do so.

- Stop interruptions by effectively communicating your needs with others.

- Figure out all the details ahead of time, so that nothing will be a surprise.

- Ask for clarification about anything you do not understand.

- If you do not believe someone is correct, do your homework before you take a stand.

- Recheck your goals and priorities on a regular basis to be prepared for the next step you want to take with your life.

Going from one goal to the next

The most self-satisfying thing in your life will be to reach a goal you've set for yourself and cross it off your list. Pause for a moment and take some time to reflect on what brought you to that goal and how you were able to achieve it. Remember what you've learned in the process and be sure to apply it to whatever goals you want to reach in the future. Glory in the moment!

Then take a deep breath and move up the other goals on your list. Look at your deadlines and projections and see that they're all still in line. If they're not, then juggle them, and adjust the timelines so that your financial matters will meet your expectations.

66
Great actions bespeak great minds.
—John Fletcher
99

Once you have taken the time to pat yourself on the back for a job well done, once you've rechecked the rest of the goals on your list and assessed how much longer and what it will take to reach them, then it's time to set your sights on the next goal. Be assured that, with what you've learned, the next goal will be even easier to reach. And as you become a skilled time manager, you'll have more and more satisfaction and less frustration, more goals met and more time to spend on the things that really matter.

Just the facts

- Everyone, even the most indigent people, have daily and lifetime goals.

- Setting career goals means being realistic and preparing for each step of the process ahead of time.

- All lifetime goals basically depend on financial goals to make them come to fruition.

- Being proactive means anticipating problems and solutions for them.

- Once a goal is met, it's time to reflect on the learning process and to move on to the next goal.

Getting More Done
In Less Time

GET THE SCOOP ON...
How to identify procrastinating tendencies ▪
How to stop putting things off ▪
Understanding the psychological and physical
implications of procrastination ▪ How to utilize
short to-do lists ▪ How to break the habit and
reward yourself for your accomplishments

PART IV

Handling Procrastination—the Devil and the Burnout

Chapter 8

L et's face it. Everyone procrastinates. Even the people who meet deadlines 99.5% of the time do a little procrastinating. We put off calling our mother because we know she's going to know something's wrong as soon as she hears our voice. We put off going to the dentist because we don't like hearing that drill. We put off asking our boss for a raise because we're afraid we're going to get turned down. We put off doing the filing because we know it'll take all day. And we put off writing that paper for history class because we're simply not sure where to start. And it's frightening.

That's it in a nutshell. One of the biggest reasons why people procrastinate is because somewhere deep down inside they're a little bit scared of something—whether it's their mother, the dentist, their boss, the job, success or failure. But don't think you're the only one who does it. You are far from

❝

Procrastination is
the art of
keeping up with
yesterday.
—Don Marquis

❞

alone, and there are just as many reasons for procrastinating as there are people who procrastinate.

Why do we procrastinate?

First of all, let's define procrastination. It's a habit, and habits are things that we repeat several times before they're ingrained and *become* habits. But habits can be broken!

When you procrastinate, you are avoiding or putting off something you need to accomplish. Often we have very good intentions, we might even include that item in our agenda, on our master list of things to do, and cancel it later. We never purposely intend not to do something; it just happens that way. But putting things off becomes a habit and when that habit starts interfering with the way you handle time, it starts becoming a problem rather than an occasional occurrence.

Do you procrastinate? Answer these simple questions to see if you should be aware of the warning signs:

- How many times do you shove a project aside before finally tackling it?

- Do you wait for exactly the "right" moment before asking a question and often miss the chance?

- Do you often miss birthdays and other holidays because you've put off buying cards and/or presents?

- If the doctor or dentist can't see you right away, do you put the appointment off?

- Do you make plans with friends/family for months in advance, then cancel at the last minute?

- Do you make excuses not to make that phone call/write that letter/pay that bill?

- Do you let the filing/laundry/dishes pile up until they're about to tip over?

There are, as we've stated already, many reasons for procrastinating, but some are common to just about everyone. Sometimes just knowing the reasons is enough to help you find the time and energy to get past them. Sometimes it's not, but let's see which type of procrastinator you are.

Psychological issues

The three major psychological reasons linked to procrastination are dislike, fear, and doubt.

It's clear to everyone that if we dislike doing something, we'll put it off and put it off. My husband has a strong dislike of waiting—for whatever reason. As I write this, he just came back from the bank. I'd sent him to put some money in the savings account, but because the line was too long, he decided not to do it. Now the money lies on the kitchen counter and I will be the one who needs to make a trip to the bank to do the job he has now put off due to his own procrastinating nature. The result? A job that could have been accomplished in five minutes will now stretch out to several days because I'm on deadline and won't be able to get to the bank until Monday since this is Friday and the bank won't be open tomorrow.

Where does his dislike come from? Largely, it's a lack of patience due to his Attention Deficit Disorder. I could waste time and argue with him about why he should have stayed there and made the deposit, but that doesn't make sense. His dislike is a psychological condition about which I can do nothing—except to understand it.

Watch Out!
Once you've identified the areas in which you procrastinate, be aware that you're probably following a pattern established long ago. Every time you're about to put something off, just tell yourself "do it!"

WHAT TYPE OF PROCRASTINATOR ARE YOU?

Type of Procrastinator	Description
Patty Pressure Cooker	She enjoys the adrenaline rush she gets from putting things off to the last minute.
Philip the Perfectionist	If he can't do it exactly the right way, he won't do it at all.
Alpha Afraid of Everything	Fear gets in Alpha's way. She's afraid she'll fail and in being afraid of failure, she's also afraid of success.
Gloria Gonna Go Away	Gloria's convinced if she waits long enough that everything (including the IRS) will disappear.
Donnie Doin' Somethin' Else	Donnie would rather be doing anything except what's supposed to be done. He seems too busy, but in reality, he's simply doing empty jobs.
Ollie Overwhelmed	Poor Ollie's forever saying, "I have too much work and not enough time." The truth is that Ollie doesn't manage his time well.
Regina Rejects Responsibility	If everyone else does Regina's job for her, then she won't have to. She was probably spoiled as a child.

And that's where I was going with this section: You need to understand the psychological reasons behind your own procrastination.

How do you tackle the tasks you dislike? Put them first on your list of things to do, swallow hard, and do them. Once you're done, give yourself a gift—whether it's as simple as a five-minute break to take a walk outside or as expensive as a new watch. Do whatever you can afford and whatever you believe is appropriate (in other words, match the gift's size to the size of your dislike).

Fear, the second on the list of the three strongest reasons why people procrastinate, is actually a double-pronged restraint. Fear can stop us from taking chances and it can also be the reason why we do take chances. Fear can save us from doing something that will harm us or it can stop us from grabbing an opportunity that might never be offered us again.

Many times, fears begin with childhood experiences. If you've ever watched toddlers, you will notice they have no fear whatsoever of hot stoves until the first time they touch one. Then they have the knowledge that they might get burned and that being burned doesn't feel good, so they won't reach for that stove again. Whether we remember the exact incident that caused our fears, we are acting out of fear when we put off speaking in public because we might be ridiculed or when we don't walk out on that dance floor because we might stumble or when we put off asking the boss a question because we're afraid of authority figures.

Sometimes, conquering fears that are deeply inbred and born of abuse require much more than making a to-do list or pushing yourself past the moment of indecision. If the fears you are feeling are truly impeding your ability to make it through

Unofficially...
Winston Churchill feared taking the tests required to get into Sandhurst but worked past his fears and actually took the entrance exams two times before he finally passed and was admitted.

your day, then you need to admit the possibility that a trained professional might be able to help you. Taking that first step and seeing someone is the first step on the road to emotional health. Take it! You're worth it.

Third, doubt causes some to procrastinate simply because they don't know whether they can complete a job or whether the job they do will be accepted by others. Will we be able to finish all the filing by 5 o'clock? Will I be able to walk across that floor and ask that girl to the senior prom? Will I be able to swallow my pride and apologize for my faux pas at the Thanksgiving table?

You won't know until you try, and the fact that you tried is the first step to conquering your procrastination.

Fear of failure vs. fear of success

Are these two fears the same? Many think so. The truth is that the fear of success brings with it a new fear: If I do this once, can I do it again when expected? Fear of failure, however, deals only with the first time you attempt to do something. You're afraid to even try to begin with, and you don't usually think about what you might do if success comes knocking at your door.

These fears can be crippling and can be the main reasons why people procrastinate. Look at how you might fit into this category by taking the following mini quiz.

If you answer yes to any of the questions, you've probably been putting off taking the steps necessary to succeed because down deep you're afraid of what's going to happen when you get there.

How do you get past this? First of all, make sure you know that it's okay for you too succeed. You're

FEAR OF SUCCESS QUIZ

	Yes	No
Am I entitled to success?		
Do I deserve it?		
Am I afraid of living up to everyone's expectations?		
Will I hurt someone else if I succeed at this task?		
Will I make someone angry if I get this promotion/ sell this book/make this money?		
Will someone who needs me be left behind if I get this job/ this promotion/this raise?		

right to expect some positive feedback when you do something right. Your work is worthy of praise and there's no reason why you shouldn't get it. And if your success is going to mean someone is left behind, there's no reason why you can't reach back and help them to succeed too. Remember what F.D.R. said: "The only thing we have to fear is fear itself."

The next thing you need to do is learn how to build your self-esteem. Nothing will give you more time in your day than getting past the many excuses you'll make for not accomplishing your tasks.

■ If you think about what you've already accomplished, you'll feel stronger about tackling the next project.

■ Tell yourself you're okay, that everyone on this earth is worthwhile. Use the popular adage, "God doesn't make junk!"

■ Maintain friendships and relationships with positive, upbeat people. When you're around depression, it'll seep into your own self-worth and convince you that you should fail. Don't go

Bright Idea
When you're afraid of failure, remember to take baby steps. Little steps mean little successes and will prepare you for the bigger successes you're capable of. Little failures are also *just* little failures. We can survive those.

Watch Out!
Identify your most "up" time of the day and use that time to undertake your most daunting task. When you're most energetic, you can do anything!

there!

■ Keep your goals realistic. Don't set your sights on the type of company Donald Trump has if you're just opening a card shop.

■ Realize that every time you make a mistake or every time you experience a small triumph, you're adding to your store of knowledge. And everything you learn is valuable.

■ Accept your foibles, quirks, and mistakes. They make you human!

Attention deficit disorder and other impediments

Dr. Glenn Barruw, a specialist regarding A.D.D. and A.D.H.D., has been working with parents and children in Florida who have been diagnosed with these disorders. He states that children who were initially spotted as having A.D.D. were considered "hyperactive" or "unable to focus." He has discovered that each of the children had individual needs and focused on the education, family, child, and therapy. Through training, behavioral therapy, and a support unit that includes teachers and employers, the A.D.D. person can be helped.

A.D.D. is caused by a chemical imbalance in the brain, a medical condition. It might affect adrenaline and neural transmitters. The person with A.D.D. may not be able to maintain control over his or her impulses because the proper messages aren't getting to the brain. In short, a person with A.D.D. (a genetic disorder) cannot stay attentive or focused. Sometimes the signs include the lack of ability to follow directions, disorganization, the inability to accept no for an answer, the tendency to become oppositional, and the inability to follow through on starting and finishing tasks.

How can this disorder be treated or helped? Barruw states that organizational skills need to be developed. The anxiety an A.D.D. student/person feels when faced with a project is incredible. They have to know what is expected of them and the steps they need to take to accomplish the task. They need a beginning and end—a deadline. If they're given too much work at one time, they simply shut down because of fear of failure.

In order to figure out what issues need to be treated, the person should be treated. Most can be trained through behavioral therapy, though some A.D.D. patients are treated with medication. But most important, the family needs to be aware of the problem and educated as to how to deal with it.

To learn more about how to deal with A.D.D. and its links to procrastination, check the Attention Deficit Disorder site on the Web (http://www. attn-deficit-disorder.com) or write to:
The A.D.D. Family...From Heartache to Triumph!
c/o New Net Media, Inc.
1355 S Boulder Rd. Suite F-259
Louisville, CO 80027

I hate what I'm doing!

If you have a job you absolutely detest or must study for a subject that simply doesn't interest you, the likelihood that you will procrastinate is incredibly high. Often, it's because the subject matter is not engaging or perhaps you hate your supervisor/ professor, or you are too smart for the menial tasks you've been asked to perform.

Take advantage of the boredom you feel and you'll be able to get past the hatred. Let your mind wander when you're doing a menial task. Think about what you'll challenge yourself with once

Moneysaver
Take some of the tests for A.D.D. online or go to your nearest school and ask if there are any organizations that will test you or your child for free.

you're done with what you *have* to do and you'll find yourself rushing to finish it—simply because you want to get to what you really love.

How many of you have fallen in love? Nothing seems boring when the person you love is waiting for you at the end of the day. Though time may seem to drag until you see each other again, one part of your brain is occupied with the fantasies of what you'll say or do together, and before you know it, that drudgery you were dreading is over.

Here are some tricks for getting past the boring, frustrating, irritating jobs we all must do on a regular basis:

Timesaver
Your goal: Finish each job as it comes across your desk. That's right: finish it! Don't just start it—complete it.

- Trick yourself. Think of this job as the first step to the ski vacation you're going to take this weekend. If you don't do this, the snow will melt and you won't be able to ski.

- Don't waste time dreading a job. Do the job that is most unpleasant first, then work your way into the rest of the day. (It's like eating the oatmeal in your bowl first and leaving the apples or other treats on the bottom for last. Same thing with ice cream sundaes—the hot fudge always tastes best when savored last.)

- If your whole day is something you dread, then do something that will give you a warm, fuzzy feeling at the beginning of the day. This works well for people in sales who can't take the constant negative answers they must deal with all day long.

The results of procrastination

If you procrastinate, you need to realize the effects of your action (or, in this case, inaction). Although you probably already know but are putting off actually admitting to the results, here they are so you can't ignore them anymore:

- **Anguish, anxiety, and stress.** These negative emotions will eventually result in physical illnesses, such as headaches, stomach aches (and, possibly, ulcers), heart attacks, neck and back strain, and many other illnesses.

- **Ruined friendships and relationships.** People who are consistently made to wait for you to either meet them someplace on time or do something you've promised are eventually going to lose their faith in you—and might become quite angry. Do you want to waste your time trying to explain yourself to them?

- **Unfinished work.** This is the most obvious. If you procrastinate, obviously something will remain incomplete or unaccomplished.

- **Penalties and punishments.** Whether you lose that promotion you desire at work or your professor decides to lower the grade on your paper because it's late, you will definitely suffer some kind of discipline as the result of your choice to put your work off until another time.

- **Extra work.** When you put off what you should do today, you'll have twice as much to do tomorrow.

- **Lost chances.** Not making a decision can sometimes result in the loss of an opportunity you might never get again.

One thing at a time—and finish it!

Getting started is always the most difficult, but once you get the ball rolling on a job or task you need to accomplish, the best way to keep working is to finish

66

Success is peace
of mind which is
a direct result of
self-satisfaction
in knowing you
did your best to
become the best
you are capable
of becoming.
—John R.
Wooden, *Practical
Modern
Basketball*

99

that job! One thing at a time. You'll discover it's not
as bad as you thought it would be and you will begin
to feel that sense of accomplishment when you go
over one hurdle. You can do it and once you know
that, it'll make the next hurdle seem even easier.

You've probably heard the 'one day at a time'
adage that Alcoholics Anonymous uses. Do you
know why they do it? Because alcoholics are the
worst when it comes to procrastinating. They can't
quit drinking today because the sun's shining or
because their dog died or because it's Saturday or
because they have someone coming over for dinner
tonight. The excuses are endless. So, each morning
when someone who's practicing the AA traditions
wakes up, the first thing he or she says to himself/
herself is, "Today, I won't drink." One day at a time.

Your job is to tell yourself. "I'll do this one job."
Just one job. One project. One task. You can handle
that, right?

If you find yourself tending to hit the wall, take a
two-minute break and keep it to two minutes. Walk
outside to get the mail or do a run around the block.
Go down the hall to get something copied, but do
something as you're taking your break. Just remember: only one or two breaks for every two hours
worked. You do need them to refresh yourself, but
don't get carried away!

Create to-do lists that get done

When you create a to-do list, make sure you keep in
mind that once you write something down, it *will* be
done. There are no questions in your mind. That list
should be a contract with yourself.

At first, make the list short. Don't expect more
than you're able to do. If you create a list of twenty
tasks, all of which will take at least twenty minutes,

you've gone way past your eight-hour workday. In doing so, you've essentially built in a procrastination factor for yourself.

Keep track of what you are putting on your list. Be honest with yourself and be realistic. Ask yourself the following questions:

- How long will each project take to complete?
- Do you have all the ingredients you need to complete the project?
- How much time do you have to work on your tasks today?
- Is the project a large one?
- Will it take more than one day of your time?
- Is your workspace clear and ready for this particular kind of work?
- Are you giving yourself a break or a gift if you complete this project?
- Does someone else expect you to finish this project?
- Can you count on that person to remind you? Or to compliment you when it's done?
- Have you set reasonable deadlines for yourself?

Create a to-do list of everything you need to do, then break it down into smaller chunks. Remember to estimate how much time each project will take and how important it is to accomplish each. Once your list is created, then go back through and number each project. If a job will take longer than a day, split the time in half and see if you can do a little today and a little another day. See the following example to see how I've done it.

Timesaver
Even five minutes is enough time to complete a project. Pick a task on your list that's a quick one and start with that. Make that phone call. See—it only took a couple of minutes and you can strike that job off your list!

MY SAMPLE TO-DO LIST

Activity	Approximate Time
Complete two pages of my novel	1 hour
Call student who missed class	2 minutes
Create handout for tomorrow's class	1 1/2 hours
Filing	5 hours
Clean cats' litter box and feed them	5 minutes
Plan party for Gail's movie premiere—including phone calls, shopping for food, cleaning house	10 hours
Write recommendation letters for two students	1/2 hour
Enter photos for Bobby's auction on Web page	1 1/2 hours

Whew! Too much to do in one day. I want to quit right now, but I won't. Let's look at what I can accomplish today. First, I need to prioritize. Creating the items I need to hand out for tomorrow's class is first, so that needs to be done today. The cats definitely need to be fed and their box needs to be changed. I should also call those students and write those recommendation letters. And if I don't enter Bobby's photos on the Web page, he won't be able to start his auction tomorrow. The rest can wait until tomorrow. Here's the revised list, written in the order I'll accomplish the tasks (from the most irritating to the ones I love to do).

Bright Idea
Print up four week-at-a-glance calendars on your computer. Pencil in your appointments and tack them on your office wall or refrigerator. When one week is done, tear it down and your next one is there, already begun for you.

PRIORITIZED SAMPLE TO-DO LIST

Activity	Approximate Time
Cats' food and litter box	(5 mins)
Bobby's photos/Web page	(1 hr/30 mins)
BREAK for coffee	(5 mins)
Call student	(2 mins)
Recommendation letters	(30 mins)
Handouts for class	(1 hr/30 mins)
TOTAL time	3 hrs/42 mins

Great, I can do 15 minutes of filing, then I'll reward myself with half an hour or so of working on my novel! (*Hint:* Always save the best for last.) Maybe later this evening, I'll make a few phone calls and start sketching out plans for Gail's party—but first, I'll break that big project down into smaller steps and create a list just for that.

The point of creating a list is twofold: It shows you what you need to get done and proves not only that you can do it, but that you have the time—and in the case above, time to spare!

Reasonable deadlines and bite-sized projects

Everyone should have an erasable calendar on a wall or desk where they can see it and check it on a regular basis. Mine is on the wall beside my desk and it is a three-month calendar because I'm usually looking ahead to future deadlines. Three months is about all I can handle at one glance. However, I do have a year-at-a-glance calendar in my day planner and that tells me all the major projects I need to accomplish.

For procrastinators, a week-at-a-glance calendar is a lot less intimidating and proves that taking one step at a time accomplishes many things (including keeping yourself focused on just finishing one thing at a time). Smaller deadlines are also easier to handle.

That large project for Gail's party was more than I could handle in one day, so I broke it down into several days. The following list shows the result.

As you can see, it was a good thing I spread it out over a few days, huh? It would have given me a major anxiety attack if I'd tried to do all this in one day, because—as you can see—it was too large a job and I underestimated it to begin with. By breaking

Moneysaver
If you give yourself X amount of time for shopping or any task where you find yourself spending more time than necessary, get a stopwatch or alarm clock. Stop as soon as the alarm goes off— and save yourself not only money, but time!

GAIL'S PARTY PROJECT (APPROXIMATE TIME: 8-10 HOURS)

Day	Activity	Approximate Time
Sunday	make phone calls to invite people	1 1/2 hours
Monday	create menu and shopping list for ingredients	1 hour
Tuesday	shop for nonperishable items	2 hours
Wednesday	cook dishes that can be frozen	3 hours
Thursday	clean the house	3 hours
Friday	shop for perishables	1 hour
	cook the rest of the dishes	2 hours
	final prep of house	1 hour
	decorate, dress, and get ready for guests	2 hours
	Total time	16 1/2 hours

this large project down into a week-long job, I accomplished a little every day and probably had a better time at the party!

Working seamlessly from one task to the next

If you're having problems getting started, promise yourself you'll work on one task for ten minutes. Chances are, once the ten minutes have passed, either you will have finished the project or you'll keep going until it's done.

Once that task is accomplished, start the next one. You might not finish it, but at least begin. If someone offers you some help, take advantage of it. If you see that delegating part of the project will help you finish it sooner, then do so. Ask for help now—not later.

When you're putting off starting the next project, listen to why you're procrastinating. Is it because you're not prepared? Do you need a break? Have you not thought through the process necessary to complete the job? Take a minute, put everything down, close your eyes, and imagine yourself working on the assignment. How are you doing it? What's the first step, then the next? What will it look like when you're finished? Take a few deep, cleansing breaths. Rub your shoulders a little, then open your eyes and start again.

Take a break. Do your work in small chunks and you'll not only be more productive, but you'll also be less tired when you're finished.

When you get a phone call, take it. While you're talking, sort through what you've already done and either toss what you have accomplished away or into your filing box. Don't put the phone call off until later unless you have to set aside more than a couple of minutes to deal with the question being asked.

Don't schedule yourself too tightly and don't put too many things on your to-do list. Also, expect problems and interruptions. When you know they might be part of your day, dealing with them as they happen will be easier.

Getting the irritating job done first

Let's examine why you consider the job irritating to begin with. The Irritating Assignment/Task/Job Form is a mini-form that will help you put things into perspective. Make a few copies for future use.

> 66
> Procrastination is the thief of time.
> —Edward Young (1683-1765)
> 99

THE IRRITATING ASSIGNMENT/TASK/JOB FORM

Name the assignment/task/job:

Reasons why you don't want to tackle this job:

1.

2.

3.

Reasons why the job needs to be done:

1.

2.

3.

The procedure you need to follow to do the job:

1.

2.

3.

The tools you need:

1.

2.

3.

How you'll complete the job:

1.

2.

3.

Date/Time you'll finish the job:

Your signature

By signing this mini-form, you are essentially making a contract with yourself. You are the only one who needs to know this, but if you do, you will make sure it's done. Who wants to wake up in the middle of the night thinking of what they've put off doing?

Rewards and breathers

C. Northcote Parkinson states that "Work expands to fill the time available for its completion." His studies prove that given half the time and half the staff, the same amount of work could be done. Yes, that's a danger for those of us who already feel overburdened, but perhaps it's also the impetus we need to overcome the tendency to procrastinate and become productive.

If doctors procrastinated, more people would die from infections left untreated, symptoms left undiagnosed, diseases left to fester. That's the same thing that happens when you leave your work undone. It won't go away, even if you think it will.

As we've stated throughout this chapter, rewards and breathers are the only ways you might get through that long list. Here are some suggestions for how to make your work easier and to make procrastination disappear.

- Put off getting that cup of coffee for five more minutes. Then when you do get it, cradle it in both hands, sniff in the aroma (take three good long whiffs), sip at least a third of the cup, then stroll slowly back to work.

- Keep a small candle or a little bottle of cologne at your desk. Light it for a few moments when you're feeling like you just can't do anymore— or take a whiff of that cologne when you're feel-

Watch Out!
Every time you find yourself saying "I can't" or "I won't be able to..." replace those phrases with "I will" or "I'll try."

Unofficially...
Thomas Edison
was once asked
to collaborate on
a futuristic
novel. He wrote
down some ideas
of what was to
come, then lost
interest in the
idea. Some of his
predictions?
Plastic, apes that
could be taught
to talk, and trips
to Mars.

ing stressed. Even better, sprinkle a few drops on your unlit light bulb, then turn it on, lean back, and think of a rolling surf or the whoosh your skis make cutting through newly fallen snow.

- Take a walk down the hall to that colleague who always has a smile or a joke. Time yourself for a quick two-minute conversation, then go back to work with a grin on your face.

- Go to the bathroom, look in the mirror, and tell that person looking back at you, "You'll make it. I have faith in you."

- Think about that boss/husband/child you're angry with and don't want to work for and imagine them naked with crossed eyes. Guaranteed to lift your spirits!

Just the facts

- Procrastination can ruin friendships, relationships, jobs, and your health.

- Sometimes getting things done is as easy as promising yourself to work for ten more minutes.

- Finish one job at a time. Then start another.

- Set a deadline and make a mini-contract with yourself to meet it.

- Attention Deficit Disorder is a genetic problem that can be dealt with through therapy and/ or medication.

- Expecting too much of yourself can actually cause procrastination.

- Giving yourself breaks and rewards helps productivity.

GET THE SCOOP ON...
How to maximize your time ▪ How to deal with
telephone interruptions effectively ▪
How to handle social interruptions ▪ How to
communicate that you don't want to be interrupted ▪ How to sidestep electronic interruptions ▪ How and when to tell interrupters no

Interruptions

We often complain about not having the time to get a job done, yet it's been proven time and time again that we waste time constantly. Watching television, waiting in line, holding on the telephone...but the truth of it is, interruptions are the worst time-wasters—and the hardest to deal with.

Interruptions happen eight times per day, on the average, and last approximately three minutes each. If you figure that out, it adds up to about 2-3 hours a day of wasted time. You can control those interruptions with a little persistence and planning.

Utilizing every moment

People who know how to manage their time do so by utilizing every moment. They do more than one thing at a time, they don't waste time, and they deal with interruptions in a way that helps them to be more productive. They also plan, plan, plan. And they know when to say no.

66

The world is so fast that there are days when the person who says it can't be done is interrupted by the person who is doing it.
—Anonymous.

99

Classifying interruptions

You're just about ready to finalize that deal and Sally from the office next door pops her head in to ask you to lunch. But she doesn't stop there. Soon you're talking about what happened yesterday, pontificating about what will happen tomorrow, and before you know it, an hour has passed by and the deadline to finalize the deal is *now*.

You've got two more shelves to clean and the spring cleaning will be finished, but little Billy comes in crying that there's no one around to play with—even though you can see all the neighborhood kids through the kitchen window. You convince him to go back outside, but two seconds later he's in again. This time he's just trying to get your attention. You spend a few more minutes with him, then glance at the clock to see it's 5 p.m. and you don't have dinner started. The shelves are left dirty, and you're feeling like tearing out your hair.

You're determined to take the weekend to do your taxes, but just as you begin, your mother-in-law calls and wants to talk. Even though you tell her you've got to get the taxes done, she continues telling you about her day at the beauty parlor. As she talks, your eyes return to the waiting IRS form and the pile of receipts, and by the time she's finished, there's only half an hour left before you have to head out to pick the kids up at the soccer game—and tomorrow is the 15th of April. You'll have to get an extension—again!

Interruptions are people. Pure and simple. There is nothing that interrupts you that is not somehow connected to a person. That ringing telephone has a person on the other end. That doorbell is being rung by a human being. That clog on the roadway is being caused by cars driven by people. The reason we all get irritated and tend to spout off when things get out of control is because we feel we can't control interruptions. Since there are always people behind the interruptions, most of us have a hard time dealing with them.

There are three different kinds of interruptions:

- Urgent (i.e. the car has rolled down the driveway and trapped your child underneath).

- Important (i.e. the boss tells you to drop the project he told you to finish yesterday and work on the one he has in his hand).

- Irritants (i.e. phone calls about nothing important when you're trying to complete a task).

The urgent interruption must be dealt with immediately, and most of the time, it cuts a chunk out of your day, but you have to deal with that.

The important interruption can often be handled by asking yourself to prioritize. Do you need to put off one project to complete another? Do you ask your boss to prioritize the projects for you?

The irritants can be handled with a little discipline and some modern technology. And one little word: no.

Telephone interruptions

Somehow, we've trained ourselves to jump whenever the phone rings. We often find ourselves running to answer it, so the first thing you need to do is decide whether you'll answer the phone before it rings. If you've decided that what you're doing is more important than that ringing phone, then remind yourself that when it rings, you've decided your priorities and will deal with the phone calls later.

Moneysaver
Listening to a salesperson's spiel pretty much guarantees them you're going to buy something. If you don't want anything, say you're busy right up front. It saves money and time!

66

For three days after death, hair and fingernails continue to grow but phone calls taper off.
—Johnny Carson

99

Some of the ways to deal with telephone interruptions are simple, while others require some stick-to-it-iveness.

Think about the following:

- Turn the ringer off on the phone and have the answering machine pick it up.

- Program the answering machine to pick up the call on the third ring; that way, you won't have to listen to the phone ringing and ringing before it's answered.

- Install a caller-ID feature so you can decide before you pick up the receiver whether the person on the other end is someone you need to speak to immediately.

- Use voice mail and ask callers to leave specific information.

- Have the call automatically forwarded to a co-worker or another number so you don't have to bother with the calls at all.

- If someone else is fielding your calls, let them handle the call—which means they not only get the name and number, but the nature of the call so that when you ultimately return it, you can do so quickly and effectively, answering the caller's questions with a minimum of fuss.

- Utilize the contact portion of your planner to keep track of who has called you, when you've returned the call and a brief description of what was said so that you don't have to field the same questions—or ask them.

- When you do answer the phone, tell the caller you only have a few moments to talk.

- If you must answer the phone while trying to juggle a child, it's best to offer him or her a snack. Keep small activities near the phone area so you can hand them to a toddler to keep him/her busy while you're taking a call.

- Place a clock or an egg-timer near the phone so you'll be aware of how much time has gone by during the conversation.

- Think about making phone calls from a pay phone. People are less likely to keep you on long when they can hear noise in the background.

- Don't waste time listening to telemarketers. If you're not interested, say so up front. You won't offend them and why should you be afraid to? They're wasting *your* time, not vice versa.

- Establish working hours, especially if you work at home. Let people know you'll be busy between 8 and 3, but if they want to call back after 4, you'd be delighted to talk to them.

- If someone makes a habit of calling at the wrong time of the day and doesn't take a hint, ask them to meet you at a time when you can both relax and talk—and make sure you tell them ahead of time that you have "an hour for lunch, between 1 and 2 on Saturday" so that they'll be aware of your time constraints ahead of time.

When making calls, plan what you'll say before picking up the phone. For instance:

- Make a few notes about the questions you need to ask and stick to them.

- When you begin the conversation, let the person know why you called and how much time you have to talk.

Bright Idea
Keep a bell next to the phone for those times when you need to get off but can't. Ring the bell and pretend it's the door or your oven timer.

- As you near the end of your list, remind the person "That's about it, so before we hang up...."
- Don't waste time socializing. Do your business and hang up.

If all else fails, you might have to resort to some "tricks" to get out of your long phone call. Some of the ones we've used—and have noticed others using—include:

- Set a timer to ring so you can announce, "I am out of time now and need to get back to work."
- Suggest the caller schedule an appointment with you to discuss the issue more completely.
- Politely explain that you need to hang up immediately, then do so.
- When everything else fails, tell the caller you have another call coming in and should take it because it's long distance, your boss, or your kids.

People interruptions

Most socializing is unnecessary, a type of mating dance we do that is all hot air and no substance. Why do we talk about the weather? It's not something we can control, yet we insist on sharing our feelings about it with almost everyone we meet or talk to during our day. And why do we think that if we pass someone in the hall or office that we need to share a tidbit or two with them? Give them a simple smile and cheery hello, and continue walking. You won't be marked as antisocial, but you also won't waste time.

There are many ways to slow down or stop people from interrupting you so that you can maximize your productivity and limit time-wasting socialization.

- If at all possible, have a secretary or receptionist screen the visitors who walk into your office. At home, install a peephole in your front door—and keep the door closed when you're working—so you can look through and decide whether the person on the other side is someone you want to be interrupted by. Solicitors are trained to push past that half-open door, but if the door isn't opened at all, you can save the time and persistence it takes to convince them you don't want to buy anything.

- Check the layout of your office. Sometimes something as simple as turning your desk around so that your back faces the door will stop people from interrupting you. And if you're not looking into the hallway, you're less likely to lose your concentration. Do you really need to see who's going by?

- Move as far away as possible from water coolers and coffee machines. If possible, keep the food and beverages in a separate room at the end of a hall so that the only time people will congregate there is when they really need something, rather than using it as a central hub for the office. Or better yet, keep a small coffeepot in your office (out of sight) so you can make a quick cup whenever you want one—and save the time of going to the coffee shop or the machine down the hall.

- Let your family and friends know that you're working if you have an office at home. Whenever you talk about what you're doing, call it "work." Remind them that you're in the office to produce a product that makes money to keep a roof over your head.

Unofficially...
Many politicians have made a habit of dealing with the lobbyists in Washington, D.C. while they're walking to and from meetings. The ones with the longest legs usually outrun the constant interruptions.

- **Use the door.** If people continue to interrupt you no matter how many signs (both physical and psychological) you've given them, then it's time to close the door. Put a sign on it that simply says, "Working—Please Don't Interrupt." And if you don't have a door, devise a little signal that you can use with co-workers or family members to tell them you don't want to be disturbed. The Hallmark Card company employees stick a flag on their desks. If it's at half-mast, it's a signal that the person behind the desk isn't available at the moment (whether they're sitting in plain view or not).

- **Wear earphones.** Whether you're listening to a "white noise" CD or just getting a break from the sounds of the office, if you're wearing earphones, people will automatically get the hint that you don't want to be disturbed.

- **Stand up as soon as someone comes into your office**—and continue standing. Don't invite them to sit. Better yet, don't keep an extra chair in your office—this will discourage people from wanting to stay and visit.

- **Walk.** If someone continues to talk even after you've given them all the signals that say you need to work, tell them to walk with you to your next appointment, the coffee machine, or the rest room, then walk right back to your office, pause briefly at the door, shake their hand and go back to work.

- **Meet the interrupter with a pre-planned statement.** "I have only a minute," or "You can't believe how busy this day has been," is the perfect screen when you need to let a person know you simply don't have time to meet with them.

■ Employ a rescue tactic. If you know certain people are going to interrupt and you have an ally around the office or home, develop a signal you can give which will alert your ally to create a diversion or "remind" you of something you need to work on right away.

■ Office hours. Post your available hours on the outside of your door and don't open your door unless you have time to deal with "droppers by." You can be accessible to your family, friends, associates, students, but you don't need to have your door open every minute.

■ Disappear. If nothing else is working, take your work to your sister-in-law's house or the coffee shop. When I knew I had to get papers corrected one busy spring afternoon, I piled them into the car and took myself to the beach, sat in the parking lot and got more work done there in two hours than I would have at home in eight.

High-tech interruptions

There's nothing ruder than a pager going off in the middle of a theater. If you must carry a cell phone or pager, at least turn down the volume when you're in a public place and make sure you answer it immediately.

The umbilical cord that once connected us to the phone has now extended and reaches us in a number of other ways. One of them is the pager; another is e-mail. Some computers are set up so that each new piece of mail that arrives is announced by a ring or beep or pseudo-human voice. Do we need to attend to each new message the instant that it arrives? Probably not. What this does is produce yet another interruption to pull us away from the work at hand.

> **❝**
> There is nothing so annoying as to have two people talking when you're busy interrupting.
> —Mark Twain
> **❞**

What can we do about these high-tech interruptions? A number of things that include:

- Turn off the e-mail sounds. Schedule your mail check several times a day and don't bother with e-mail at any other time. If you answer that noise every single time, you're going to be interrupted an average of ten times a day. Can you afford to waste three or four minutes ten times a day?

- If you're busy and cannot be interrupted, turn on the answering service for your cell phone or have the messages forwarded to another number. Or, better still, simply shut it off.

- Get a cell phone or pager that vibrates instead of rings. If you are otherwise occupied, it's easier to ignore a vibrating phone than a ringing one.

- When you're in social circumstances, it might seem cool to you when your cell phone rings, but everyone else will be annoyed if you take time out to answer each call that arrives. Shut it off. If you can't trust that the people who call will call back, then have your voice mail service or answering machine take the calls.

- Set time limits on your calls and take them only during certain periods of the day.

Communication with those who interrupt

We've talked about some types of communication already, but you might need to practice a little. Most people have trouble letting others know when they're encroaching on space and time, but if you are serious about managing the hours in your day and becoming as productive as possible, then you'll need to be effective. Sometimes just the language you use and the way you say what you need to is

Unofficially...
While performing onstage in a Broadway show, a well-known actor heard a cell phone go off in the audience. Stepping out of character, he walked to the edge of the stage, asked them to shut the *** thing off, then continued with the play.

enough. At other times, you'll need to use a little diplomacy. And sometimes we all need to be budding psychiatrists.

Here are a few tips for communicating effectively with interruptions and the people who create them:

- As soon as you turn to face your interrupter, ask what you can do for them today. The greeting will remind them of the reason they're interrupting and be a gentle prod to get to the point. Quickly.

- Whenever you need to keep a call short or stop someone who's constantly interrupting, do it with a smile.

- When you're finished with a conversation, ask if there's anything else you need to discuss. Most of the time, the answer will be no, then you can smile, say goodbye, and be on your way. But if there is something else, the person has the opportunity to discuss it and also gets the clue that you're finished.

- Think about verbal clues that you need to sign off. "You must have important things to do…" *or* "I need to get back to work," *or* "I've taken up enough of your time," are all considerate ways of letting your caller or visitor know it's time to get back to what you were doing before the interruption.

- If you truly cannot deal with that person, tell them. Saying, "I can't really help you right now, but I'll spend a minute with you to point you in the right direction," is better than promising them you'll help later. Or stressing yourself out to help now.

> **66**
> Far from saving time, such devices as personal computers and fax machines have simply created more for people to do…and in a speeded-up life, it can be difficult to find time for community-building.
> —*Creating Community Anywhere* (133)
> **99**

■ Negotiate to talk another time. If you say to someone, "I'm really busy right now, but I can continue this conversation around 2:30 this afternoon or at 10 tomorrow morning," you've left them an opening and satisfied their need to get in touch. Remember to follow through if you make an appointment with them and give them the time they need! This is also a good ploy with children who need your attention. Telling them that you'll play a game with them until the clock hits a certain point gives them the time they need and also lets them have a choice of playing now or waiting until later.

Expect distractions and build in time for them

One of the best ways to deal with interruptions is by heading them off at the pass. Begin your workday before everyone else gets there, or stay after everyone leaves. If you're one of the first ones in the office, you have the luxury of getting your priorities straight and your "to-do" list created before the phones start ringing and people start demanding pieces of your time.

If you're the type of person who'd rather burn the midnight oil, you might be able to get lots more accomplished when everyone else has gone home. However, if you have a family, you might have some explaining to do!

Expecting distractions simply means that you don't try to fit a fifteen-minute job into fourteen. Instead, give yourself twenty or twenty-five minutes. If you do that with each chore, you'll find you're accomplishing everything you need to and are not as stressed by those last-minute interruptions. As a result, everyone around you will recognize your

Bright Idea
Keep a toy clock near the phone and when you get an important call, give the clock to your kids so they can watch the time for you. It'll keep them busy so they won't interrupt and also time your call.

productivity and be impressed with how well you seem to handle it all. It's only when we try to cram too much into a short period of time that we feel we don't have enough hours in the day to finish our work.

When interruptions are intolerable

There are times when you simply can't be interrupted and you need to make those times clear to the people around you. If polite hints and smiles don't work, leave a note on your door (in all caps) that you should not be disturbed. Children, other family members, and co-workers should be warned ahead of time, if at all possible, when you cannot be interrupted. If you've made yourself clear, in a concise, non-combative way, you should be able to handle the reins and manage your time.

However, there might be someone who simply doesn't understand. Don't lose your cool—having an argument will not only waste time, it will also eat away at you while you're trying to work and as a result, decrease the quality of your work. Psychiatrists have proven beyond a shadow of a doubt that when people are preoccupied, the chances of their making a mistake are doubled.

This is the time you need to remember how to focus on your goals. Get out your list of chores/jobs for the day and remember how much you need to finish before you quit. Is it worth getting upset with someone who doesn't share your vision? Is it worth losing the time it takes to explain it to that person? If not, close your door or simply turn your back, and pay attention to the work at hand. Shut everything else out. Firmly and politely tell that person you don't have time to talk right now, but you'll deal with them later—when your work is done.

Watch Out!
If you know you'll be exceptionally busy, take care to stay away from people who are notorious talkers. And watch your temper! It's more likely to flare when you're feeling pressed for time.

"Do not disturb" signs are a necessity!

Because people cannot always understand how we can be visible, yet not accessible, a "do not disturb" sign is a necessity. It's your choice whether you make it a humorous one, a polite suggestion to call or come back, or a direct "do not bother me, I'm busy." Whatever the case, make sure you hang out that sign for all those people who will not "get it" otherwise.

We are so used to hearing people say they're busy, that sometimes we just tune it out. But you can't tune out a sign on a door.

Explaining briefly to others

Once you've laid out the rules for yourself, it's time to explain to others—briefly—how you intend to work and what you need in order to achieve the completion of your tasks or to reach realistic deadlines. In the office, this might be as simple as calling a five-minute meeting and telling everyone about the imposing deadline and how important it is to keep the interruptions to a minimum. At home, that same five-minute meeting could revolve around the kids' need to understand that Mom's got to package up all the household goods in two weeks for that big move to Oregon. The home office worker might need to send a quick e-mail to all friends and correspondents to let them know that because he or she has an office at home, it's much more difficult to garner the time to work—and working for oneself is working for the hardest taskmaster of all.

Whatever the case, a brief explanation ahead of time or a reminder while in the midst of a crunch is often enough to communicate your needs to those around you—and to explain why you might not be as accessible as they'd like you to be. If this is something that's ongoing, everyone will eventually get

Unofficially...
The writer Carolyn Chute (*The Beans of Egypt, Maine*) was at a conference in Portland, Maine one year and was trying to finish a book by deadline. She hung a skull-and-crossbones sign on her door that read "Interrupt and Die." Everyone laughed, but she got her privacy.

the hang of it. If they don't, it's time for a quick private conference, and a sterner reminder.

Just the facts

- Interruptions happen at least eight times a day and last about three minutes, effectively wasting almost an hour of your work time.

- You don't have to answer the phone every time it rings. Getting an answering machine or voice mail will stop some interruptions.

- Explaining your needs to someone while keeping a smile on your face will keep them from disturbing you.

- Turn the sound off your e-mail system so that you're not notified each time a message comes in.

- Hanging a "do not disturb" sign on your door can be an effective way of alerting people when you're busy.

Timesaver
Letting someone know exactly how much time you have ("I have three minutes until my next meeting") will clue them in that they need to do their business and skedaddle.

GET THE SCOOP ON...
How and when to delegate work ▪ What to pay
part-time and contract workers ▪
How to hire help ▪ What the 80/20 Principle
really means ▪ How to let your workers do their
jobs efficiently

Asking for Help Doesn't Weaken You

We all have had moments when we've cried out, "This is all too much. Not only do I need an extra 24 hours a day, I need four hands!" Your stress level goes up, the adrenaline starts to rush, ulcers start to form and the chances of a heart attack go up and up and up. Every moment seems more precious and fleeting than the one before. The kids start to call you by another name, your friends don't bother to call at all anymore, your boss is hinting that he's interviewing other people for your job, and you've discovered gray hairs where there shouldn't be any.

Have you taken on too much? Are there any projects or jobs you can ignore or get rid of? If not, it might be time to get someone to help you out.

When is it time to hand over some work?

How hard is it for you to admit that you can't do it all alone? So many of us are determined to prove we're super people that the thought of some-

Unofficially...
John Kenneth Galbraith, a well-known educator and economist, once stated that he thought the people who had less interesting jobs should be paid more than those who have fun at work.

one else doing part of a job (or all of it) is absolutely repulsive. We think of it as failure or believe that people are going to say, "Look at her. She needs a housekeeper to help her! She must be really lazy or think she's Mrs. Vanderbilt."

The first step toward being able to have the strength to delegate is to realize that time management means *you* control how you utilize your time. If you realize it's out of control, then *you* control whether you're going to do something about it or let it start controlling *you*. When things get out of control, stress takes over, and when stress takes over, the mind shuts down. When the mind shuts down, there's no way anyone can think clearly enough to do the preparing, prioritizing, and scheduling necessary to work. That's the time to ask for help—and to shove aside the feelings of inadequacy.

Figure it this way: It's wiser to ask for help to get your jobs/chores/assignments accomplished than to fall farther and farther behind as you struggle on by yourself. Who's going to respect someone so dogmatic that they get stuck on a treadmill going nowhere? Get the monkey off your back and start moving in a sane, time-sensitive direction.

What are the benefits of delegating some of your work to someone else?

- Time will be saved.

- Jobs will become easier to accomplish.

- Your subordinates/workers will be allowed time to accumulate knowledge and experience.

- Workers will have a more positive attitude when given jobs that make them stretch their current skill levels.

When do you delegate?

- As often as possible
- Whenever staff changes
- When your business is being restructured/ reorganized
- When special events occur
- When you are overwhelmed by details
- When you need to redistribute tasks or reformat goals

It's hard to find good help

Yes, good help is hard to come by, but sometimes you don't have to look very far. The first place to consider is right within the confines of your own family and circle of friends. Is your mother willing to take over some occasional childcare? Does your best friend go by the bank where you need to make a deposit? Is one of the kids in the neighborhood willing to mow your lawn once a week?

Sometimes all you have to do is spread the word that you need help babysitting, keeping the house clean, doing some filing, sealing some envelopes, or fixing the car, and someone will tell you about their brother, aunt, or best friend who has exactly the talent you desire. But sometimes it takes a little more hunting.

When it comes time to interview, it's good to have a formal application. If you're a small business or a householder simply hiring childcare or housekeeping services, you can still work up a form for your potential employees to fill out.

Here's the information you need to know:

1. Full name
2. Address and phone number

Timesaver
Take a couple of minutes before you go to bed to think about how you'll delegate work the next day. While you're sleeping, your mind will work out the details.

Moneysaver
Advertise in the local free newspaper when you want help for a small job. Most ads are free or close to it.

3. Phone number of nearest relative/friend, in case of emergency

4. Proof of Citizenship (employers have gotten into serious legal trouble hiring illegal aliens)

5. Experience

6. At least three names and numbers of references

When you sit down to interview a person:

- Have a list of at least 5-10 pertinent questions ready and ask the same questions of each person you interview.

- Make notes on their application about the way they answer so that you'll be able to remember them after they've gone (it's amazing how easy it is to forget the first person you've interviewed when you're interviewing more than 3).

- Have them describe their strengths and weaknesses. This gives you a chance to hear them speak and to also get a feel for the things they feel are most important.

- Ask if they mind if you check their references— and watch them as you ask! Someone who's nervous about that question should definitely be stricken from your list.

- Remember that the work they are about to do for you will reflect directly back on you in some manner, so check their references!

- Give yourself at least an evening to think about your applicants and weigh the pros and cons of each before you hire someone. Whether you're inviting someone into your office or your home, you want to be sure they're the best person for the job—and you'll save yourself time and heartache by taking a little more time to make your decision.

How much do you pay?

Before you reach for the phone or holler into the next room to hire some help, consider how much you can afford to pay vs. how much the going rate for the job might be. A couple of minutes of research can save you lots of money in the long run.

One of your first considerations is how much your own time is worth. If you're making $5 an hour, you certainly can't afford to pay someone else the same. However, if you're making $125 an hour, you also can't expect someone to pick up part of the duties for your position for $5 an hour.

Second, consider what the going rate in your area is for the job to be performed. A quick check of the local newspaper will tell you what house-keepers and bookkeepers are charging, but might not give you any idea what a babysitter will charge. However, a phone call to the local high school's guidance office might help you to nail down a firm hourly wage for babysitting.

Third, think about the type of worker you want to hire and the skills they will need. If you're expecting a college-educated worker, you should be prepared to treat them in the manner to which they're accustomed.

Save yourself the time and energy you'll waste by hiring the wrong person by going to the right source from the beginning. As I said before, we all need a little help occasionally. Make sure you get the right person for the right price.

According to the National Average Wage Index, yearly income has risen from $2,799.16 in 1951 to $27,426.00 in 1997. From the chart they've created, it's easy to see that the average annual income has risen approximately $1,000 a year. When you consider that, you realize that what a worker might have

> ❝
> By working faith-fully eight hours a day, you may eventually get to be a boss and work twelve hours a day.
> —Robert Frost
> ❞

been paid the last time you hired someone could be drastically different today.

What you pay for help will vary from area to area. For example, in rural areas, childcare services are less expensive than in urban areas, where childcare workers are in high demand. Consider the old adage: You get what you pay for.

Secretary

A secretary can be defined as simply someone who answers your phone and greets clients, or someone who runs your appointment schedule, writes letters, files, meets/greets clients, keeps the books, and supervises other office staff. Their duties are many, their talents expansive, and they can often manage the office while the boss is away. Some of the secretaries who work in large corporations hold Master's degrees in business, accounting, or computing. Others are high school graduates who have worked their way up through the ranks.

How you pay a secretary depends on what he or she will do for you. Here are some samples derived from a recent search on the Internet:

- In 1997/98, a study of what secretaries who worked in Florida's school districts were paid revealed that their hourly wage ranged from $5.50 to $21.13. The range depended on school-district location, the qualifications of the secretary, and the length of service in the district.

- In Marinette, Wisconsin, a 1994 labor evaluation of wages in the manufacturing industry showed that receptionists started at $6.45 per hour and made an average of $7.57, a clerk/typist started at $6.22 per hour and made an average of $8.11, and a secretary started at $7.76 per hour and made an average of $8.79.

- A community college in Texas in a 1999 ad for an administrative secretary advertised that the person would start at $6.97 an hour and would be expected to perform the following tasks: the full range of duties as assigned including serving as receptionist, providing information and assistance to students, staff, and the public, typing, scheduling appointments, and filing. The job required a high school diploma or GED.

- The Santa Lucian Government (in the West Indies) released a list of wage statistics which stated that secretaries earned an average of $7.55 per hour, worked an average of 7.90 hours a day, and 43.8 hours per work.

- A virtual secretary service that can offer any type of service you need and customizes its experience to suit you, charges $50-100 per job, depending on the details.

Unofficially...
Most executive secretaries have been paid very well, but when their bosses get into trouble, they are the first on the firing line.

We have tried to provide statistics from varying areas to show the differences in salary ranges. Remember that some of these jobs also supply benefits to their secretarial employees.

You should take into consideration the following when deciding what to pay your secretary/clerk/receptionist:

1. Minimum wage

2. Benefits you will offer

3. Person's duties

4. Person's experience

5. Is job temporary or permanent?

Housekeeper

Though housekeeping is usually considered a lowly position, you must not discount the fact that you will allow this person into your house, possibly to have access to your most intimate and private places. You need to trust that person above all else! This is a position where an interview and reference checks are invaluable. Nothing will waste more of your time than chasing down someone who steals from you.

In a recent search on the Net, the following was discovered about housekeepers:

- A domestic agency in Illinois that advertises they do all the screening and guarantee their personnel, offers housekeepers, butlers, live-in companions, food consultants, at various rates, depending on the job and the hours.

- The Wyoming Job Bank recently advertised for a housekeeper starting at $6.00 an hour.

- A housekeeper for the Department of Natural Resources was reported as having an annual income of $16,986.00.

- The North Carolina General Assembly Legislative Services Office advertised for a housekeeper to work from 3p.m.-11p.m. Monday through Friday for an annual salary ranging from $17,105 to $24,697.

- In Kentville, Ontario, an ad for a housekeeper states he or she will be paid $8.00 an hour.

- Jobs for Tigers lists several housekeeping positions starting at $4.75 per hour to $6.10 per hour. The listings are part of the services for Fort Hays State University in Kansas.

- We hire a housekeeper for occasional cleaning jobs and pay minimum wage.

For your information, the average housekeeper expects to wash floors, clean bathrooms, do laundry and general cleaning. The hourly rate does not

Watch Out!
It's better to hire a housekeeper you personally know or one from a reputable agency that will back its personnel than to search for one by placing an ad in a newspaper and striking out on your own.

usually include washing windows, lifting heavy objects, taking care of children, driving, or cooking.

Babysitter/Child care

Child care is one of the most expensive things you'll have to pay for in your adult years. Prices are higher in the North and East than in the South and most rural areas. According to Ann Douglas, author of *The Unofficial Guide to Childcare*, "parents in Dallas get away with paying an average of $4210 per year for full-time childcare for a three year old, parents in Boston end up speding $8840 per year. According to the Children's Defense Fund—the source of these statistics—the corresponding figures for Boulder, Oakland, and Minneapolis are $6240, $6500, and $6030 respectively." Other books on the topic concur with these prices.

The breakdown roughly goes like this:

- Putting an infant or toddler into the hands of a caregiver will cost you more than the care for a preschooler or child already in school.

- The price of childcare for younger children is largely regulated by the government, which states only a certain number of infants can be cared for in a home.

- Hiring someone to take care of your children in your home or theirs is a lot more expensive than sending them to a childcare facility.

- Live-in sitters' wages are approximately the same as for sending the children to someone outside the home, but you're also paying for their room and board.

Remember the hidden fees: If you're late, you pay extra. As stated before, prices for childcare differ depending on where you live and the ages of

Bright Idea
Although they're not officially housekeepers, a professional organizer will make your life easier. To find one, contact the National Association of Professional Organizers, 1033 LaPosada Drive, Suite 220, Austin, TX 78752.

66

Children have
more need of
models than of
critics.
—Carolyn Coats

99

your children, but according to Douglas, the following are averages:

- Professional nannies: $2,000-4,000 per month.

- Au pairs: $115-125 per week, plus room and board (you might also be responsible for airfare and some education expenses).

- Full-time caregivers: minimum wage.

- Childcare center: $90-125 week (depending on the age of the child).

- Family center: $75-105 (depending on the age of the child).

- Half-day preschool programs: $15/day.

Personal buyers/shoppers

Though most people believe personal shoppers are only for the wealthy, there are a number of ways to get shopping done for you when you simply can't fit it into your busy schedule. If you make a detailed shopping list, most supermarkets will put together your order and often deliver it for a small fee. You can also hire a retired person to do the shopping for you. Check with your local volunteer organization to see whether they offer that service.

Today, many business executives or overwhelmed housewives, elderly people, and young, upwardly mobile professionals hire personal shoppers. Most department stores and grocery stores offer a service to those who are infirm or unable to shop. If you give them a list of the items you desire, they will dispatch store personnel to accumulate your order and cash it out for you.

A quick surf through the Net and we discovered:

- Bloomingdale's New York store offers a no-obligation, no-charge service to its customers.

You relax in the lounge on the fourth floor while its personal shoppers and fashion experts find what you need.

- Xplore Shopping on the Net offers instant access to the most popular shopping sources and even offers you your own personal shopper.

- A personal shopper based in Paris will purchase whatever beauty products, perfumes, or gifts you'd like from Paris and ship them to you— anywhere in the world.

- A European personal shopper will match a broken dish to the original German china pattern, will shop for special gifts you might not be able to get anywhere but Poland, and offers a free online catalog.

It appears that most personal shoppers make their money on commission by taking you to the places where they get a portion of the sale; however, a lot of the stores offer this service for free. The charges appear to range from absolutely free to thousands of dollars, so you're on your own regarding how much you can afford.

Accountant/Bookkeeper

If you're like most families, arguments thrive when money is mentioned. One way to dodge the arguments and save time is to hire an accountant. Depending on your needs, an accountant will charge you either by the hire or by the chore. If you can't afford an accountant, contact your local college and see if there are any accounting majors who are looking for an internship in household accounting. Most times, you can hire college students for minimum wage and you'll get the benefit of their knowledge of the most up-to-date computer programs, while offering them the opportunity to put their newly learned talents to work.

Most of us need to hire an accountant or a bookkeeper at only one time during the year: tax season! But those who have a small business or feel that they need help managing their finances might feel that it's money-smart and time-wise to hire someone good with figures to help out. You can either hire a human being to help you out or invest in an accounting program—or a virtual accounting/ bookkeeping service online. Whichever way you decide to go, be sure that the person/service is reliable. Asking for references is *not* out of the question. Remember that many wealthy and knowledgeable people have lost their shirts to wily accountants.

According to sources on the Net:

- An ad for a full-charge accountant for a company on the Oregon coast states the salary would be $36,000 per year.

- The Experience On Demand online newsletter states that beginning accountants make approximately $28-35,000 per year. Accounting partners make $100,000 and up. Bookkeepers start at approximately $22,000 a year. Payroll accountants start at approximately $21,000 a year.

- School Reform News states that the average annual salary of an accountant in a small firm is $36,000.

Considering that the accountant/bookkeeper would be working a 35-hour work week, you can approximate an hourly salary to be $20. Add a few dollars to that amount if you want to hire an accountant/bookkeeper for just a small job, and you

Bright Idea
Start a file each January 1 and divide it into categories like 'insurance,' 'home expenses,' 'travel expenses,' 'medical expenses,' etc. Each time you pay a bill, file the receipt in the appropriate slot—and save time, money, and frustration next April 15.

can probably expect to pay $25-45 an hour, depending on the job and your geographical location.

Lawn and Garden Services

Often the first thing we let slide when we get busy is mowing the lawn. Sometimes we can get lucky and a neighborhood kid will start up a small business. That way, you can help out an enterprising youngster and get your work done more inexpensively. But if you live in an area where that isn't the case or if your lawn requires more maintenance than just a weekly mow, you might want to consider hiring a service that specializes in lawn and garden maintenance.

Some sample prices:

- In Florida, where lawn and garden services compete with each other to keep lawns green and gardens blooming all year round, the average weekly charge is approximately $25. That includes mowing, trimming, feeding, weeding, and some miscellaneous work. Usually the service only comes out once a week.

- A lawn care service in Aurora, Colorado offers tree and hedge trimming, gardening, lawn cutting, and landscaping, and charges by the job rather than by the hour. Estimates are free.

- In San Jose, California, a landscaping service there charges on a weekly, monthly, bi-monthly, or one-time basis. They offer mowing, trimming, edging, weed control, yard clean-up, installation of sprinklers, and full landscaping services.

- A landscape company in upstate New York offers all types of landscaping and gardening services, has a tree surgeon on the premises,

Timesaver
For the smaller projects and regular maintenance work, check out your local newspaper and yellow pages. Do some comparison shopping before locking yourself in with one service and check with neighbors and friends to see who they'd recommend.

sells flowers and vegetable plants, as well as trees and shrubs, and builds stone walkways and retaining walls. All jobs are priced individually.

From *my* research, commercial landscaping companies appear to be more expensive than the home-grown mom-and-pop enterprises; however, they offer a lot more than just mowing and gardening services. Depending on your needs, you might want to consider the larger companies for items such as walkways, large tree removal (especially since they are liable to have better insurance for their workers—you don't want to be sued if a tree falls on a worker in your yard), deck building, and large landscaping projects.

Paying taxes and insurance

If you hire a worker, you are responsible for paying social security, state, and federal taxes. The easiest way to handle these details is to simply hire someone from a temporary agency. However, if you can't do this, make sure you get the necessary information from your worker (i.e. name, address, phone number, social security number, and Green Card info, if the worker is not a U.S. citizen). Play it safe—call the IRS to get the right forms and information about how to report your worker's earnings. It'll be different for each employer, depending on how many people you're hiring, how long they will work for you, and how much they earn, so I won't attempt to give you the details here.

Unemployment compensation should be attained for those who will be in your employ for an extended period; however, it's not necessary for temporary workers. Worker's compensation is required for people who are doing a job on your property. If you hire contractors, they usually carry their own worker's comp; if you hire individuals, you are responsible to cover them in case they have an accident on the job. Sometimes your homeowner's insurance will cover people who come into your home to work, but to be safe, make a call to your insurance agent and get the particulars.

Free help? Bartering for work

Bartering has been around since people first started figuring out they could trade with each other. We have used it quite often in our lives, and we're still surprised at how easily we can do it. It never hurts to ask!

We've bartered for the following:

- Written small-business brochures in exchange for accounting services.

- Mowed a neighbor's lawn in exchange for pet-sitting.

- Babysat with a friend's kids for a share of their orange crop.

- Exchanged several pounds of zucchini for a couple dozen ears of sweet corn.

- Helped a friend move in exchange for her bookkeeping help during tax time.

- Taught someone how to use a computer program in exchange for some housecleaning.

Be creative with your bartering. You never know when your lawyer will need a pet-sitter (you) in exchange for lowering his bill, or if your doctor could use some secretarial services to give you a free physical. And don't forget you can always trade physical items. Does your next-door neighbor collect Hummels? If she has doubles of one you'd like, you can always trade some of your autographed

Watch Out!
Don't try to get by without reporting what you've paid an employee to the IRS! No matter what anyone tells you, make sure of your responsibilities by calling the IRS themselves.

books. That pecan pie your cousin makes would be a great trade for your pickled beets. And the old television you were going to put on the curb for next trash day can be traded to your handyman neighbor for his old mower.

Use bartering to save yourself time and money. It's an old trick that's still worthy of much use!

Utilizing family and friends and the IRS

How does hiring family and friends help you at tax time? The IRS prints many fine brochures on the subject, so I won't attempt to list all the rules and regulations here. Save yourself some time and a headache by finding out when you need to pay employment taxes and when you don't. The rules change every year, so make sure you keep up with them.

Some suggestions:

- If you hire help on a contract basis, it's more likely that you won't have to worry about tax liabilities. However, the lines in the sand are finely drawn, so check with your tax accountant or lawyer.

- If you hire someone to work in your home, make sure you get all the necessary information you need to provide worker's compensation.

- If you hire family, you can often save tax money. Again, check with your accountant or lawyer for details.

Determine what to delegate and to whom

Think of delegation as a gift: You're giving yourself time off and freedom from the stress of finishing certain projects in an unreasonable amount of time, and you're also giving the person to whom you delegate the opportunity to prove themselves worthy of achieving goals with less help from you.

66
It takes a village.
—Hillary Rodham Clinton
99

Ask yourself the following questions:

▪ Am I comfortable enough with this person's qualifications to let them do the job?

▪ Does my employee know what needs to be done?

▪ Can I afford the time, resources and money to repay the employee properly for the job I'm asking them to do?

▪ Do we agree on the standards necessary so that the job will be done on time and at a price acceptable to me?

▪ Am I committed to seeing my worker succeed?

▪ Does the employee seem as committed as I am to his/her success?

Letting go once you delegate

After you've decided to delegate a job to someone else, letting go and letting that person run with it is the next step. It's akin to putting your car on cruise control when you're driving on the highway. Do you touch the brake? Only when another car cuts you off or you need to switch lanes, or you see that state police car in the distance with its lights on. In other words, only when you need to.

Your staff—whether you are just dealing with family, a small group of employees, or a mega-corporation—needs to be given full responsibility for the work that you delegate. That means, you need to have the confidence that they'll succeed in whatever jobs you hand over to them. They need to know that you are abdicating your responsibility and that they need only come to you for coaching or when a problem arises.

Watch Out!
The IRS suggests you hold on to canceled checks, pay stubs, receipts, and bank account statements for at least seven years.

Bright Idea
Outsourcing, the
90s definition for
delegating, is
the perfect way
to farm out work
rather than to
hire a whole
team or delegate
the work to
someone else in
the office.

Stepping back from the plate and letting someone else pitch a few balls is tough, but a good manager must be able to do so. That's where coaching comes in.

Coaching your staff means showing them the way to not only do the job you assign to them, but to do it well and within the time frame you've set up. Communication is the key here. If you follow the simple steps below, your needs will be clear and the employee will know exactly what's expected of them.

1. Draw up a timeline for the project.

2. Determine what steps will be taken to finish the project.

3. Figure out how long each step should take.

4. Project a deadline and build in a little extra time for problems.

5. Sit down with your employee and spell out all you need from them.

6. Reassure them that they will do a great job.

7. Tell them that if there are any snags, he or she should specify all the resources they might need to overcome the snags before coming to you with the problem.

8. Train them—briefly—in the skills they might need to complete the job.

9. Remind them of the preparations they'll need to make and give them an overview of time management.

10. Ask them to repeat what you've discussed and open the floor to questions.

What if you've done everything you think you should and the job still isn't done right or your subordinates are resisting the delegation? Perhaps he or she hasn't had enough experience to accomplish the task you've set before him/her. Maybe they fear your criticism. Maybe your priorities aren't theirs?

If you see that the jobs aren't being done properly, consider the following:

- Have I chosen the right person for the job?
- Have I clearly defined the parameters of the task and exactly what the outcome should be?
- Have I supported my workers and offered them advice?
- Have I evaluated their work and given praise?
- Is the worker acting independently?
- Is he or she admitting to mistakes or wrong decisions?
- Has he or she told me about problems that have arisen?
- Has the worker discussed the needs of the job with other workers/staff members?
- Have I rechecked my own goals as well as those of the workers?

Focus on the important

Letting a worker know what's going right with a job is just as important as telling them when something is going wrong. If a manager is fair with an employee and let's them know in no uncertain terms how he or she feels the work is going, then the channels of communication are kept open and everyone is kept happy.

However, if you lose sight of what's important and start nitpicking, everyone (including you) will be miserable. And we already know that if people are unhappy, they focus on that and lose the will to

Unofficially...
Blanchard and Johnson's *One Minute Manager* suggests that a very simple way to "give yourself and others 'the gift' of getting greater results in less time...[is to] set goals; praise and reprimand behaviors; encourage people; speak the truth; laugh; work; enjoy and encourage the people you work with to do the same as you do!"

manage their time wisely. If they lose that will, then the job won't be done correctly, and if the job isn't done correctly, nothing else will matter.

Continue to set goals with your workers. Take that moment in the morning to make a list of things to do and urge your workers to do the same. Also remember to take time out for praises when a job is well done. You'll get more and better quality work when you consider the employee as a human being who needs to be reassured and set on the right path as much as you do. And if a reprimand needs to be made, make it short and sweet. A harangue is time-consuming and degrading—to both you and the worker.

Initiate the 80/20 rule

Vilfredo Pareto, an Italian economist, discovered a truth about time and workers' input/output that remains solid to this day. A hundred years ago, he did a study on income and wealth patterns. What he discovered is that there is a "predictable imbalance" that shows up in every area of life. Called the 80/20 Rule or the Pareto Time Principle, it directly relates to time management in that it states that 80% of time spent poorly equals 20% of desired results, while 20% of time spent wisely nets 80% of the desired results.

It's been proven that:

- 80% of production volume comes from 20% of the producers.
- 80% of the useful information on the Web comes from 20% of the sites.
- 80% of what makes you happy in this world comes from 20% of the people with whom you are close.

- 80% of the sales you make will come from 20% of your cold calls.

- 80% of the accidents are caused by 20% of the cars on the road.

- 80% of the lottery winnings paid out are the result of 20% of the bets.

Timesaver
80% of the work you produce is a direct result of 20% of your time.

How does this relate to you and your employees? Think of it this way: If we can focus on that magic 20%, we can transform ourselves, our careers, our businesses, and as a result, have a direct and positive impact on the people around us.

The following is a comment on the Y2K problem, what some expect it to do to the world's computer banking systems, and the relationship of that problem to the 80/20 Principle:

"Example: If you thought there was an 80% chance that your bank would fail tomorrow, would you pull out only 80% of your money? Or would you pull out all of it? If you thought there was a 20% chance that it would fail, would you pull out 20% of your money? Or would you pull out all of it? If you decide to pull out any of it, you will pull out all of it if you can." (http://www.garynorth.com/y2k/detail_.cfm/2281)

The ABC analysis

Some managers and workers use the ABC Analysis to figure out which tasks are urgent, which are important, and which can be left to free time.

- It's figured that 15% of the most important tasks (A tasks) are actually worth 65% of the goal.

- B tasks make up approximately 20% of the total and are worth 20% of the value in managerial tasks.

■ And C tasks make up the largest percent of the tasks (thus take up the most time) at 65%, but contribute only to 15% of the value.

What does this say to you? The C tasks are the ones you can most easily farm out to someone else. Personally, filing and menial tasks take up the majority of my time, but they are neither fulfilling nor do they help me reach my goal of finishing a book. So, if I'm feeling stressed and I need some help getting through my projects, I'll hire a clerk to deal with the huge pile of filing, while I concentrate on the actual writing.

For homemakers, jobs like washing the windows can take all weekend, but that job hardly contributes to what actually makes the house run. Why not hire someone else to do the windows while you cook the meals, a far more productive chore that takes far less time?

By utilizing the ABC analysis to divvy up your work into three easily recognized categories, you can decide whether you need to pass some of your chores on to someone else.

What's the easiest way to put this into action?

1. Make a list of all your activities for the time period for which you're going to hire a worker.

2. Figure out the importance of each task and number them accordingly.

3. Evaluate the tasks according to the ABC Analysis. In other words, the first 15% of your list of tasks are the most important, thus they are A tasks and can't be delegated. The second 20% are B tasks, which are important, but might be handed to a trusted worker. The third percentage, the 65%, are far less important and can be delegated to someone else.

How do you decide which are A tasks? Ask yourself the following questions:

- Will this task be important in meeting my goals?

- Can I accomplish several different goals by completing one task?

- Which task will garner the most recognition or importance for my company/department/group?

- Which task will cause me the most stress or negative feedback if I don't attend to it right away?

- What do I stand to gain by completing this task?

He is great enough that is his own master.
—Joseph Hall

The Eisenhower principle

President Dwight D. Eisenhower took the ABC Analysis one step further, by adding a W—which stands for wastebasket. When determining how to meet his goals, he divided his tasks into four categories:

- Immediate/Important: The tasks that need to be tended to right away.

- Immediate/Less Important: The jobs that are demanding, but can wait a moment.

- Less Immediate/Important: Those tasks that can wait, but which will become problematic if put off too long.

- Less Immediate/Less Important: The chores that can be relegated to the wastepaper basket or given to someone else without a worry. These are often the tasks that make a person feel overworked and underpaid.

Give time-consuming jobs to others

Utilizing one of the principles defined earlier in the chapter, you need to analyze which of the jobs

Moneysaver
Figure out what you're making an hour and what it would take to pay a worker to do your easier tasks. Chances are you'd make money by paying someone else.

you're responsible for are taking up the majority of your time. Those are the tasks you can easily delegate to someone else. Keep the important jobs for yourself. They will be the ones for which you are entirely responsible, thus you don't want to pass on that responsibility to someone else.

Here's a sample checklist that you can use to determine the priority of each task you have on your plate:

PRIORITY CHECKLIST

Date	Priority	Task	Delegated?	To?
5/6/99	A	Write book	No	
5/6/99	A	Call realtor	No	
5/6/99	A	Call college	No	
5/6/99	B	Plan lunch	No	
5/6/99	B	Answer mail	No	
5/6/99	C	Wash clothes	Yes	Bobby
5/6/99	C	Clean windows	Yes	RentaMaid
5/6/99	C	Mow lawn	Yes	Bobby

Some of you might prefer do your priority list on a weekly basis or even on a monthly basis. You might also want to add dates for when each project starts and finishes. Or, do a separate list for each project, so that you can be in charge of the important elements and parcel out the more time-consuming chores to others.

Pare back or combine meetings/appointments/errands

A last, simple way to cut your work time is to seriously consider whether meetings are worthwhile and how you can combine appointments and errands. Don't just sit waiting in the doctor's office; balance your checkbook!

Look at the other chapters of this book for more explicit suggestions.

Just the facts

- Don't wait until the last minute before deciding to delegate your work. If you think about what you need to do first thing in the morning, you can delegate a little every day.

- Secretaries, housekeepers, babysitters and other contract workers are paid different wages depending on where they're located, what their experience is, and what the job consists of.

- The 80/20 principle relates to every aspect of our life. Why work 80% harder to reap a mere 20% benefit, when you can have someone else do some work for you?

- By utilizing the old barter system for exchanging services and goods, we can save ourselves time, money, and a great deal of energy.

Types of Lifestyles
and Their Needs

GET THE SCOOP ON...
How to arrange your schedule and your family's
■ How to organize your house so that you won't
waste time looking for everyday items ■
How to create meals that are quick and healthy
■ How to find help when you need it most ■
How to keep the finances from rocking the
family boat

PART V

Parents—New, Used, and Single

A lmost 75% of parents work outside the home these days. Because of the extra stress that causes within the family, time management skills are much more important than they were in the days of Ozzie and Harriet. It seems like we do more and more in the mere 24 hours a day that we all have, and we hear everyone around us saying, "I just don't have the time," or "If only I had another 48 hours." What it all boils down to is managing the time we have in a way that allows us to get the most important things done first and to prioritize the rest.

Balance in the home

One of the best ways to improve your use of time is to use the 4 Ds of time management:

- Do it
- Dovetail it
- Delegate it
- Delay it

...even on weekend days with larger amounts of free time to spend, television manages to capture almost 37 percent of free time.
—*Time for Life: The Surprising Ways Americans Use Their Time* by John P. Robinson and Geoffrey Godbey.

They are more or less self-explanatory, but here are a few helpful hints to make the 4 Ds clearer:

- Make a to-do list each morning as you're having your coffee and then number the top 3 that you should do first. Look at the big tasks and break them down into smaller, bite-sized chunks. Consider your energy level (some of us are morning people, while others have the greatest energy spurts after dinner) and get the big jobs done when you have the most energy.

- Do two things at once. Fold the laundry while you're watching television. Call your mother while you're doing the dishes. Iron the clothes while you're helping the kids practice their spelling.

- Give easier jobs to the kids. Agree with your mate that he/she will do one household task while you tackle another. And give everyone a break: Will it matter ten years from now if the house wasn't perfectly clean?

- How important is that household task? If it can wait, let it. Put off scrubbing the tub until you have a rainy weekend.

How can one little baby demand so much?

Most new parents are so excited about the possibility of having a baby of their own that they are not prepared for the amount of time and energy that new person will demand of their lives. A couple's schedule can be totally thrown off when a baby begins teething or has a night of sleeplessness (and what baby doesn't?). If a couple realizes before the birth that their lives are going to change, they can often make allowances beforehand. One thing to remember: Your schedule is no longer yours. It's the baby's.

A lot of the timesaving techniques to implement after your baby's born will also be adaptable when they begin to grow. If you start off on the right foot, you'll learn quickly that saving time in the family is just a matter of preparedness. Here are a few simple things to remember when the children are still infants:

■ Keep two or three bottles filled and ready in the refrigerator at all times. When you use one, replace it with another. If you line them up on the right side of the refrigerator, there'll be no guessing which one is the freshest.

■ Arrange the baby's sleeping area so that the bassinet or changing table is right next to the crib. Keep the items you need to change the baby within arm's reach (i.e. diapers, sleepers, t-shirts, bibs). Don't store anything in the other room or you'll have to bring baby and all to get the items.

■ Keep a full package of diapers on hand at all times. Also replace all other necessities as you use them—and *before* you run out. You don't want to get caught short without diapers, formula, baby powder, or lotion in the middle of the night.

■ Fill a small bag with baby aspirin, teething ring, a thermometer, and other infant medicinal needs and keep it in a drawer close by the crib (do not keep it where other children might be able to reach it). Also replace those items *before* they run out.

■ Do a load of infant laundry each morning as you're making your first pot of coffee or the baby's bottle. If you keep up with the laundry

Timesaver
Offer help when a family member seems to be struggling with his/her chores. Do it once, lay on the praise for a job well done, then step back. Next time, chances are they'll do the job alone.

Moneysaver
Buy diapers, formula, and wet-wipes in bulk instead of in smaller units. Watch the Sunday papers for sales and buy once a month instead of every couple of days. Not only does this save money, but you'll find it saves time.

on a regular basis, you'll save time otherwise wasted trying to find an outfit when the child spits up for the tenth time that day (infants go through clothes more quickly than at any other stage of their lives).

▪ Change the baby's sheets while he/she is in the playpen or infant swing, quiet and happy.

▪ Keep a traveling bag packed with a clean set of clothing, blanket, diapers, wet-wipes, powder, and other essentials so that you can simply grab it on the way out the door to do errands or visit. When you return to the house, wipe the bag down and replace what you've used in the bag before putting it away.

▪ Schedule at least an hour every three or four days for yourself. Ask a relative or friend to watch the baby while s/he's sleeping so that you can get some household chores or errands done (or sneak in a nap).

▪ Nap when the baby does!

Can you still have a life with children?
When children are a part of your life, organization is the best way to save time. Develop a routine. Children need to know when they'll be able to count on you and giving them the discipline of a schedule is the easiest way to let them know they count.

▪ Ask yourself whether there are certain times of the day or days of the week when you do regular jobs. If so, mark them down on your master calendar.

▪ Give your kids an idea of the times when you'll make yourself available to play with them, help them with their homework, take them places.

■ Schedule a day each week when you'll do all the shopping, laundry, or cleaning. Often, you can be shopping while the laundry is in the dryer and can vacuum while the wash is going. Practice dovetailing your activities to save time.

The worst and best time of day is the morning when everyone is rushing to get to jobs and school. You don't want to start off the day by yelling at the kids, so the best way to begin on a positive note is to give yourself extra time to take care of the first-hour-of-the-day frazzles.

Bright Idea
When doing errands, bring an activity bag for your children. Fill it with small toys, books, and snacks. It will keep them busy, which will keep them happy, and you can get more done.

1. Go to bed a half hour earlier.

2. Pack your briefcase and the kids' bookbags the night before. Leave keys, purse, and lunch money in a specified place near the door.

3. Have everyone choose their clothes the night before.

4. Get up first so you don't have to share bathrooms.

5. Rouse everyone at least 1 1/2 hours before leaving to alleviate rushing around and prevent forgetting last-minute items.

6. Let the kids make their own lunches.

7. Share the morning chores with your spouse and kids.

8. Have breakfast! If you can't eat at home, take a piece of fruit or a muffin with you to eat on the commute.

9. Set your clocks 5-10 minutes ahead to keep you on schedule.

10. When you arrive at work ahead of time, give yourself a treat later on.

Watch Out!
Remember to follow through when you promise children something. Don't waste time arguing. If you go to the store, remind them ahead of the time that you're shopping for food and not for toys.

When junior's soccer game is at the same time as the big meeting with the boss

There will be times when you won't be able to do two things at once. And someone will be disappointed. Try to schedule your week on Mondays. Fit your children's activities into your work schedule or give them at least fifteen minutes when you first arrive home from work. Make sure they know that's *their* time. They wait for you and look forward to seeing you and are usually easily appeased. Get down on the floor and play a game with them, color a picture, talk about school, but focus on *them.*

Once your "together time" is up, help get them started on activities they can continue without you. Let them know how much time is left before you start your own work, so they'll be prepared when you are ready to walk away. As stated before, get into a routine. By giving them the same amount of time every evening, you will discover they will be less likely to interrupt you later in the evening when you try to do some work you've brought home from the office or attempt to catch up on housework.

Cooking, cleaning and caretaking

According to all the surveys done on how much time families spend on household chores, cooking and cleaning take up less than 10%. It doesn't seem so, does it? Thankfully, this is one area where time is easy to save—and I don't mean by going out for fast food!

Since most families have weekends off and a greater percentage of weekend time is spent watching television, that's the best time to get some of the meal preparation for the rest of the week done. It's also the time to enlist all members of the family to clean the house.

Agree to make a regular weekly schedule for your family (remember the 4Ds) and brainstorm with family members about other ways you can save time in the household. Remember, this is a joint effort!

Microwave and other quick meals

Most families find themselves eating on-the-run, but are they eating healthy foods and is it really saving time?

Consider this: There are many meals that can be made in one minute or less. You have that much time, right? Here are some ideas:

- Keep a piece of fruit with you at all times. You can eat it at any time, at your desk, while driving, while waiting on the phone.

- A glass of milk and cup of orange juice give you 30% of your daily calcium needs and 162% of your vitamin C requirements and take only 19 seconds to prepare.

- A strawberry yogurt frappe (frozen strawberries, strawberry yogurt, nonfat milk and a dash of vanilla) mixed in a blender until smooth is delicious and takes less than a minute.

- English muffins can be used as the basis for a quick pizza (tomato sauce, mozzarella cheese, Italian herbs), a tuna melt (tuna and cheese), or a peanut butter melt (peanut butter and banana).

- Put a piece of turkey on a lettuce leaf, add a carrot stick, roll it up, and eat.

- Pita pockets can hold just about anything: a piece of leftover meatloaf, some veggies, peanut butter and bananas, salsa and cheese, tofu and tomatoes.

Unofficially...
Nutritionists state unequivocally that breakfast is the most important meal of the day, yet most people tend to cut that one out. Studies indicate that people who skip breakfast accomplish less work, are more likely to catch common colds, and are slower to make decisions.

Bright Ideas
Keep some low-fat snacks packaged and ready to go in the refrigerator for kids to grab on the way to soccer practice and for a quick snack for parents who don't have time to package a full meal. Some examples? Frozen bananas, lowfat crackers, rice cakes, vanilla wafers, and raw veggies.

Plan your meals a week ahead. Take the time you'd be watching television on the weekends and prepare an extra large batch of tomato sauce and spaghetti. Not only will it feed your family that evening, but you can package up small amounts in sealable bags and throw them in the freezer for later that week (meatball sandwiches on Tuesday?) or the next.

Planning one week's meal agenda not only saves time but also saves money and helps you keep your family from falling into a nutritional rut. *Plus* the added timesaver of giving you an exact list of what you need at the grocery store that week.

The following Weekly Meal Planning Chart gives you a format for making sure your family gets the milk, meat, grains, fruits and vegetables they need to stay healthy.

Organizing the household

We often waste moments every day looking for keys, glasses, or deciding what to wear. If the household is organized, these wasted moments will be saved and will add up to a few extra hours every week. Here's a few simple suggestions for you to consider.

■ Hang all sets of keys on a rack somewhere near the front or back door. Get everyone in the habit of putting their keys there instead of throwing them on the counter or table.

■ A basket on the table or counter could be used as a receptacle for eyeglasses and the day's mail. If the family knows that's where those items will be found, everyone will go there first.

■ A large divided folder hung on the back of a kitchen door can serve as the place where all incoming bills are filed.

WEEKLY MEAL PLANNING CHART

Food Group	Sunday	Monday	Tuesday	Wednesday	Thursday	Friday	Saturday
Dairy							
Meat							
Grain							
Fruit							
Veggie							

■ A message board on the refrigerator can be used to keep track of members of the family, appointments, and events like "today's soccer game—4 p.m.—high school field."

■ A pad of stick-it notes and a cup full of pens and pencils next to each phone in the house will save time for taking messages. The notes can be stuck to the refrigerator or that person's bedroom door so he or she can see them.

■ A large erasable calendar for scheduling activities, games, appointments, lessons, family gatherings, and other activities should be hung where everyone can reach it. Each person should put their initials next to their events so that other family members will know what everyone is doing.

The Kitchen

It's all too easy for this room of the house to become disorganized and too much time is wasted looking for a particular size bowl or storage container. Use these three simple words to keep your kitchen an efficient and timesaving room: clear, clean, and condense.

Go into your kitchen right now and ask yourself these questions:

1. What do I need in here?

2. What haven't I used in the last three months?

3. What do I use every day?

The items you need should be kept closest to your working space.

■ If you have a kitchen appliance on the counter that you don't use on a daily or weekly basis, find someplace under the counter to store it.

Timesaver
The "message center" in the kitchen should consist of: one large, yearly calendar; one cork board (at child level); push tacks, a pencil hanging on string, a pad of paper; list of phone numbers for emergencies (including Mom/Dad's work numbers, police, fire, hospital, poison control center, and a neighbor or other family member).

■ Keep unused items like extra muffin tins, bowls, or old glasses in the bottom shelves or in a closet where they won't have to be pushed aside in order to get to the items you use on a regular basis.

■ Go through all those recyclable plastic tubs and old jars. Toss the ones without covers. Stack the rest by size. Keep only three of each.

■ Hang the tongs, kitchen utensils, and pans you use on a regular basis near the stove. This will save space and time looking for them.

■ Store the cookbooks you use regularly near the preparation area. Put the rest in a closet or cupboard. Toss the recipes you have never used.

Bright Idea
After cleaning out the kitchen, put aside all the items you don't need and give them to the kids to have a yard sale. Not only will it keep them busy on a weekend when you might need to do some office work, but it'll give them spending money.

The Closets

How many moments have you lost in the morning or when you're ready to go out, simply looking for that certain pair of slacks to match your top—and when you find them, you disvover they have a spot on them, so you're back to your original search? Organizing your closets will save you precious moments when you're trying to run out to catch the bus, take the kids to school, or get to that important meeting with your boss.

Rule #1: Don't put a stained outfit back into the closet thinking you'll get to it later. Send it to the cleaners! And if it's torn, either repair it or get rid of it.

Rule #2: How long has it been since you've worn that piece of clothing? More than a year? Give it away or throw it out!

Rule #3: Keep the clothes you wear most often in a place that's easy to reach.

Moneysaver
Most department stores have sales on closet organizers. Buy several different kinds and build them into closets throughout the house. While you're doing so, sort out the stuff you don't use and give it to the kids for a yard sale.

Rule #4: Move seasonal clothes to the back of the closet or pack them in boxes and store them on top shelves. Put that prom or wedding dress in a box and store it. Same with baby's first shoes and christening dress. Get it out of the way!

Rule #5: Examine how much room you need to hang dresses. If you have only a few, think about adding a bar or shelves below so you'll get twice as much storage space.

Rule #6: Get rid of bulky dressers or drawers by incorporating a drawer system (or shelves) into your closet.

Rule #7: Store everyday things at eye level.

Rule #8: Buy or make closet organizers to maximize your space. Nice boxes or zippered bags work well to keep things organized and out of the way. Get a shoe rack for the door.

Rule #9: Look at the height of your closets. Is there some space above the highest rod or shelf? Then pack boxes up there or make another shelf to store those items you never use.

Rule #10: Once you've straightened the closets, take the time to repaint them—and make sure there's a light inside so you can see what you own.

One of the companies that makes closet kits and other housework-saving items is Closet Masters. Closet Masters, 10626 York Rd., Cockeysville, MD

e-mail: clomas@erols.com

http://www.closet-masters.com

The 15-minute cleaning spree

When you see something that needs to be picked up or cleaned, do it. Right then. Train the rest of the family to do the same thing. Once every other day, set your kitchen timer and do a "15-minute cleaning spree." Choose one room and ruthlessly go through it as quickly as you can. Throw things away, wipe down counters, toss clothes in piles to be cleaned, strip a bed, wash a couple of windows. If you make this a regular habit, you'll eliminate the need to spend an entire day off cleaning the house. It's amazing how much you can do in fifteen minutes if you concentrate on just doing it.

Quality caretaking

It has been proven in many surveys that women spend almost half their family time on cooking, cleaning, laundry, and the rest on childcare. Men spend time doing errands and taking care of household repairs, doing outdoor jobs and house-management activities. Naturally, all those duties don't include child rearing, which should be a 50/50 proposition.

Since your children are your most cherished assets, you need to take the time to make sure that whatever caretaking is necessary is the best you can afford. Because both men and women are parents, both should be involved in the choice of a caretaker. To save time, Child Care Aware, a national organization devoted to helping parents choose quality child care, lists the following five steps to finding child care:

1. **Look.** Visit child-care homes or centers and ask yourself tough questions about your first impression. Remember, this is the place where your child will be when you are not able to be

> **❝**
> Few tasks are like the torture of Sisyphus than housework, with its endless repetition: the clean becomes soiled, the soiled is made clean, over and over, day after day.
> —Simone de Beauvoir
> **❞**

Watch Out!
Make sure you leave addresses and phone numbers with child-care providers: yours, your spouse's, another family member or friend, as well as your doctor's. Also arrange for regular conferences with care-takers. Don't let problems build up.

the major caretaker. Visit the home or center more than once and stay as long as possible to get a good feel for what the place will be like for your child.

2. **Listen.** Do the children being cared for there sound happy and involved in activities? Are the teachers/caretakers' voices well-modulated, calm, and patient? If it's too noisy, the kids might be out of control. If too quiet, there might not be enough to keep kids occupied.

3. **Count.** How many children are in the group? How many staff members? The smaller the ratio of staff to kids, the better care your child will get. That's especially important for babies and younger children.

4. **Ask.** Questions to the staff members will tell you what kind of care they are able to offer your chil-dren. Make sure they have the knowledge and experience needed to care for your child—espe-cially if your child has special needs. It also might be best to find out whether the center/ program is accredited by the National Associa-tion for the Education of Young Children or the National Association for Family Child Care.

5. **Be Informed.** Take part in any community efforts to improve child care and make sure you know about the programs already underway. For more info before making your decision, call Child Care Aware at 1-800-424-2246.

Delegating

Families should work together, but often the only way they can do so efficiently is when the main care-taker of the family (usually one or even both of the parents) realizes they can't do it all. That's the time to delegate.

Delegating isn't always easy. It means someone will lose a little of the control he/she might have had over the household. It also means certain jobs might not get done as well or as quickly as they used to. But if you want to find some time in your busy schedule, the best way to create some is by giving some of the easier tasks to other members of the family.

Communication is one of the most important factors when delegating, and there are several ways to do this:

- Tell or show them.

- Leave notes in a specified place (the refrigerator is usually good—get a small erasable board).

- Work with family members. Together, you'll get twice as much done twice as quickly.

- Make a list. Use it as a mini-contract.

To divide the household responsibilities, it's often wise to consider the tasks and decide who will get each job. Consider using the chart below and keep it in a place where each member of the family will see it. Each task should be assigned to one or more members of the family (you might also want to make up a daily schedule so that tasks can be assigned to different family members on different days). Not only will the chores be done with a minimum of argument, but each person will automatically know their responsibilities, as well as those of the other members of the household.

Creating a task list like the following sample will help you organize your family and get the housework done with a minimum of fuss.

Unofficially...
Rosie O'Donnell, talk show host and entertainer, often stocks her office with toys and snacks for her kids so they can visit her while she works.

Timesaver
When it's on sale, buy hamburger in bulk. While you're repackaging it in meal-sized quantities, throw some hamburger into a skillet with some oregano, salt, pepper and tomato sauce. When done, package and freeze it. Instant meals!

SAMPLE TASK LIST

TASK	Mother	Father	Children
Rising first		X	
Preparing breakfast	X		
Taking care of dishes			X
Preparing lunches			X
Making beds	X		
Emptying garbage		X	
Caring for pets			X
Preparing dinner		X	
Daily to-do lists	X		
Shopping	X		
Vacuuming		X	
Sweeping/ cleaning floors	X		
Laundry	X	X	X
Picking up toys/ clothes			X
Miscellaneous tasks	X	X	X

Shopping efficiently

One of the biggest time-wasters is something we're all guilty of: stopping for a moment on the way home from work to pick up last-minute items. Without fail, this is when the supermarket or drugstore is at its busiest, and as a result, you spend more time in line and in the aisles, trying to get around everyone else who has had the same idea you have.

Get yourself into the habit of shopping once a week—yes, that's what I said: once a week. And do that shopping later or earlier than the rest of the crowd. Go to the grocery store first thing in the morning or after dinner. Not only will you have the pleasure of having the aisles to yourself, but you won't have to waste precious moments in line either. Also, if you get there first thing in the morning on a sale day, you're liable to get everything you need in one fell swoop—and stock up on those items you always need, those items that you have to stop for on the way home during the week.

Purchase extra quantities of sale products and store them in places you don't normally use. Canned items can go in that small area under a staircase. Dried goods can be stacked under a bed. Not only does buying in bulk save you money, it also saves you time.

Preparing for special occasions ahead of time

Keeping track of birthdays and anniversaries on your yearly family calendar helps to keep track of important dates, but what happens when those dates are on top of you and you don't have time to buy a gift? One solution is to maintain a drawer full of "all occasion" gifts. Make it a habit of picking up the package of stationery you see on sale at the local department store when you're in there for the annual white sale. Perhaps you don't have someone to give it to at that moment, but you can tuck it in your "gift drawer" for sometime in the future. Another idea is to save all those well-intended gifts you've received but can't use. Instead of tossing them, put them in the "gift drawer."

Saving time with finances

Often we put off balancing the checkbook or filing taxes simply because the job is daunting. Make it easier on yourself by being organized right from the very beginning. If you've filed your paid bills by

Moneysaver
Shop for next Christmas at the beginning of the year. Take advantage of all those 50-75% off sales. Perhaps you haven't a clue who you'll give the gifts to, but it will save you valuable time and money to have a stash of them put aside for the rest of the year.

Unofficially...
During a July, 1998, PBS documentary titled "Affluenza," several experts stated that we have no free time because we work too much and we work too much because we've bought too much. In other words, families are in over their heads.

category throughout the year, when it comes time to please the IRS, your work is almost done for you. Often the best way to save time at the end of the month or the end of the year is by taking a few moments to be organized throughout the week.

This might also be the time to do the math and decide whether that second job is an expense or a gain. Oftentimes, when couples figure out the expense of an additional car, child care, shopping quickly instead of carefully, meals out, a work wardrobe, insurance, etc., the extra income dwindles to nothing.

Timesaving budget forms

A basic record of your assets and liabilities not only helps you figure out your budget, but will also give you an idea of how much your household is worth at a glance. Here's a simplified form. Yours might end up being more complex, but this one is quick and easy.

ASSETS AND LIABILITIES

Cash on hand	$
Savings accounts	$
Mutual funds	$
Stocks	$
Bonds	$
Life insurance	$
Other assets	$
TOTAL	$
Outstanding debts	$
Credit card debts	$
Mortgage	$
Miscellaneous	$
TOTAL	$

Keeping records

The easiest way to keep track of family expenses that you might be able to take off your income taxes at the end of the year is to write them right into your daily calendar. A simple note like "Dr. Swartz—Billy's ankle—$75" will alert you that you went to the doctor on that day and spent that amount of money. You can do the same with any deductible travel expenses, home-office supplies, long-distance telephone calls, and other deductible expenses.

Bills filed right save time

For those bills you've already paid, find an accordion folder and label each section with the categories you normally divide your taxes into. Here's an example:

- Mortgage/household expenses
- Car expenses (including insurance and repairs)
- Medical, hospital, pharmacy
- Utilities (electricity, gas, water, heating/air-conditioning)
- Checkbook/banking expenses
- Donations
- Moving expenses
- Clothing
- Taxes
- Home office expenses

If you file your bills as you pay them, you'll discover hours of saved time when April 15 rolls around. And, if you need to prove your expenses at any time before then (for buying a house or credit purposes), you'll have everything in one place.

Moneysaver
Get a checkbook with a built-in calculator. Not only can you then add/subtract checks more accurately, but you can whip it out when waiting in line and balance your checkbook in moments.

Computerize your finances

Most banks have computerized checking and savings these days. If you keep those records online, chances of making errors are kept to a minimum. It takes only a moment or two to log online and check your daily balance.

In addition, you can arrange to have your regular bills paid automatically. Not only does this save time, but it will also save overdraft charges, postal fees, and the irritation of having to sit down once a week or once a month to write out the bills.

Credit cards—the false timesavers

If you need to use a credit card, remember that whipping it out when you're in a hurry will cost you move money in the long run. Most credit cards charge at least 12% interest—some charge as much as 20%. If you find you're in a hurry and need the ease of a credit card, check with your bank and see if you can get a check card that also works as a credit card. You can use them anywhere and it'll save you hundreds of dollars over a year's time if you use it only to withdraw money from your checking and/or savings account, rather than using the credit card that will add a minimum of 10% on to every purchase you make.

Getting help when you can't do it all alone

If you discover you still don't have enough time to handle all your duties and responsibilities, consider getting some help. Most often, you can trade some of your time with friends or family, but when you can't, there are plenty of reasonably priced services that will do the following for you.

Caretakers and car pools

We've already discussed child caretakers, but there are also other options:

■ Check with your local library to see whether they have reading hours during the morning or on Saturdays. If they last an hour, you can do some short errands while your child socializes and is entertained. Remember to get back on time! Library personnel aren't babysitters.

■ Most working moms or parents who are going to college have learned that working in a group often takes the stress off each other and frees them up to do the work/studying they need to. Arrange with several friends to hold a weekly playtime when one parent takes the responsibility for three or four friends' children. For a couple of hours, each member gets free time in exchange for taking the responsibility themselves at a pre-arranged date.

■ Check with the local Y to see whether they have after-school programs or drop-off times when parents can leave children for a short period.

■ Church groups often offer summer Bible-study programs or sponsor groups like Brownies and Cub Scouts. Not only do the children learn, but it's a way for parents to schedule much-needed breaks for themselves.

Laundries

For those families who can't keep up with the laundry, most Laundromats offer wash-and-fold services. For approximately 75 cents per pound, you can get your laundry washed, dried, and folded. This saves an incredible amount of time. Check with your local Laundromat or dry cleaners.

Unofficially...
Two women in Connecticut worked with the local newspaper to found the W.I.N.-W.I.N. Foundation, which stands for (When in Need-Where in Need). Its goal is to give a break to families raising disabled children—if only for a few hours each week.

In addition, most local newspapers feature a section in which at-home mothers or retired homemakers advertise their services. For a small fee, they might even pick up your clothes and drop them off.

Just the facts

- Preparing for an infant before he or she arrives will save time and headaches later on. Buy items like diapers, baby food, and formula in bulk.

- Create a large calendar where all family members can write their appointments, games, and other plans so everyone will know each other's schedules.

- Don't waste time shopping at the busiest time of the day and try to keep grocery trips to a minimum by buying everything in bulk.

- Organize kitchen space and closets with racks and shelving. Toss out anything you haven't used in the past six months.

- File your bills and receipts neatly so that you don't waste hours looking for them when you need to do your accounting.

- Create play groups with friends and other family members so that you'll have spare time for running errands.

GET THE SCOOP ON...
How to balance work time with personal time ▪
How to recognize when you're losing touch
with your goals ▪ How to streamline your road
to success ▪ How to deal with the guilt and
anger caused by simply not having enough time
to keep up ▪ How to use computerized tools to
meet the demands on your time

The Career Person

We make decisions every moment of every day. Sometimes those decisions concern spending time reading a book, watching a baseball game, organizing a meeting with clients, or making love to our significant others. Work-time decisions are different, and they *always* focus on how we're going to spend our time.

Often work-related time is decided for us—we don't get a say in when a project is due; the boss does. And as the world around us speeds up with the advent of timesaving devices, our own time needs change and evolve. The road to the top becomes fraught with tougher and tougher decisions, most dependent upon how we manage the career time we have.

Some choose to let the career steer them and to follow in whatever direction necessary to achieve their career-oriented goals. Some go the other route: The career is secondary to personal goals. Some feel they have no choice, that the decision is made for them rather than by them. That's not the case. The choice of how you spend your time is yours and you can manage it if you know what your ultimate life goals are.

When work takes time away from family and friends

More and more often, we hear people complain about being torn, unable to decide between the hours they need to spend working and the time they want to spend with family and friends. "Play" time is often the last thing to be written into the daily planner, and stress levels rise until we scream, "I need 48 hours in a day, not 24!"

We hear stories about people who have lost touch with their family because business demands are so great that they can't take an hour or two to see Ryan's soccer game or to spend time with friends who have long ago stopped inviting them to parties. We might feel that what we're doing to succeed in business keeps us going from the time we wake up until we fall into bed at night—only to get up and do the same thing over and over again. We are those people who work forty hours a week at a regular job, then spend the weekends trying to catch up on work-related reading or studying for the next college degree we need in order to climb up the ladder of success.

Answering the following questions should prove whether you're one of those career people who need to begin practicing some more productive time-management skills:

- Have your friends stopped calling?
- Does your family wonder what you look like?
- Do you feel you're not enjoying life to the fullest—or at all?

66
There are risks and costs to action. But they are far less than the long range risks of comfortable inaction.
—John F. Kennedy
99

- Are the strains of trying to satisfy your own needs and those of your loved ones keeping you in constant conflict?

- Are some of the balls you're juggling starting to fall to the ground?

- Does what you're doing take more time than you think it deserves?

- Do you find yourself scrambling just to catch up, never getting ahead?

- Have you discovered you're never finishing a project you begin?

- Do you feel you need to hire someone to simply help you meet your own responsibilities?

- Is it all too much?

If you've answered yes to any of the above questions, you're probably a person who needs to really examine the impact time management might have on your career—and your life. And if both your career and your personal life are important to you, maybe you need to ask yourself one final question: If this were my last day on earth, would I wish I had spent more time at the office or with my family and friends?

At what price?

Most of us don't have the option of leaving work in the middle of the afternoon to fit in a round of golf. If you do, that's great! Taking time out to play some sort of game (even if it's with co-workers or people with whom you're discussing business) works off some of the adrenaline build-up that people who work 24/7 accumulate.

Doctors have known for years about what happens to people who exist in high-pressure environments. They've treated heart patients, stroke

Unofficially...
Anais Nin, writer and world-renowned diarist, stated often in her journals that she longed for personal time when she could spend uninterrupted hours with her husband. She guarded that time selfishly and advised others to do the same.

victims, and people with ulcers for centuries, and every doctor in the world will tell you that almost all of those diseases can be cured by a simple adjustment in lifestyle.

The "fight or flight" syndrome (a survival mechanism from our ancestors) causes a rush of adrenaline which, in short bursts, is healthy for the system. That's what gives mothers the strength to lift heavy items off their children, what spurs a warrior into action against a much larger foe, what will save a woman from a rapist. It's a strength we need in times of danger. However, when that rush of adrenaline is continuous, it's poisonous. Career people who live on the edge on a regular basis—whether it's as a stockbroker, watching the rapid roller-coaster of highs and lows, or as a self-employed businessperson who needs to monitor small business sales and employees seven days a week—are all victim to the diseases, both physical and mental, caused by that constant rush of adrenaline.

That "fight or flight" syndrome can also cause us to become so stressed that our vision becomes extremely limited. We no longer see how others feel about what we're doing. We can't recognize the change in a loved one's tone of voice, can't see the disappointment in a child's eyes, can't connect with our friends when they need to "just talk." When that happens, relationships start to crumble. If we're in a marriage, our spouse may decide that since our job is more important than he or she is, what's the use of continuing. Time to solve these problems becomes more and more precious—and more difficult to find. The more pressured we feel from those around us, the more likely we are not to efficiently utilize the time we have.

Divorce rates skyrocket when the career takes over. Old friends disappear. Kids grow up believing Mommy or Daddy just doesn't care. The results of this kind of disillusionment can be catastrophic. Currently, the divorce rate is at approximately 50%, up from 43% in 1988. Is that directly related to the fast track many workers are on? It's hard to tell, but it is obvious that people expect more of relationships these days—and when relationships are interrupted by one partner's work schedule... someone suffers. Most of the time, it's you.

By learning how to manage the time we need to spend to forward our careers effectively, we also learn how to give time to those relationships that matter most. When we discover the secret to that delicate balance, we have truly discovered the secret to living a full and enriching life.

How important will this be five years from now?

Every time we get into a situation where we need to make a choice between work and home, the one question that ultimately forces a decision is: How important will this be five years from now? Your answer to that question will depend on your individual needs, but whatever that answer is will also determine how you spend the days of your life.

If you want to get to the top of the corporate ladder, you need to streamline your energies. Planning, preparing, prioritizing, and controlling should be words common to your vocabulary.

You should keep the following steps in mind constantly. Every day you devote to your career and every moment you think about how that career dovetails with your personal life, you should:

1. Keep your goals—daily, weekly, annual, and lifetime—clear.

Watch Out!
When stress becomes chronic (long-term), rather than acute (short-term), the likelihood of heart attacks rises dramatically. Take time to smell the roses!

2. Check in with yourself on a regular basis and re-establish your own needs.

3. Weigh your career needs vs. your absolute necessities.

4. Ask yourself if you're satisfying yourself and those you love whenever you take time away from your career for your family or time away from your family for your career.

5. Control how you spend your time by practicing good time management *every day*, not just when you feel stressed.

Saying no to others means saying yes to yourself

Moneysaver
When asked for a favor, ask yourself if it'll save or make you time, guilt, or money. It may seem cold, but when you put everything into those categories, it's often easier to make decisions about what you should do.

Think about the quality of your life. Take a moment and sit back in your chair, go over the pros and cons of your life, and consider what it is that you're missing. You can come up with something you want, but do you have everything you *need?*

As you're reading this book, your immediate answer might be, "I need more time to do what I want." We all do, but do we allow ourselves that luxury? Most of us don't. The trick is to evaluate what your needs are and how you might meet them. One of the most positive ways is by learning how and when to say no.

The single, most-effective word you can say is 'no'. Remember that when others try to determine how you should spend your time. If you have trouble saying 'no,' then practice. Realize that by saying 'yes,' you are essentially moving your own priorities aside in order to accommodate someone else's— and by doing so, your work/free time is cut even shorter than it already is.

Ask yourself the following questions:

1. If I don't finish the project/task/I've agreed to, what are the consequences?

2. Is *not* finishing going to be more strenuous than saying 'no' from the start?

3. Is the request something that fits in with my own priorities and goals or will it take me away from a project I need to complete?

4. Can I delegate the project to someone else?

5. Am I hesitating to say 'yes'?

66

The only man who is really free is the one who can turn down an invitation to dinner without giving any excuse.

—Jules Renard

99

Don't feel you have to make an excuse every time you say 'no'. Just say it and shut your mouth. If the other person pressures, you can make a simple statement like "I have too much on my plate right now and wouldn't be able to do that job justice," or "I'd rather not do that right now, but let me make a suggestion...," or "Now's not a good time, but why don't you call me in a week/month/year."

Handling the guilt and anger

In today's world, most couples who live together also work, sometimes carrying on lives that barely connect. It can be incredibly frustrating to try to find quality time when schedules don't mesh at all. Sometimes, one person ends up doing more than his or her share of housework or child care while the other seems caught up in business. Situations like these cause one partner to be angry, while the other usually manages a load of guilt. Each one tries to find the time to make all ends meet—often unsuccessfully. How do you handle the guilt and anger? Through planning and a lot of compromise.

Here are some suggestions:

1. Sit down and write out all the things you need to do.

2. Agree on who will take which chores, then post the list where everyone can see it.

3. Agree that if either of you has a work-related emergency, the other will take over—and arrange some way to repay the person who has taken on the extra work.

4. Make sure #3 doesn't happen more than three times in a row.

5. Decide exactly what is and isn't necessary around the house. If you don't need to iron the sheets, *don't.* Send out a load of laundry to the cleaners on occasion.

6. Don't buy a house that requires gardening upkeep unless that's a natural relaxation technique for one of you. Remember how time consuming gardens are!

7. Get rid of your guilt about take-out food or leftovers. It's okay to have pizza occasionally. Not only does it save time and energy, but most of the time it costs the same as a home-cooked meal.

8. Create ways to socialize that will combine your business and personal friends. That way, you'll both get to see the people you care about.

9. Instead of inviting people for dinner, invite them for dessert or a quick potluck, where everyone brings their favorite meal. That way, you can entertain without having to plan for days ahead of time.

10. Plan time for "dates." Most working couples forget the reason they got together in the first place—they enjoyed each other's company. Schedule times when you can both get together to relax. Make it a date and keep it!

In addition to taking care of the daily routine, make sure you keep in contact with yourself and your mate about important matters. Don't converse about urgent things in brief moments before you both head in separate directions. Take the time to sit down face-to-face or schedule a drive where the two of you are alone in a car without other interruptions. Surprisingly, doing this in the car forces people to make decisions and also allows the freedom to say how you really feel because no one can walk away and you're both looking forward or out the windows. It's amazing that more psychiatrists don't recommend the car as a safe place for couples to work out the details of their lives.

And perhaps most importantly, when you get everything done on time and your life feels more in control, build in some rewards. Once you meet a goal, give yourself a gift, whether it's simply lying on a chaise lounge under a tree for an hour listening to the squirrels chattering to each other or a fancy meal at the nicest restaurant in town. You deserve it—and life is too short to keep rushing around without taking time for yourself.

Taking control of work hours vs. personal time

Let's talk about control. Not the "bad" kind of control where one person is in charge and every one else had better shut up and listen, but the "good" kind. The kind that allows you to get your work done and still have time to relax and enjoy life. That's what it's all about: life. No one will remember that you worked every night long past when everyone else had left. They'll remember that you were a good father, friend, mother, daughter, partner, or person. In order for your life to be well balanced, you need to personally take the reins. That's control.

> **"**
> I don't know what the definition of success is...but I know failure is trying to please everybody else.
> —Bill Cosby
> **"**

Watch Out!
Don't waste time trying to control other people. You can't control other people's expectations of you, but you *can* control how you respond to those expectations.

Who and what can we control? We can control ourselves. That's it. No one else and nothing else. That said, you need to remember that there are a lot of things we can't control.

Remember, the reality is that when you are in the workplace, you are dealing with other people, and when you have to cooperate with those people, there are a lot of factors that are purely and simply out of your control. Expect that and accept it. If you do, you'll be able to control the moments of your life that are important to you. It will also make it easier for you to realize your goals if you know that other people will occasionally be part of the obstacles you need to bypass in order to achieve what you perceive to be success.

However, when you are expected to lead people, the equation changes somewhat. Then the control ultimately depends on how *you* manage things. The way you manage things ultimately determines how you manage people. And the way you see things determines what you do in order to get the result you want.

Whether a worker or a leader, the balance between work hours vs. personal hours is a tenuous one. Recognizing the fact that none of us have total control over our lives is the first step toward gaining the necessary control over how we spend the time we *do* have control over.

Imagine this scenario: You enter the office at 8:30 a.m. on Monday morning and the following is what awaits you:

- Meeting at 9:00 with management to establish a scheme for getting new clients.

- Four urgent phone calls must be made before noon.

- Twenty e-mails must be answered, three of which are urgent, ten are important, and the rest can wait.

- Two memos must be written—and they're key to a new marketing campaign, so they must be handled with care.

- Afternoon meeting with a client who's unhappy with the way her account is being handled.

- Mail must be answered.

By noon, you've added four more items to your stack of things to do: reports generated by the meeting with management and problems that arose from the three phone calls you were successful in making. You skip lunch to catch up on the e-mail, and by three, you're getting an anxiety attack about writing the memos. Five o'clock comes and the stress from meeting with your unhappy client weighs so heavily on you that you shove the mail aside and put your head in your hands for a moment. Your head throbs, and when the phone rings, you consider letting your voice mail pick up. But you must answer, and it's your husband asking what he should pick up for dinner. With a sinking heart, you tell him you won't be coming home for dinner. Silence. Then he reminds you this happens on a regular basis and he's beginning to feel like you aren't married anymore. All of the irritations of the day boil over and before you know it, you're arguing. Can you head this problem off at the pass? *Yes!* If you'd taken about ten minutes early in the morning and scheduled your day, created a to-do list approximating the amount of time each chore would take and building in time for interruptions, you could have had a clear picture of what was expected of you during the day and planned how you would handle it. You could

Bright Idea
Figure out how your job functions for you by charting the time it takes you to complete various tasks. Give each one a priority, then an estimated time, the goal time, and the actual time completed.

have prioritized your chores and approached the day in a manner which would have allowed you not only to accomplish all your work, but to get out of the office on time.

What are the questions you should ask yourself?

1. What are the most important tasks I need to accomplish?

2. What can I put off until later or pass on to someone else?

3. Which activities are the ones I can do while I'm doing something else?

4. Are the meetings necessary or can they be handled with a phone call or an e-mail message?

5. How can I rearrange my schedule to get the maximum amount accomplished and take care of the urgencies?

And—how can I do it all and still leave time for myself?

Taking five minutes to plan and prioritize can save you hours later on. In the meantime, the important thing to remember is to try to accept your own imperfections before they begin stressing you out so much that you can't learn the simple skills you need to balance the scales.

Thankfully, the need for stress reducers at work has finally been recognized. Some companies have instituted such benefits as on-the-job masseuses, health clubs, retreats, and seminars on time management. They know, probably better than we know ourselves, that a worker who feels they have no time to accomplish all that the job requires will probably turn in a lower quality of work—simply because there isn't enough time to do a good job.

Some simple ways of taking control are to:

Unofficially...
Millionaire steel magnate Andrew Carnegie once paid a consultant $64,000 for advice. The consultant gave Carnegie two ideas: Write down what you have to do today and do the most important thing first.

- Take advantage of those stress-reducers. Enroll in a workout class and remember that the hour every couple of days that you spend working out will give you more energy to deal with work-related activities.

- Treat yourself to an occasional day off to catch up with your family.

- Remember that if you effectively manage the hours you spend in the office/at work, you can also do the same with those hours you spend at home.

- Keep in mind that the only person you can control is *you*.

Do you work well with others?

Though we've stressed over and over again the importance of being able to control your own use of time, the career person may also need to be able to work with and control others and how *they* use time.

Working with people is inevitable. Even if you're working at home on the computer, sooner or later you'll have contact with someone else—either via e-mail, a chat room, or some sort of instant messaging service. In order to achieve your career goals, you must deal with people and realize what kinds of dealings are time-wasters and how you can best focus on saving time.

We won't get along with everyone we work with—that's a fact of life. But if you can manage to see their strengths, as well as their weaknesses, you can figure out how to work effectively with them. Or how to teach them to work effectively with you. Once you achieve that kind of understanding, you will automatically save yourself hours of otherwise wasted time.

66
You cannot always control what goes on outside. But you can always control what goes on inside.
—Wayne Dyer
99

Watch out for:

- Morning chatters—especially on Mondays.

- Afternoon chatters—those who want to get out of work early.

- Drop-ins—people who don't respect others' time or space.

- Meetings—especially meetings where the agenda is never clear and discussions last far longer than necessary.

- Lunches—especially when the planning for where to go and when often takes longer than what you need to discuss.

- Online chatters—those who think a "quick" chat during the work day is okay.

Watch Out!

Socializing is one of the greatest time-wasters—and it can happen in an office with a hundred people as quickly as in an office with two—and even when you're online.

You have control over exactly how much time you spend socializing. Sometimes a quick glance at your watch is enough to signal the other person that it's time to go back to work. Sometimes a stronger signal (such as a sign on your office door) is necessary to let others know you need to work. And sometimes you need to utilize impersonal tools like voice mail. Whatever the case, sidestepping is necessary—and often quite difficult. But if your priority is to finish work by 5 and get home to your family or friends, then you need to control how you spend the hours at the office.

Let's take each of those situations and see how you can save time.

1. Early morning chats. Instead of joining the others at the coffee machine, pick up a cup on the way to work (or bring it from home) and disappear right into your office. Get into the habit of shutting the door or indicating you're busy for

the first ten minutes of the workday. Use that time to plan your daily strategy. By the time you're done making a to-do list, the early-morning chatters will be at their desks and you can get your second cup of coffee, then go right to work. I'm not saying you need to be anti-social; just watch out for those prolonged conversations by the coffeepot.

2. Afternoon chats. Save your filing and straightening-up activities for the end of the day. If someone wants to come in to wind down, you can file while you talk. But keep working! Getting two tasks accomplished simultaneously is one of the ways efficient people get their jobs done.

3. Drop-ins. Think of people who don't respect your work time or space as akin to drive-by shooters. They're stealing bits of your life and you need to protect yourself against them. If your desk is in plain sight, figure out a signal code with your fellow workers. Putting a flag in plain sight on your desktop might work. Often, simply keeping your head and eyes down indicates that you don't want to be disturbed. If that doesn't work, try putting on a pair of headphones. You can listen to "white noise" or nothing at all. No one needs to know the difference, and you'll be giving yourself the privacy you need to accomplish your tasks.

4. Meetings. If you're leading the meeting, make up an agenda of items to accomplish and stick to it. Use phrases like "moving right along" and "let's table that until later" to signal to others that you are there to do a job and intend to get it done as quickly as possible. If you're not the

meeting leader, suggest to whoever is that they might want to let others know what the meeting agenda is ahead of time so that everyone will have their remarks/comments prepared and things will move smoothly. If the meetings happen on a regular basis, perhaps the office needs to set a time limit. And if you make these suggestions, chances are management will notice and appreciate you.

5. Lunches. When planning lunch—whether business or personal—mention to your partner(s) that you have from 12-1 or 1-2. Schedule a certain amount of time and make sure you keep within that time frame. If the lunch is a business lunch, move it along as you would a meeting. Suggest having food delivered so that the lunch-meeting will be more productive. Once you get into a restaurant, the natural tendency is to drift into social conversation, which will lengthen the meeting time and reduce your productivity. If the lunch is personal, remind the friend you're with that you need to get back to work. And remember not to drink! Drinking during the day reduces your productivity in the afternoon.

6. Online chatters. If you simply don't have time to talk, don't open your messaging box at all when you get online. Or, program your messenger with an automatic response like "I'm away from my desk right now. Will get back to you later." Another alternative is to quickly answer the person, then add that you'll send a longer, regular e-mail message later when you have more time.

Bright Idea
If you have an office door, put up a sign— perhaps something humorous like "Interrupt Now and You'll Be Fired" or "When the Computer's Clicking, Don't Come Knocking."

Utilize the tools of the computer age to maintain a "social" life

There's absolutely no excuse for working individuals to miss out on a social life, especially when we have so many computerized tools to help us do the work we need to accomplish to maintain our desired level of success. Though we have mentioned a few here, there are new timesaving devices coming on the market all the time, and if you take advantage of the work they can do for you, your stress will decrease and your free time will increase.

Can't juggle both personal and business schedules? Enter everything you have to do on an electronic palm organizer. Let the computerized calendars remind you of birthdays, meetings, baseball games, and deadlines. They can even prompt you to return phone calls.

Don't have time to chat with friends or family? Use a cell phone to have your quick catch-up conversations while you're in a traffic jam or waiting to pick up the kids after school.

Do you feel like you've lost touch with friends/family who live far away? Schedule half an hour late in the evening to create a long e-mail, then cut and paste to send it to your favorite friends and cherished family members. You won't waste time saying the same thing over and over again, and you can keep them up-to-date on what's happening in your life.

Determined to get more work done before watching your daughter cavort on stage in the school play tonight? Use a hand-held dictating system while you're caught in traffic—or better yet, try ViaVoice, Lemout & Hauspie's Voice Xpress, Naturally Speaking or Dragonspeak's mobile recorders. You can dictate directly into the recorder,

Timesaver
Turn on the optional "clock" for your messages so that you can easily see how long you've been online. Sometimes that one simple act is enough to curtail your own tendency to waste time chatting.

Moneysaver
Remember to keep your planning time to a minimum. Getting into the habit of spending 5-10 minutes at the beginning of the day planning your projects will save you money.

then simply plug it into your computer at home. While you're playing, the recorder downloads the dictated memos, reports, and letters into your computer. All you have to do is edit and print!

Can't figure out which project to do first or how to complete two at once? Use your computer to generate a PERT chart. Designed by the U.S. Navy to monitor the Polaris project, PERT stands for "Program Evaluation and Review Technique." It's used to help people visualize and keep track of several projects simultaneously. Create a time line chart that stretches as long as your projects, then write in the steps it will take to complete both projects; or, you can order a program which works with Microsoft and other technology from PERT Chart Expert® online.

Ever get cut off while you're online? When you get back on, a simple way to find out where you've been is to hit Ctrl-H. It will give you the history of the websites you've visited and make that research much easier. Usually, a computer will save the history of where you've been for approximately a month or so—and save you lots of time when you've forgotten that piece of information you desperately need to include in your memo to the boss.

Only have an hour to make two hours' worth of calls? Batch your calls, plan carefully, dial yourself and you'll be saving time planning, calling, and the time of one or two other people in the process. If the line is busy, hit redial, and if you discover that certain people are available only during regularly scheduled hours, note it in your planner so you won't waste time calling when that person isn't there.

Playing telephone tag with family, friends, and co-workers? Utilize your answering machine to its greatest advantage. Leave a message about when you'll be available to take calls or leave a detailed message about whatever's going on in your life. When my husband was in the hospital undergoing heart surgery, we had ten or twenty calls to answer in the evening after getting home from visiting him. Instead of repeating the same message over and over, I found it was easier, less time consuming, and more satisfying for those who were calling if I left a message with his status on the machine each morning. A few years later, my father had the same operation and my mother left the same kind of message on her machine. When you're under stress like that, it's exceptionally difficult to stretch for another hour at home and make phone calls to loved ones. With the detailed messages we left, everyone knew what was going on and we were free to rest once we'd returned home. What was most important was that we remembered our priority: to stay healthy and relatively stress-free so that we could take care of our husbands.

Can't connect with people no matter what you try? It's time to write a letter. In this day of computerized machines and voice mail, sometimes people simply cannot deal with another faceless message. If they have a good, old-fashioned piece of paper in front of them, it might get the action you require. So, when all else fails, use the U.S. Postal Service.

Just the facts

- Setting goals first thing in the morning helps you plan the day and prioritize tasks.

- Dual-career couples must schedule time for each other, just as they would for a business appointment.

Unofficially...
Many artistic people worked on multiple tasks simultaneously. Leonardo da Vinci took notes with one hand while drawing with the other.

- Pausing briefly before agreeing to a project can save time and unnecessary stress.

- Using an answering machine to deliver a specific and timely message to each caller saves hours of telephone time.

GET THE SCOOP ON...
How to save time before school starts ▪ How to
establish priorities ▪ How to dodge procrastination ▪ How to study effectively ▪ How to
make research quick and easy

The Student

Chapter 13

S tudents are among the most "scheduled" people on the planet. Beginning with grammar
school, students have classes held at regi-
mented hours, homework that must be done on
time, sports and other extracurricular activities to
attend, and with all of that comes the stress of trying
to manage time. As students age, their time becomes
even more important, and it's not uncommon for
junior and high school students to experience stress
and stress-related illnesses because there aren't
enough hours in the day to accomplish everything.
Is that true, or is it just that you, the student, haven't
figured out how to *find* more time by managing the
hours you do have?

Yes, we understand most students work. Yes, we
understand what it takes to make it through high
school and college. Yes, we know you also want to
have a life. And you can! But you must learn to manage those hours in order to get your work done and
create some breathing time for yourself. Here's how.

Unofficially...
Wilma Mankiller, mother, wife and the chief of the Cherokee nation, went back to school in the late 1960s. In spite of family responsibilities, she found time to take extra classes at San Francisco State to learn how to use the library and to expand her vocabulary.

Creating a time plan

Successful students always plan ahead. You might ask at this point: How can I plan ahead if I don't know what I'm planning for? That's a good question, but you can start getting some items together to help you put the wheels into motion once you get into class.

Firsthand experience, both as a student and instructor, has shown many that one of the first aspects to student success is to assess your expectations. *your* expectations, not the school's or the teachers' or the coach's or your parents'. Yours.

Ask questions of yourself, such as:

■ How much time do I normally need to study?

■ What do I want to do with my free time?

■ What's most important to me: a degree in computer science or a great season on the football team?

■ What bad habits could get in the way of my studying effectively, and do I have the fortitude to fix them?

■ What are my best attributes, and how can I utilize them to my advantage?

■ Where will I need help, and how will I get it?

Be honest with yourself. Analyze where you've gone wrong in the past and why. Although you'll never be perfect, you can improve. And if you go into a new situation—whether it's a new grade in the same school or whether you're entering college for the first time far from home, you're wise to go in with a good knowledge of who you are and what you're capable of from the beginning.

Then, list your goals (see the table on next page) and put that list somewhere where you can see it. It's okay to make changes to it, by the way. All of our goals change as our life progresses.

LIFE GOALS/PRIORITIES LIST

Life Goals	Priority
1.	
2.	
3.	
4.	
5.	
6.	
7.	
8.	
9.	
10.	

Step 1: When you've finished filling in the blocks, go back and list them 1 through 10 depending on priority.

Step 2: Then, take the top four priorities and establish them as a goal that you'll work toward during the current year.

Step 3: Now list several choice activities that will help you achieve those goals. For example, Goal No. 1: Finish in top half of class

▪ Produce papers/homework on time.

▪ Give myself the gift of free time for each 'A'.

▪ Attend writing workshops.

▪ Meet with study group once a week.

Once you've done some self-examination, you'll have to do some pre-school work. Don't groan. Sometimes shaving some time off up front will save you hours—or days—later on.

Moneysaver
Order general supplies from an office supply catalog that will give you a discount.

Things to buy (or make) now:

- A computer (if you can't buy one, find out where the computer lab is on your campus and visit it before school starts!).

- Printer ribbons/cartridges (a case is better than buying just one).

- A calculator.

- A dictionary and thesaurus.

- A calendar (preferably two of them—one for your book bag and the other—a plastic, erasable one—for your wall).

- An assignment notebook (either a paper one or a hand-held computer with a scheduling program).

- A lightweight notebook with dividers.

- A divided pocket insert which will fit into your notebook.

- Pencils, pens, and highlighters.

Why buy these things now? Because this little shopping spree will save you time later on when all your fellow students are crowding the aisles of the bookstores and department stores during the first week of school. You'll already be at home entering dates on your calendar and getting ready for your first assignments.

Another thing to remember is that you can check out the bookstore as soon as you register. See if the books for your classes are in and beat the rush for the best and cheapest used copies!

Next thing to do before the first day of classes is to take a thorough tour of the campus, even if it's small. Know where the library, computer lab, class-rooms, cafeteria, and bookstore are. Familiarize yourself with how long it takes to get from one place to another. On the big campuses, classes are usually scheduled ten or fifteen minutes apart, but you might have a class at one end of the campus and the walk to the other end may take fifteen minutes or more, making you consistently late. Better to know that now! Even finding out where the bathrooms are in each building will save you time later on.

Okay, do you feel comfortable now? Then, let's start school!

Start at the beginning of the semester

At the beginning of each semester/quarter/year, the teachers/professors usually hand out some kind of schedule or syllabus. Some are kind enough to add a breakdown of what will be required during each class period you attend. Others will simply inform you of the dates when big projects or papers will be due. Get as much information as you can. If the dates aren't available, go to the teacher/professor after class and ask if they have an idea when their biggest tests or papers will be due so that you can start blocking out time for them. Not only will this impress those denizens of higher learning, you'll be doing yourself a huge favor as well.

Once you have some kind of idea what the class is going to expect of you, get yourself a calendar for the entire period (i.e. most semesters are approximately 16 weeks long, so you'll want a five- or six-month calendar). Take the time to sit down and map out the calendar. Mark all important due dates, as well as other events (i.e. football games, dances, vacations, holidays), so that you can see the whole picture at a glance. Don't wait to do this! Do it during the first week of school, because once the ball starts rolling, you'll be so busy with assignments, you

Bright Idea
Check your college/school's Web site and take a virtual tour of the campus. You might also find invaluable information about registration, Web site addresses of faculty members and counselors, a study skills site, and an additional bonus: discounted tickets for school events and local attractions!

Moneysaver
Make copies of your schedules on the campus copy machine rather than buying several calendars. Then place one schedule in each notebook, in your room, and on your refrigerator (or somewhere where roommates/family will see it). If you work, make a copy for your boss so he or she won't schedule your hours during class times.

won't have a chance to create this type of organized schedule for yourself.

When you have the big dates inked on the calendar (preferably in red or a color that will stand out), then you can start counting days or weeks between the larger assignments. Note which ones can be started right away (i.e. reports for which you can gather research materials now), and which ones will depend on material supplied in class.

Another thing to do now while things are still quiet is to visit all of your teachers/professors. Introduce yourself and address anything that you believe might be an issue during the semester. For example, if you know you have a problem reading quickly or that math has never been your best subject, talk to the professor about it. He or she might be able to suggest sources to help you study or might offer tutoring (a huge timesaver, not to mention a great way to raise your grade). Discuss the instructor's expectations and how you might meet them. In general, get a better feel for the assignments and how you can prepare to complete them.

Plan ahead for major projects/papers

Now that you know what you have to look forward to, it's time to sit down and figure out how much work each project/paper is going to demand of you. Be honest with yourself. Examine the projects/papers you are least interested in first. If you get them out of the way, you'll feel a sense of accomplishment that will buoy you and make it even easier to meet your deadlines for the other assignments.

On your erasable wall calendar, note the amount of time in between now and your big assignments.

SAMPLE MONTHLY STUDENT CALENDAR

Sunday	Monday	Tuesday	Wednesday	Thursday	Friday	Saturday
1.	2.	3.	4.	5.	6.	7.
8.	9. Psychology test	10.	11.	12. Algebra test game	13.	14. Homecoming
15.	16. End of withdrawal period	17.	18. Composition essay due	19.	20.	21.
22.	23.	24. Doctor's appointment	25.	26. Thanksgiving	27. Holiday	28. Holiday
29. Holiday	30. Back to school. Sociology paper due					

When you've figured out your monthly commitments, it's time to create a weekly calendar to break your time into more reasonable "bite-sized" chunks. This is the place where you'll schedule your classes, time to eat lunch (yes, you must eat!), study time, free hours, sleep time, extracurricular and social activities. Hour by hour.

Analyze how many hours you will need for that end of the semester biology project, to study for the mid-term history exam, and to create the essay for composition class. Now, go back to your monthly schedules and write down your study/writing time for those large projects.

Most experts believe that each hour of class time equals three to five hours of study/homework time. When you create your weekly schedule, build that in—and remember that the larger projects take twice that amount of time, so consider that now instead of later. Get the jump on as many of those larger projects as possible.

Make a commitment to yourself to keep to your schedule and remember that in order to get everything accomplished, the only time that is flexible is free or social time. All your other "appointments" with yourself must be kept if you are going to succeed in managing your time.

Schedule more time than you need

How am I going to do that you might ask. Easy. Don't wait until the last minute to do anything. If you do, Murphy's Law guarantees that something will go wrong. The library won't have the book you need for researching your political science paper; the computer lab will be jammed with other students; your study partners will suddenly come down with the flu; or your printer will run out of ink.

Unofficially...
One of the most prominent American businessman of our century, Lee Iacocca, learned early in his career that time management was of the utmost importance. In his autobiography, he stated that, even though his school days were full of extracurricular activities, he still "managed to graduate twelfth in a class of over nine hundred."

SAMPLE WEEKLY STUDENT SCHEDULE

Time	Monday	Tuesday	Wednesday	Thursday	Friday	Sat/Sun
6:00 A.M.	Eat	Eat	Eat	Eat	Eat	SLEEP!
7:00	Study	Study	Study	Study	Study	"
8:00	Commute	Commute	Commute	Commute	Commute	"
9:00	Class	Study	Class	Study	Class	Study
10:00	FREE	FREE	FREE	FREE	FREE	OR
11:00	Lunch	Lunch	Lunch	Lunch	Lunch	Play
12:00 P.M.	FREE	Class	FREE	Class	FREE	
1:00	Study Group	Study Group	Study Group	Study Group	Study Group	All
2:00	Study	Clean	Laundry	Study	Clean	Day
3:00	Class	Free	Class	Free	Class	
4:00	FREE	FREE	FREE	FREE	FREE	
5:00	DINNER	DINNER	DINNER	DINNER	DINNER	
6:00	Study	Class	Study	Class	Study	
7:00	TV	TV	TV	TV	TV	
8:00	TV/FREE	TV/FREE	TV/FREE	TV/FREE	TV/FREE	
9:00	Prep	Prep	Prep	Prep	Prep	
10:00	Prep	Prep	Prep	Prep	Prep	
11:00	Sleep	Sleep	Sleep	Sleep	Sleep	SLEEEP!

If your paper is due Friday, start writing it the weekend before. If it's done early, great. Look it over one more time on Wednesday and get it typed Thursday. Not only will it be ready on time, but you will be less stressed.

You have a research project for statistics due in two weeks and an exam in chemistry tomorrow? Which takes priority? The exam, of course! But you can study in the library for fifteen minutes, then look for some books for your statistics project. Give yourself ten minutes to get the books, then get back to studying chemistry. If you break down your study habits this way, not only will you be able to accomplish two things at once, but you'll remember more of what you study.

Never leave any project until the night before—or even two nights before. Coasting along and thinking you don't need to worry about something because it's a week or two away will only serve as a time impediment for you.

GRAB YOUR WAY TO SUCCESS

G	Goals	Set a goal.
R	Responsibilities	Determine your responsibilities.
A	Analysis	Analyze where your time goes.
B	Balance	Balance work, class, study, and leisure time.

Remember this simple acronym (Source: *The Confident Student* by Carol C. Kanar, Valencia Community College).

Expect the unexpected

The computer printer always runs out of ink in the twelfth hour, and when you're pressed for time, the clock inevitably moves faster than it should and nothing mechanical ever works the way it's expected to. If you've scheduled yourself fairly and blocked out more time than you need, you can avoid some of the worst time-wasters (i.e. getting halfway through printing that Composition essay and running out of ink; oversleeping on the morning of the big Statistics exam because you spent too much time studying the night before; hurrying to meet your professor and getting a flat tire). The key to sidestepping these problems? Preparation!

If you know you have a couple of long papers due next week, take the time on Saturday or Sunday and pick up an extra ream of paper and an additional printer cartridge. Set your alarm clock for half an hour earlier than necessary on those days when you have a big test or a meeting with your professor. That way, if you oversleep, you'll still be on time—and if you get that flat tire, you'll be able to change it and still make it to your professor's office on time.

In other words, plan ahead. Give yourself a little more time than you need, and don't leave *anything* until the last moment!

Making the most of class time

Most students don't realize how much time they waste in class when they are not actively engaging in what the instructor is saying. The simple act of keeping a pen in hand while a lecture or demonstration is being given keeps the student interacting with the material. And when you're interacting, the brain is in gear—and keeping the brain in gear is all-important in school!

With pen in hand, you can underline passages in a text, jot down quick notes about the material being reviewed, write yourself a reminder about an assignment that's due, or create outlines for a formula you might have difficulty remembering later.

Moneysaver
Check the Sunday newspaper for sales on the items you normally need and take advantage of the sales when they happen. This not only saves you money, but it'll save you time—especially when you run out of ink the night before a big project is due!

Watch Out!
Forgetting important things can waste incredible amounts of time. Always pack your book bag the night before, so you can grab it and go. Jot reminder notes to yourself and place them somewhere obvious. Use Post-its ® in bright colors and always keep a packet with you.

Whatever you're doing with that pen, it'll be your quick start to remembering what you need to know in that class in the future—and will help you avoid the time trap of daydreaming in class. The best part is that those notes you took, the diagram you made of that amoeba, or the quick sketch you drew of the cannons Napoleon used in the French Revolution will be just the right tidbit to bring back the details you'll need for that big final exam. It's no wonder that students who sit up front and take copious notes are the ones who get the best grades.

Highlighting/annotating

As you're reading texts, you should always have a highlighter handy. Use it to emphasize key points, to indicate which definitions are important, and to draw your eye to facts you'll need to know later (i.e. dates, formulas, statistics, lists). You should also highlight any words you're not sure of—as you're reading them. *But* be careful. Highlight *only* the important text. It's easy to get carried away.

Later, go back and review the meanings of those words and write a brief definition in the margins. Not only will this save you time, but you'll also add new words to your vocabulary list as you go.

You should be actively reading the text, engaging with it as you would with a professor. Note any questions, comment on any surprising information, disagreements, and note any parallels you might draw in the margins of the book in pencil. As you find the answers to these questions, you can erase your comments. Writing them down commits them to your memory and will also serve as a basis for class discussion (something the teachers really appreciate!).

Don't worry about losing the value of the book. Textbooks don't sell for much and for the extra couple of dollars, you're getting an invaluable study tool. If you're really trying to save money, write in pencil.

How to retain what you read

There are several different methods that have proven to help you remember what you've studied. The most important factor is that you read the material with curiosity. This is called active recall. If you use a highlighter and annotate, as suggested above, you will be practicing this technique. In addition, asking and answering questions helps students grasp and retain important information.

The SQ3R Method increases your reading speed and understanding. Here's how it works:

- S = Skim

- Q = Question

- 3R = Read, Recite, and Review

Skim—Quickly glance over the heads in the section and make mental note of them. Read the summary at the end of the chapter, if there is one. It will give you an idea of the important topics covered. Skim the whole chapter. Write questions and comments under the definitions and headings you skim.

Question—As you read quickly, try to anticipate questions your instructor might ask from the task and attempt to answer them.

Read, Recite, and Review—close the book. Write a short summary of what you've read. Answer questions out loud. On 3 × 5 cards, write down new terms and concepts, then review them once more before closing the book and going on to your next homework assignment.

Unofficially... College athletes like Daunte Culpepper, star quarterback of the University of Central Florida Knights football team, have an incredibly tight schedule. To save time, Culpepper worked closely with an instructor/tutor to write essays for Freshman Composition classes.

Timesaver
Keep your 3 X 5 cards with you at all times. Review them while waiting in line at the grocery store, bank, on the bus, or when you have an extra five minutes at lunch. If possible, share them with your study group and have your peers question you about terms and concepts. A few moments will save you hours later!

Are you studying effectively?

Half of the problem with retention is that students aren't prepared to study. Use the following checklist to make sure you utilize your reading/studying time to its fullest.

- Are you studying at the same time every day? Create a schedule with specific times and places to study. After class or before class is the best time—and choose a well-lit place with a desk or flat surface. Don't set up your bed as your study area. Beds are for sleeping.

- Have you decided exactly what you need to do? Make a short to-do list before you begin.

- How important is the homework task? Each step you take in completing a project brings you closer to your ultimate lifetime goal. Remind yourself of that and motivate yourself the same way a prizefighter would. If you do this, you'll win!

- Is your study space organized and cleared? Straighten it up. Take out your books, your pencil and paper, turn on the computer. A neat work area will save you the time wasted while looking for your "tools."

- Are you ready to begin? Then begin! Start. Don't shuffle papers. Don't make that extra phone call. Just open the books.

- Do you find yourself daydreaming? Remind yourself that daydreaming is one of the greatest time-wasters of all. *Focus.* Pull yourself back every time you find yourself drifting. If you find you can't, take a mini break, but come right back!

- Are you scheduling regular breaks for yourself? Studying for fifty minutes, then taking a ten or fifteen-minute break is more effective than attempting to work for two or three hours straight. Give yourself the "gift" of a quick walk outside or another hot cup of coffee. Then return to the project.

■ Are you finished? Do one more small task. Push yourself to go the extra mile. Then congratulate yourself, schedule your next study time, and straighten up your study area.

■ Are you making this a regular habit? Don't study for a couple of hours on Monday, then plan on returning Friday. Do a little bit every day!

■ Are you scheduling yourself too tightly? Leave some time for interruptions and make sure you give yourself time for social activities. If you have those to look forward to, your regularly scheduled study times will come more naturally.

Remember: Students who have a regular study/ work pattern are more likely to succeed.

Use your school's resources

Most schools have a division of student affairs or a student handbook that contains time-scheduling ideas, study-skills suggestions, and the addresses/ phone numbers of various counseling offices on campus. They are there to help you and can offer everything from tutoring in English or Math, help with legal problems, assistance to students who have learning disabilities or language problems, and counseling for psychiatric, academic, or financial issues.

Taking a few moments to scan what your school has to offer can save you hours of heartache later. Of particular assistance to all students are advisors

Bright Idea
If you find one particular subject daunting, tape the lectures from that class. Listen to them while driving or taking a shower. The mere repetition of the lecture will make it easier to understand the subject matter. And don't wait until the night before the exam!

66

Students can avoid spinning their wheels by seeing their professor for direction at the start of a project.

—Gail Radley, English Lecturer, Stetson University

99

and professors who can offer knowledgeable suggestions about how to make your academic career a satisfactory one for you.

Contact your professor/teacher

When a professor/teacher begins a class, he or she will inform students of their office hours, phone numbers, and e-mail addresses. If you haven't already taken the time to visit your instructors when the semester begins, then schedule a few moments to see them when they assign the first project. The following is a checklist that will help with that visit.

- Tell the instructor how much time you'll need and make an appointment with him/her during class.

- Make a list of all questions you want to ask and check them off as you ask them.

- Bring your books and a copy of the syllabus to the office.

- Ask the professor to list the three most important aspects of the assignment/test and how best to accomplish them.

- Write down the answers and refer to them later when you are completing the assignment.

- Thank the instructor for his/her time and ask if you can check in with him/her later in the semester with any other questions.

The writing center and other tutors

Almost every school in the nation has a writing center which offers one-on-one attention to a student's writing assignments. The tutors, normally students like yourself, have the skills to offer help in the subject matter, as well as the experience necessary to offer advice about how to attain better grades.

Often, they are pros at managing their time. How else could they manage classes and their jobs as tutors? Take advantage of them!

Things to remember when working with the writing center and other tutors

- Schedule an appointment ahead of time. Don't waste precious moments sitting and waiting for the next available tutor.

- Bring your assignment, as well as whatever handouts the instructor gave you, to the appointment.

- If you know you have problems with comma splices or algebraic equations, tell the tutor up front. That way you can get specialized instruction in that area rather than wasting time on others.

- Ask the tutor to send a form to your instructor to prove you've attended a tutoring session. Most instructors appreciate the extra time a student takes to get help.

- Thank the tutor and get his/her name if they've been especially helpful. It'll save you time later on if you work with someone you already know.

Counselors are invaluable

Learning how to deal with the act of putting something off is often difficult to handle. Procrastination is a problem every college student deals with at one time or another. The reasons for procrastinating are many and sometimes are best dealt with through counseling. Academic counselors are highly trained professionals used to dealing with this problem, as well as any others you might encounter during the time you spend in school.

Timesaver
Tutors at writing centers help you identify priorities for revision, so you can work on the most important things first.

Whether you simply have a problem expecting perfection from yourself, put off attempting tasks that are daunting because you have a learning or language impediment, are trying to deal with the adult learner's problems of juggling a family/job and school, or are dealing with grief, abuse, pain, or physical disabilities, the school's counselors are there to help you.

Some of the advice they might offer you will be simple, while other suggestions might require more attention. Here are some of the strategies advisors use to fight procrastination.

Procrastination: The king of time-wasters

How many times have you put off paying a bill or studying for a test or calling a friend about a problem you've had? We've all procrastinated doing something unpleasant (proof: when was the last time you scheduled a dental checkup?), and as a result, we've gotten a shut-off notice or ended up burning the midnight oil for the next day's biology exam or have had to do some fancy explaining to a friend. Has any kind of procrastination ever saved you any time or alleviated any stress? Be honest. Procrastination not only wastes time—it pushes you to the outer limits of stress.

Want to conquer procrastination? Think about the following:

- Consider the benefits of completing the task vs. the stress of procrastinating.

- Set reasonable goals for yourself. A simple daily to-do list often lets you see goals in smaller, more manageable (and less intimidating) chunks.

- Begin! Simply start doing something. Once you do, you'll find it's easier to keep going.

- Ask for help from family, friends, instructors, supervisors, and counselors. If you get a little help, it will go a long way toward building your confidence—and might save you a lot of time.

- Accept your mistakes. No one is perfect. You learn by making errors. Use them to better yourself and remember that it's better to try than to do nothing.

- Learn how to say 'no'. Think about what someone is asking you for a moment. Consider whether you have the time or energy to do it, then be honest. You come first.

- Think ahead. Remember that one forgotten item can throw off a whole day and one moment of scheduling can save you five.

- Curb your social time. Spend half an hour with a friend, then check your watch and announce it's time to go home and study. He or she probably has something to do, too!

- Remember your priorities and stick to them!

Learn how to research effectively and quickly

In today's world, more people do research on their computers than anywhere else. As a result, students have fewer library skills than ever before. If you're one of the people who believe that everything you need, you can find on the Net, you might be right. However, have you ever considered how much time you're wasting when you don't research effectively? And what about those pieces of information that you can't find on the Net?

Using the library to your advantage

Today's libraries utilize computers as well as some of the old card-catalog type of indexing. Since there

Watch Out!
80% of material learned is forgotten within 24 hours. If you review before that, you'll remember more. You'll also decrease the stress of cramming later on.

are several different kinds of filing materials, the best suggestion I can make is to schedule time at your library to get an orientation. The half hour it will take to either visit with the librarian or follow a guided tour (available at all university libraries) will save you many hours later on. Being familiar with the system used by your favorite library will help you scope out the general subject area you're interested in without spending hours on the computer or in the card files.

Naturally, the library contains more than just books on the subject. How to find it all? Check out the reference desk. Usually, the library will provide a series of handouts placed near the desk. Designed to help steer students to the available resources in the library, the handouts are filed by subject matter and will direct you to the places in the library where books, magazines, periodicals, journals, and other written materials on your subject are stored. Sometimes that's all you need to get started.

If you need more, go to LUIS or WebLUIS, for example, on your school's library computer. LUIS (Library Users Information Services) is designed to let a user do a search for a title, author, or subject. It can also link you to other libraries where you can borrow a book through interlibrary loan if your library doesn't have the particular title you desire. WebLUIS offers a more complete listing of all the printed material available on your subject, as well as audio/visual aids.

For the first timer, I suggest taking a few moments to do the tutorial offered for WebLUIS. In only fifteen minutes, you'll learn how to do a more constructive search, how to order books and other materials without leaving your computer, and how

> **"**
> When he assigned our first term paper, my professor suggested a free library class on cutting Internet research time. I laughed but took it anyway [and] discovered specialized search engines which helped me find the information I needed to get the paper done sooner.
> —Steve, University of Central Florida freshman
> **"**

to make the library system work for you in less time. And that's what this is all about, right?

Study groups: why three heads are better than one

One of the newest innovations on college campuses is a program called LINC (Learning in Communities). A major reason this program has met with critical acclaim is that it addresses the needs of first-year college students by placing them in two classes simultaneously. By going to the same classes with other students, LINC members are more likely to form study groups with fellow students who share the same classes. Not only does this help students overcome the anxiety of college life, but it improves their grades.

If you have trouble in math, for instance, studying with a partner who is as determined to succeed as you are makes learning easier. You can talk about assignments, work out problems, and prepare for tests. With two study partners, you enjoy the benefit of being able to meet even if one is sick, and your chances of understanding a difficult new equation are doubled.

Does this save time? You bet! Think about all the hours you might spend if faced with a difficult physics theory or trying to remember important dates for a history exam. If you have someone in the same room with you who not only has the same books and has heard the same lectures but also has as much at stake as you do, your cooperation is invaluable. You are more likely to comprehend difficult lectures if you can voice what you don't understand to someone else. Even if that person is also confused, together you can work it out.

Consider this: Your strengths might be your study partners' weaknesses and vice versa. Put those strengths and weaknesses together and you are supporting each other rather than failing on your own. An hour spent with a study partner has been proven to be more beneficial than three hours spent studying alone.

There definitely is strength in numbers!

Surfing the Net without drowning in the information sea

It used to be a pleasure to get on the Net, do a search and come up with a couple-hundred answers to your question. Now inexperienced surfers have to wade through thousands of "hits" when doing a search. Nothing is more time-consuming than trying to figure out which of those hits will be the most useful for you.

Though there are plenty of books on saving time on the Net, one of the most helpful tools is knowing which search engines are the best for your project.

CHOOSE THE BEST SEARCH ENGINE

Search Engine	Strength	Weakness
AltaVista	Complete coverage of Web, powerful	No browser directory
Infoseek	Searches Web, Usenet, and e-mail addresses	Small index
Lycos	Index rivals AltaVista's, some pop-up menus	Limited Booleans
WebCrawler	Fast	Searches only titles or summaries
Yahoo!	Best browser directory	Limited logicals for searching

Timesaver
Restrict your Net search by using Booleans. By adding *and, or,* or *not* to your search string, you'll finesse your search and be more likely to hit upon the actual topic you're researching.

Research isn't the only thing you can do online. You can also enter chat rooms, subscribe to newsgroups (which is a huge timesaver when it comes to accumulating research for an end-of-the-semester project), and e-mail anyone who also has an e-mail address.

Some instructors allow students to e-mail small projects to them. Check with your professors to see whether this is acceptable. It will save you time if you're ill and need to get an assignment in, and it will also answer those middle-of-the-night questions when it seems like you're the only person in the world up studying.

Just the facts

- Getting supplies and preparing yourself mentally *before* school begins saves hours of heartache later on.

- Calendars and to-do lists are effective ways of letting you see your academic life at-a-glance and allow you to juggle priorities.

- Utilizing the expertise of instructors, counselors, writing centers, and other tutors not only saves time but boosts grades.

- Make sure you choose a well-organized and quiet place to study where you won't be interrupted.

- A quick class in how to do research in the library and/or on the Net will make you a more effective student.

Watch Out!
Surfing the Net can be addictive. Keep a close watch on the time you spend chatting online to friends. Close your Instant Messenger when you're done and answer your e-mail after you're through studying.

GET THE SCOOP ON...
How to determine your need for creative time ▪
How to get time to create from family and
friends ▪ How to schedule big projects and meet
deadlines ▪ How to find an agent ▪ How to get
into colonies/retreats

Time for the Creative Person

Chapter 14

E very creative person, whether he/she is a
writer, an artist, a dancer, a singer, an actor, a
musician, or a weaver of fine fabrics, knows
how difficult it is to let go of the 9 to 5 world and follow his/her dream. Our technology-driven universe
often frowns on those who choose to listen to the
songs their hearts play and to reject the 40-hour
week for something far more soul-enriching. It is difficult to argue with the logic that most people don't
make it as artists. It's absolutely true. But what would
this world be like if Chaucer, Mary Shelley, Twyla
Tharp, Michelangelo, Mikhail Barishnakov, Sarah
Bernhardt, Barbara Streisand, and Stephen
Spielberg had listened to the masses and ignored
the urge to create? If those people had chosen to
simply conduct their life in a manner that put food
on the table and paid the bills, there would be no

music to hear, no ballet to watch, no movies to make us laugh and cry, no songs to compel us to sing along, and no books to enlighten our minds. The world would be a pretty boring place.

Following the dream

If the creative urge burns deep within your soul, how do you find the time to satisfy it when there are children at your heels, a mortgage to pay, a family to feed, and your own physical needs to appease? You learn how to manage your time in order to fulfill your creative needs and your stomach simultaneously! How? Thousands (perhaps millions) have done it before you, and all it takes is passion and a little ingenuity.

Getting permission to create

The first step to finding the time to be creative is giving yourself permission to do so. Most people believe artistic urges come from "the gods" and that you must wait until you are inspired. Not so! You must allow that you have that urge, then make time to follow through. The first thing you need to do is tell yourself it is not only okay to be creative, but a necessity in your life.

Saying "It's okay" to yourself

The artistic person's greatest time impediment is him/herself. We all fear failure. The truth is that we also fear success. Before you can control time, you must control the fear inherent in creation. Will we be able to put our work out for the world to see? Do we have to? No. You don't have to exhibit what you create. You don't even have to show your own mother, husband, wife, or best friend. You can keep all those stories, paintings, songs, and feverish dances for yourself. But you must get past the fear and give

Unofficially...
Mary Shelley, author of *Frankenstein*, wrote that entire work by hand while taking care of a house, children, and her poet husband, Percy. She simply wrote at the kitchen table, kept notes in her journal, and forged on.

yourself permission to enjoy the imagination and passion for art that thrives within you. Accept the gift and do not be afraid to use it.

Here's a simple list of how to tell your inner self that it's okay to take the time to create, to give yourself the gift of the art that you love.

Only he who does nothing never makes a mistake.

- Admit that you are an artist/ writer/ singer/ actor/ dancer, and that you are not alone. Say that out loud.

- Promise yourself that you don't need to create something perfect each time you sit down at the page/ the canvas/ in front of the microphone or the audience. Allow yourself to make mistakes.

- Forget about the parent/ teacher/ friend who told you not to waste your time acting/ singing/ sculpting/ writing. Think about how good it makes *you* feel.

- Respect your fears and acknowledge them. All humans have fears. It's totally natural.

- Tell yourself it's wonderful to enjoy your creative abilities and that if you don't, you won't have a chance to experience true happiness.

- Give yourself the opportunity to discover the heady joy and satisfaction of the world of imagination. Think of it as rejuvenating your soul.

- Daydream. Visualize yourself signing copies of your new book, dancing on stage, emoting in front of an audience, singing along with your favorite pianist, drinking champagne with art dealers enamored with your newest sculptures. Feel the pleasure that warms you and note how positive that feeling is.

Bright Idea
Check out an audiotape from the library on releasing the creative spirit and listen to it in your car. When you get to your destination, take two minutes to write down three ideas you have for projects and write yourself a promise to finish them.

Getting creative time from your family, friends, and colleagues

Sometimes getting creative time is as simple as asking for it. Sometimes it requires that you word your request in a way that the people around you will perceive to be a request for what *they* need, rather than what you need. Only you know those closest to you, so choose to either ask for help or ask what they need most, then adjust your time to fit their needs. The easiest way to do it is to consider the following steps.

1. Choose five of your most supportive family members, friends and colleagues.

2. Ask them what they believe are your talents. (More than likely, your artistic abilities will be on their lists.)

3. Tell them how strongly you believe in your own creative spirit and how frustrating it is not to have the time to create.

4. Request their help in organizing time blocks in which you can write/ paint/ act/ sing.

5. Write down their suggestions while they are still talking to you.

6. State your intentions for building creative time for yourself.

7. Appeal for suggestions for how you can rely on them to help you in your quest for finding creative time.

8. Write down their suggestions and repeat them as you do so.

9. Create a "mini contract" with them, incorporating your needs with theirs, and their suggestions for how you might satisfy both.

10. Thank them for understanding your artistic urges and tell them you'll be scheduling time

for yourself and know that they'll respect your needs.

By handling the above situation with tact and diplomacy, requesting their help and respecting the suggestions they've made, you will have paved the road for those times when you will take time for yourself and not be available to them. The act of writing down the "mini contract" is important because it will remind them that you are sincere and intent on controlling the time you need for yourself, as well as appreciating the help they will offer when you need it. In addition, it also reinforces your own promise to yourself. And that's the most important of all.

Knowing what you need to be creative

Here's a little quiz to see whether you have what it takes to balance the creative side of your life with the more mundane side. Be honest now! This only works if you are completely truthful.

- Do you need to create more than anything else? (Notice I said "need" rather than want.

- Are you willing to give up some creature comforts in order to work on your art?

- Are you willing to forge on in spite of rejection?

- Are you willing to give up social time, get up earlier or go to bed later, devote weekends and holidays to your craft?

- Do the people around you support your artistic bent?

The answers to this little quiz are just as important as the soul-searching questions themselves. If you answered 'no,' to any of the above questions, you might want to consider moving on to another

Timesaver
Take five minutes first thing in the morning and jot down your daily routine. Schedule at least fifteen minutes or more for creating and be at your desk/easel/instrument at the scheduled time, ready to create. And don't worry about being perfect!

Moneysaving
If you enroll in a class in your discipline at a nearby college, not only will you be in contact with like minds, you will also be eligible for a student discount you can use to purchase the tools of your trade.

chapter. In order to manipulate your busy life in order to find time to create, you first need to be artistic almost as much as you need to breathe. Without that passion, all the time in the world won't make a whit of difference.

With that out of the way, let's look at exactly how you can go about finding more minutes, hours, and days to produce your own personal work of art.

Give yourself the space and place

It's imperative for the creative person to have a specific space in which to work. The key word here is "work." If you begin by thinking of your art as work, you will not only pay attention to it but others will too. Well-meaning friends and family tend to intrude on an artist's precious time and space.

Find the type of space in the right place for yourself and when you go there, you will instantly know that you are there to work, to create. Sometimes that place will be in your own home, but others will have to find a type of office or studio. By having that place, you will save yourself incredible amounts of time. If you schedule your creativity the way you would a job, the act of going into that office or getting into your car and driving to your studio will signal a habit. After a few days, your mind will automatically shift to "creative mode" and those wasted hours of saying "I'll write when I have a free block of time this weekend" (or tomorrow or when the kids grow up or when I have a vacation) will end.

How to find the space for you? Depending on the discipline in which you work, your space will differ. Here are some ideas for possibilities that might exist right under your nose.

- A spare bedroom can be easily made into an office or a studio—and it's extremely helpful if it has a door.

- A laundry room might be small, but with the right type of shelving can be just enough for a writing space.

- A basement room can be converted into a dance studio, art studio, music room, or office with a minimum of work. Usually, heat and electricity is all that's required.

- A garage can often be cleaned out or rearranged to accommodate an artist's studio, a writer's office, a dancer's workout space, or a musician's practice area.

- Some libraries have study rooms that you can schedule on a regular basis. You'll be the only one there, it'll be quiet, and you have a specified time within which you work.

- Quite a few coffeehouses have back rooms where a writer can plug in a laptop or a songwriter can spread out music sheets and work undisturbed. The beauty of this is that you also have someone to bring you coffee refills!

- The local Y usually has times of the day when their exercise rooms are free. If you can schedule your time around theirs, you'll have dance space for practically nothing.

- A small office in a downtown building can often be rented very inexpensively and the thought of paying rent is the strongest motivator for using the space.

- Check with your friends and family. If they have space in their home, they might be willing to let you come at certain times of the day when they're not there and the place is quiet enough for you to produce your work.

> 66
> I enjoy writing when I am in the desert. There are no distractions such as telephone, theatres, operas, houses and gardens.
> —Agatha Christie
> 99

Break each project down into bite-sized chunks

Believe it or not, one of the best deterrents to procrastination is to have a deadline. Tell yourself you want to finish that painting, create that piece of music, memorize that song, write that book, or sculpt that bust within a particular time frame. Then give yourself mini deadlines. Remember, each project began with that first, small step, that first note, that first brush stroke on the canvas. No symphony was created in one day. No well-written book was written in one week. No play went from conception to Broadway in a month. One step at a time. You can handle that, right?

Here's the way to break the project down into chunks you can handle on a timely basis.

- Give yourself a final date when you want to finish your project.

- Look at the whole project and decide what you need to accomplish every day to reach your goal.

- Make up a calendar and write down your final goal on it.

- Write down your daily goals on a piece of paper, then transfer the weekly totals to your calendar (i.e. create one page of text a day, which translates to seven pages a week in order to reach your goal of finishing that book in a year).

- Schedule that writing/painting/singing time into every day.

- Book yourself time for breaks and vacations. Make sure you write down your "life" deadlines too—those weddings you need to attend and holidays you need to spend with your family.

Unofficially...
Josephine Baker, the famous dancer, singer, and burlesque star, raised twelve orphans while simultaneously holding down an incredibly demanding stage career, with the help and understanding of her husband and friends.

- Every day, wake up and think, "I will accomplish one page of writing/one verse of singing/one sketch/one paragraph of my part in that new play." When you go to bed that night, reflect. Have you met the goal you set out for that day? If so, celebrate!

- Have another artistic friend ask you occasionally how your project is going. If you can say, I finished five pages or wrote the first stanza of the song, you can feel a sense of pride.

- Calculate where you are along the way. Make sure you re-figure how many pages you have left or how much of that aria is still unwritten so that you can do a "time check" at important stages.

- Each time you're successful reaching a deadline, give yourself the gift of another hour working at your art. You deserve it—and that hour will put you even closer to your goal!

Bright Idea
Buy ten post-cards and write on each: Have you met your deadline? Date each about a week/month apart. Mail them in an envelope to a friend and ask him/her to drop them in the mail on specific dates.

No excuses

Procrastination is the artist's worst enemy. And it's the most common malady. It's much easier to walk away from the work than to say no to a family member who needs your help moving or a friend who wants to talk on the phone. But the most successful artists have all had to face their procrastination head on—and they have all won.

Check your "time-wasters" and figure out which ones you can adjust.

- **Interruptions.** Do you have drop-in visitors or phone calls? Don't answer the door or the phone during your scheduled creative hours. If you have to, put a sign on your door that says "do not disturb" and get an answering machine or caller ID for your phone.

Watch Out!
Planning often
wastes time and
becomes procras-
tination. Don't
overplan! Simply
do it!

- **Meetings.** Which ones can you miss? Keep the meetings within their specified time limit and don't schedule them during the time you've promised yourself as artistic time.

- **Priorities.** Have you set down a list of goals? Is giving yourself time for your book, painting, songwriting, or dancing at the top of that list?

- **Workspace.** Is it cluttered? Organize everything so you don't have to hunt for what you need.

- **Focus.** Finish one task before you go on to another. Don't begin three projects at once.

- **Socializing.** The conversation with your next-door neighbor about the weather is taking valuable time away from your creativity.

- **Playing.** Computer games, television, and surfing the Net are huge time-wasters. Give yourself several hours a week to "play" and devote the rest of the time you would normally spend doing so to creating a work of art.

- **Self-discipline.** Make yourself promises to work on your art at least once a day for a short period of time. Keep those promises.

If you can spot one time-waster in the above list and use that time for yourself and your art rather than wasting it, you will discover more hours in the day than you thought possible. Remember: All you need is to make your creativity a habit and the ideas will come.

Stealing time

We often think we don't have enough time, yet it's been proven by the experts that we have more time now than ever before. We just waste it. Here's a number of ways to find moments, hours, and days in your busy schedule, simply by utilizing the time you already have.

Get rid of the time-wasters and utilize timesavers

All of us find it extremely easy to put off the act of creating by simply filling our days with other acts of "being," whether it's cleaning the house, talking to friends, tackling too many projects simultaneously, or simply watching television. It's quite easy to turn these time-wasters into timesavers, and to eliminate the reasons why you can't write that book or score that opera.

Appointments, errands, and visits

Learn to consolidate the time you spend away from your desk/easel/instrument. Many times, we have to break from the flow we've just gotten into to take Junior to the doctor or to pick up the package from the post office. Schedule your creative time in one block and do the same with your appointments, errands, and visits.

If you know you have to take one of the kids to the doctor's, think about what you can do on the way there or on the way home. Make a list of your errands and do them all at once. Perhaps you can even slide in a fifteen-minute visit to Aunt Mabel or a cup of coffee with several friends.

Visiting more than one person at a time, preferably at mealtimes, can be very satisfying. You can take care of your social obligations, eat a meal, and no one will object when the hour's up and you're back in your car on the way home to your office/studio. An unscheduled visit might waste far more than one hour, but if you meet in a restaurant, an hour is more than sufficient.

Timesaving
Bookmark a shopping source for your artistic needs. Shop online and only for specific items. This will save time spent in large department stores, aimlessly wandering and impulsively shopping. When you need something, do a search, find it, buy it, and log off. Don't browse!

Bright Idea
Keep a notebook in your car and your pocketbook or pocket. Whenever you have a few moments to wait in line at the supermarket, bank, post office, or while at the doctor's office, take it out and jot down some ideas or make a quick sketch.

Mail, cleaning the house, and other time-wasters

Once you have ordered something from a catalog, you are forever on someone's list. It's easy to be enticed by colorful ads and catalogs. Either toss them while standing at the kitchen counter sifting through your mail or relegate them to the bathroom where you can flip through them—and toss them in the barrel immediately afterwards.

Cleaning the house is a perfect excuse for not creating. If you insist on doing it (and I strongly suggest you hire someone else, if you can afford it!), give yourself a task to do in your mind while you're vacuuming or dusting. Think about the next scene in your book, ponder the color you should use to create that ocean scene, practice singing at the top of your lungs. But don't waste that time by mindlessly pushing the mop. Thinking is creating and the artists who use "walking-around time" to explore the possibilities are the ones more likely to rush into their studio or office to jot down their ideas before they lose the moment.

Utilize vacations and days off

Those luxuriously long blocks of time when you don't need to work your 9-to-5 job are often daunting. We don't know how to schedule our time off after experiencing such tightly scheduled hours when working. What do we do with all that free time? The answer: schedule!

Often, the artist is best served by spending vacations at colonies or retreats and utilizing free weekends by attending conferences or workshops. For more information about what kinds of opportunities there are and how to take advantage of them. But for those of you who will spend those off times at home, create a schedule so you can find some time to be artistic during vacations. It doesn't have to be a moment-by-moment breakdown, but simply something like this:

- Morning—Work in studio/office
- Afternoon—Lunch with family and time by ocean
- Evening—Dinner out and late evening hours planning for tomorrow's project

The perfect artistic vacation is time spent alone. A room by the ocean, filled only with your tools of the trade. No phone, no mail, no interruptions. But if you're not so lucky, ask your family or friends for two or three hours of privacy at some point every day. Perhaps early morning is your most productive time, or you might be the type who loves it when the house is quiet after everyone has gone to bed. Whatever the case, vacations are times when the muse is relaxed and you should take advantage of it.

Timesaving tools

Moments are precious and if we can save even half a dozen a week, they can add up to an hour's worth of creativity that you might not have had otherwise. Think of some of these tools as ways to rescue lost time in your artistic life.

- Pens with flashlights at their tips. Writer Susan Hubbard keeps one of these next to her bed for those nights when she awakens with an idea. They are perfect for jotting down notes at those times when you don't want to awaken your significant other or don't want to turn the light on yourself. They're also perfect for taking on trips.
- Small tape recorders. Take one on your next trip. They're perfect for thoughts you get while

driving, flying, or otherwise in transit. Simply say a couple of words that will remind you of your idea or jog your memory, or use them as dictation machines. For those who have long commutes, it's the perfect time to turn off the radio and create a new scene in your play or sing that tune that keeps going through your head.

- Dragon-Speak hand-held recorders. A new innovation for writers, this device not only allows you to dictate, but can be hooked up to your computer so that your dictation is automatically translated into a document you can save on disk or your hard drive. An incredible timesaver.

- Microwaves. Perfect way to heat up leftovers or make a whole meal when you're busy.

- Day-planners. Artists need scheduling too and day planners have proven to be the perfect way to keep all your appointments and creative promises to yourself in one place.

The best artistic timesaver is often an agent

Agents handle an artist's work, creating the freedom the writer/songwriter/artist/singer/dancer/actor needs to devote him/herself to the art they long to bring into being.

Should you consider an agent?

If you are an artist who is ready to bring his/her work to the world, then perhaps your best timesaver is an agent. He or she will handle the business end of your work, giving you even more free time to create.

An agent not only takes care of sending a writer/artist's work out to the people who matter, but he or she will also take care of contract matters

Watch Out!
Some unscrupulous agents ask for money up front from unsuspecting writers/artists/actors. Agents worth their salt make their living by taking a percentage of the artist's earnings. Don't deal with anyone who wants a fee before signing you on.

that are often not only time-consuming but mind-boggling. In addition, a good agent can be a sounding board about business matters, can offer advice on an artist's career, and can protect him/her from the disappointments associated with being rejected. There are a number of questions to ask an agent before you sign with him/her. But before you get to that step, it might be wise to save yourself some time and ask your fellow artists who they know in the business or attend a conference, workshop or visit a colony to meet agents in person. Often, years of time and heartache can be spared by simply doing a few moments of homework in the beginning.

Suggested questions to ask before you hire an agent:

- With whom have you worked in the past? Whom do you currently represent?

- What percentage do you take? Most writers' agents take 10-15% of a writer's earnings and actor's agents may take as much as 25%.

- How often do you inform clients of your activity on their behalf?

- How much guidance do you give your clients regarding where they should be in their careers? Do you do any editing?

- How soon after you get my check from the publisher/ producer/gallery, will you forward my share?

Also, check your agent's qualifications with a noted organization before signing any contract. Some of the most trusted who either list agents or can refer you to places where you can obtain information are the Association of Authors' Representatives (for print material, film, TV, and/or stage);

Moneysaving
Investing in a guide like *Money for Artists: A Guide to Grants and Awards for Individual Artists* will introduce you to the many opportunities for struggling artists to apply for awards that will offer the time and money one needs to create.

Graphic Artists Guild (for graphic artists and print-makers); Screen Actors Guild; and many others.

Artists' colonies, conferences, and retreats

If the rigors of daily living are too much, artists often find themselves looking at other options, other ways to help them find the time, space, and quiet they need in order to create. For centuries, musicians, poets, artists, theater people, and sculptors have discovered that being in close proximity to other artistic people fuels the fires of inspiration. Somehow, banding together to gives them the freedom to believe in themselves as talented entities.

Do you need to go away to create?

Your job demands your attention 24 hours a day, your family doesn't understand your creative urges, and you find yourself creating every excuse known to humankind to not pay attention to your art. What do you do? Perhaps you need to leave your home space and go someplace neutral, someplace where your phone doesn't ring, the kids don't clamor for your attention, your needs are taken care of, and you have the chance to bounce your ideas, as well as your frustrations, off people who not only under-stand but sympathize.

Ask yourself the questions below to decide whether a colony or retreat would be best for you:

▪ Are you self-disciplined?

▪ Is there a project you're longing to complete but can't because of other obligations?

▪ Do you lack professional contact with other writers/musicians/ artists?

▪ Is it impossible to find the privacy and quiet you need to create?

- Are you comfortable living in a community where you share some mealtimes with strangers and might not have access to amenities such as a phone?

- Can you find an extended period of time when you're free to go away?

If you've answered yes to most of the above, an artists' colony or retreat might be the answer for you.

Where to find retreats

Retreats and colonies exist all across the United States, as well as in other countries. One of the best listings of such places is Shaw Publishing's *The Guide to Writers Conferences*. Though the title might sound restrictive, the guide gives information on many colonies/retreats that are open to artists from all disciplines. It also offers information about admission policies, costs (if any), dates the places are open, locations and contacts.

The quickest way to get in

Most colonies/retreats have an application process that begins long before the artist is ready to arrive. Begin looking for an opening at least six months in advance, sometimes earlier for those colonies that have a following.

Here are some of the items you should prepare before you start sending out applications:

- Letters of reference. Most colonies/retreats require one or more.

- Description of the project.

- Budget for the project.

- Brief curriculum vitae.

- Statement regarding the need for colony time.

- Financial statement if applying for fellowship.
- Sample of work (either printed, published, or photographed).

Just the facts

- Creating a schedule for yourself often makes it easier to find the time to be artistic.
- Asking for help from family and friends not only helps them understand your need for creativity, but might result in unexpected help.
- Time-wasters, like television and the Net, take large chunks of creative time from the artist's life. Learn how to say 'no'.
- Agents can be great timesavers, but they take a portion of the money produced by the artist.
- Colonies and retreats offer time and space to struggling artists, and having a package of pre-application materials ready will help the application process go more smoothly.

Organize Your Work/Home Space and Yourself

PART VI

GET THE SCOOP ON...
How to plan an office cleanup ▪ How to decide
what to toss and what to save ▪
How to cancel junk mail ▪ Filing necessary documents and coordinating paper files with computer files ▪ Deciding how long to save documents ▪ How to use your In-/Out-box

The Paper Blizzard

Chapter 15

When you look at your desk, does it appear as though an avalanche is about to happen? Are you constantly shuffling one pile into another? Does it take more than 30 seconds for you to put your hand on the item you need? Sounds like it's time to organize what's commonly called the paper blizzard—and by default, yourself!

Controlling the paper flow in three easy steps

- Toss
- Keep
- Act

We might also add a fourth step: Communicate.

Before an office starts to reorganize in order to save time, all members need to be aware of what it's going to take to make the office more efficient.

Your goals:

- Get rid of clutter.
- Analyze existing office procedure.
- Decide best ways to reorganize.

Bright Idea
Hire a professional: National Association of Professional Organizers (NAPO) contact information: (512) 454-8626 or e-mail to: napo@assn-mgmt.com. Check out the NAPO NATIONAL Website. (www.napo.net).

- Save time looking for misfiled documents.

- Simplify filing by using one process.

- Eliminate duplication.

- Keep important records in safe places.

- Establish guidelines for how long items should be saved and where.

- Define responsibilities for filing and record-keeping.

- Train yourself and employees how to keep the office organized.

Time to clean!

No excuses. No more procrastinating. You can't work well if you can't find space on top of your desk. Think of it this way: where are the cleanest desktops in your organization? They belong to the most important people, don't they? Do you think it's because the corporate bigwigs have nothing to do? Just the opposite! They have much more responsibility than anyone else, and they get things done because they're organized. Thus, the clean desktops.

So, take a deep breath and let's start cleaning.

Schedule a day when you won't have to worry about being interrupted, find yourself a nice big barrel, and wear old clothes. Get yourself in the mood for cleaning and prepare yourself before you even walk into that office that what you're going to do means making quick decisions.

Here are the questions to ask yourself as you pick up each piece of paper, as you go through each file:

- When was the last time I needed this?

- Do I need it now?

- Will I do something about it in the next week?
- Can I replace it easily if I discover I need it later?
- Do I need it for taxes or any other legal reasons?

Your answer: yes or no.

Your objective: Split everything into three piles. One goes into the wastebasket, one will be filed, and the third will be put into your in-basket so you can do something about it immediately.

Make the decision and don't question yourself about it!

Cancel that pile of junk mail

Junk mail wastes more time (and paper!) than any other kind of mail. Some people like receiving unsolicited notices and catalogs or sales fliers, but most of us don't. One way to stop wasting your time reading is to stand while you sift through the mail—right next to the barrel. If you see something you haven't requested, toss it before you even open it.

Ask the post office not to pass your name on to any lists. One of the ways they do this is by using your change-of-address cards. Request that they keep your name and address private.

Some activists suggest even stronger ways of stopping junk mail.

- Send the mail back to the sender with a note on the envelope stating "remove me from list."

- Write your credit card companies and tell them not to use your name without your written permission.

- Call the 800 numbers on random solicitations and tell them to take you off their database.

Unofficially... Hemingway's writing studio in Key West was little more than a gateleg table, upon which his typewriter was placed, a few bookcases, a credenza with adjustable shelving where he stored his files, and a lounge chair where he could stretch out to think.

Timesaver
An organization
called Zero Junk
Mail (zero-
junkmail.com)
will stop all
unsolicited
brochures,
newsletters,
sales material by
contacting the
direct mail orga-
nizations to get
your name taken
off their lists.
They charge
approximately
$25 a year for
the service.

■ Call your Congressman and tell him/her you want more action taken to curb junk mail and strengthen privacy laws.

Write to the address below and ask that your name be deleted from their mailing lists:

Mail Preference Service

Direct Marketing Association

PO Box 9008

Farmingdale, NY 11735-9008

Today there are more than 54,000 mailing lists being sold on the Net, so your chances of being "spammed" or receiving junk e-mail are pretty good. What do you do about it? Junkbusters Spam-off SM will build a "no e-mail solicitations" block for your web page that should stop most of the unwanted junk mail.

Skim instead of study

When you first open your mail, skim the important items and put them aside. Sift through the rest of the pile and toss the junk mail. Put aside brochures, magazines, catalogs, and other texts you want to read later. Then return to the important matters. You should have three piles—and all done within a matter of moments.

The best way to decide whether you're going to read a magazine is to scan the table of contents. If you find an article that's interesting, circle it—or better yet, clip it and throw the rest of the magazine away (or send it to the laundromat, doctor's office, or nearest waiting room where someone else will get some enjoyment out of it).

If you seriously can't afford to order anything out of a catalog or don't think you can use anything they're selling, pitch it. And don't keep your

catalogs longer than a month. Most catalog companies publish their wares more often than you can
keep up. People who know how to manage their
time don't spend precious moments buying things
they won't ever use/need.

What to hold and what to pitch

We all know the old rule that you should only handle a piece of paper once. Maybe that's correct, but
sometimes a piece of paper will get read, filed in the
in box, then retrieved for some action, before getting permanently filed in a cabinet. That's being
handled more than once! How can you stop this bad
habit? Read what needs to be read, then file it. If
some action is required, transfer that information to
your to-do list.

Some suggestions for how to stick to the handle-
each-piece-only-once rule:

- An interoffice memo about a meeting. Enter
  the meeting date, time, and reason in your calendar, then toss the note.

- A note from a colleague asks a question. Pick up
  the phone and answer the question (or drop
  them an e-mail), then toss the note.

- A brochure for office materials arrives. File it
  with catalogs (and remember to weed out the
  old ones and toss them while you're there. Most
  have dates right on the spine, which makes it
  easy to see which are outdated).

- An interesting article catches your eye. Forward
  it to a colleague or file it for future reference.

- Instead of saving several pieces of paper or articles, make one list.

Moneysaver
Check out a mag-
azine's contents
online before
buying it. Most
of the bigger
publications now
have online sites
that give you a
bite-sized taste
of what they
offer.

❝
The brain is a
wonderful organ.
It starts working
the moment you
get up in the
morning, and
does not stop
until you get
into the office.
—Robert Frost
❞

- Recycle. If you can't bear to part with some of the finer magazines or catalogs you receive, find out whether any of your local libraries or schools are collecting them to be mailed to another country. Often organizations will package up old material for schools in foreign countries. One of the schools where I used to work did an annual collection of books and magazines for schools in Guatemala.

- Think. Before you keep something to file, remember that 80% of what's filed is never looked at again.

- Decide to stop procrastinating. Get rid of the clutter!

The timesaving filing center

Most people hate to file. We put it off until the piles are so high that we have no choice but to find a place to put it all. By that time, you can get rid of most of the items you thought you needed, simply by going through the pile and considering whether you'll ever use that piece of paper, magazine article, or annual report again.

Where do you put all these papers? There are two types of file cabinets: vertical and horizontal. Which one you use depends on what kind of space you have in your office. You can buy metal file cabinets, fire-retardant cabinets, or wood cabinets that gleam like the furniture in Thomas Jefferson's well-organized office/library. Getting a file cabinet with easy-rolling drawers and good suspension is most important. You don't want to have to dig in the back of the drawers to see the files.

Another determination you need to make is whether you need letter-size or legal-size files.

Unless you are likely to have a lot of legal matters in your life, letter size is best. Legal papers tend to be 14" long, thus take up more space, but most people don't need that extra space, so consider your own circumstances before purchasing the files.

Other options include cardboard filing boxes for those people with fewer items to file or less space (these boxes fit under most beds). You can also get portable plastic filing boxes if you are likely to want to move your work from place to place. These are all available at your local department stores (Kmart, Wal-Mart, Target, etc.).

Check with your local office-supply place and see which one is best for you.

Office supply outlets that sell furniture:

Office Max—800-788-8080; (www.officemax.com) or (www.officeworld.com)

Value America—888-510-VALU; (www.valueamerica.com)

Office Depot—800-685-8800

Best Buy—800-648-0113; (www.bestbuy.com)

Circuit City—800-395-4377; (www.circuitcity.com)

Levenger's—800-544-0880; (www.levenger.com)

When you've decided how you want to file, the next step is to create file folders that suit your purpose best and label them clearly so you'll be able to find them immediately. Most people like to use an alphabetical system, but if your projects are numbered, perhaps that's easiest for you. Or, you might want to file projects by dates so that you can toss the

Moneysaver
Open shelf spacing costs less than conventional filing methods and takes up fewer square feet. It's estimated that open shelving costs about $50 per foot while conventional files take up floor space averaging over $200 per square foot.

❝

For most men
life is a search
for the proper
manila envelope
in which to get
themselves filed.
—Clifton
Fadiman

❞

oldest ones and move the newest ones to the front of the drawer.

Label makers are available from most office supply houses and can help you create easy-to-read labels for your files. Choosing different colors will make each subject automatically recognizable. For instance, you might want to use red labels for one company's projects and blue for another's. Or use purple for quarterly reports and orange for annual. Or green for Mr. Wise's work, red for Ms. Cohen, purple for Mr. Bocca, and yellow for Ms. Elwell.

Another way of filing is to use three-ring binders. Buy separators for them so you can divide the items into date-intensive files or alphabetical or subject matters.

Hints for filing:

- Don't use paper clips when filing. They'll attach themselves to the next page and before you know it, you won't be able to find the page you're looking for.

- Alphabetize your file folders. You'll be able to find things more quickly that way.

- Inside the file folder, file the most recent correspondence in front.

- Put a label on the front of the file drawer to indicate what's inside.

- Write the label by hand with a marker. It's easier and faster than running labels through the typewriter or computer. If you have a bunch to do, get a label maker. Casio makes several different kinds for different purposes and they're available at most office supply places.

- Keep the most important files (the ones you'll refer to daily) in your desk drawer.

The daily/weekly/monthly/annual cleanup

One of the easiest rules to remember is KISS: Keep It Simple Stupid. Everything else will fall into place if you remember that one line.

Daily: Every night before you leave the office, clean off your desk. Throw out the items you no longer need, transfer important to-do items to your master list, make a pile of things you need to attend to the next time you come in, and throw the rest in your box to be filed. The only thing on your desk should be what you'll act on first in the morning.

Take five minutes before you walk out the door and file the pile on your desk. Keep on top of this organizational chore and you'll know where everything is when you need to put your hands on it. Don't keep up with it and your office will soon be teetering and tottering with piles of paper—and you won't be able to find a thing.

Weekly: Before you do your weekly filing, ask yourself if the information you're filing is available elsewhere. If you can get it on the Net or in a book already on your shelves, toss it. Your pile should go down by at least half.

Toss newspapers that are older than two days. If you need an article, clip it, and put the rest in the recycle bin. And if you haven't used or passed on that article by the end of the week, toss that too.

If there's anything on your desk during your weekly cleanup, you should be actively asking yourself whether you can transfer it into a file, or better yet, the wastebasket. Keep your paper piles to a minimum. Don't let them get out of control or you'll

Watch Out!
Check every piece of paper that's clipped to another. You don't want to throw away something important.

Timesaver
If you only have
a few filing sys-
tems, there'll be
fewer places for
you to lose valu-
able papers.
Better put your
information in
the most general
category first
than to file it
under a specific
term you might
never use again.

waste more time trying to get back into an organized pattern again.

Monthly: Once a month, go through the files in your cabinet. Toss anything that's more than six months old. If it's too important to be tossed, move it to the back of the cabinet or to an archival storage area.

Check the magazines you've received for the month. If you haven't read them, cancel your sub-scription. Clean out the magazines that are more than a month old. There'll be a new one coming in soon to replace them.

If you've gathered business cards during the month, transfer the names and addresses you'll use to your Rolodex or calendar. If you don't remember who the person is, toss the card. If the person has an e-mail address, enter it in your online address book, then toss the card.

Annually: Once a year, the storage areas need to be purged. Remove anything that hasn't been touched for a year. Toss files associated with employ-ees no longer with the company. Remove anything that has legally gone past its date. (IRS files only need to be kept for seven years; legal files only need to be kept for the statute of limitations; expired poli-cies, or guarantees should be pitched.)

Wading through the piles

Okay, you've thrown away whatever you can, and now it's time to tackle the piles that are left over.

- Remember, if you have work to do, note it on that master list you've been keeping.
- Keep the pieces you'll need to refer to in the future.

■ This is the time to make a to-do folder. Get a colorful one (preferably with sides so you don't lose anything) and write 'things to do' across the top. Keep this one close by because you'll be filling it.

■ Take another look as you go through your pile and if there's a piece of paper you can't file or know you won't attend to, throw it away.

■ Get rid of the stick-it notes. If the note is important, transfer it to your master list. Better to keep one list than a bunch of notes that might get lost.

If it hasn't been used, it's refuse

Invariably, when I go through my in-box and finally reach the bottom (I bought a deep one specifically because I have so many things waiting to be done), I discover that the stuff on the bottom consists of items I don't really need to do anymore. If it hasn't been used, it's refuse.

How long do you keep important papers? Here's a quick glance at some retention guidelines:

Save permanently:

■ Annual financial statements

■ Fixed-asset additions (improvements, retirement info, depreciation policies)

■ Income tax reports

■ Court briefs and appeals

■ Income tax payment checks

■ Corporate documents (charters, constitutions and bylaws, stocks, deeds, labor contracts, trademarks and registration applications)

■ Accounting books

Bright Idea
Keep a file index so all papers will be kept in regular files. Keep it simple, short, and have a paper copy handy, as well as a copy on your word processor. Hang a copy near the file cabinets themselves.

Seven years:

- Bank statements (checks, stubs, register tapes)
- Cancelled payroll and dividend checks
- Purchasing records
- Sales records
- Travel and entertainment records

Three years:

- Monthly financial statements (internal)
- Subsidiary ledgers
- Personnel and payroll records

One year:

- General business files and correspondence

Moneysaver
One rack with different levels and file pockets, preferably see-through, will be enough for you to keep everything you need close by. One such rack is made by WolffWire Corporation 800-748-0190 E-mail: exdesign@carrinter.net

Keep the important papers within reach

Naturally, you want to keep everything you use on a regular basis within hand's reach. A small (and we emphasize the word 'small') desktop filing rack will keep everything you need at hand.

Necessary brochures/books/manuals

Those computer books you need to refer to on a regular basis, a dictionary and thesaurus, an office directory and only one or two other books or manuals should be within arm's reach. The rest can be stored behind your desk or in file cabinets.

Other brochures/catalogs you might want to keep nearby:

- Office supply catalogs
- Travel brochures (especially if you're on the road a lot)
- Zip code directory
- CDs for computer use
- Notebooks for office rules/procedures

In-/out-box

Your in-box should be the place where you keep everything you haven't already looked at or taken action on. If you keep the items you need to deal with in your in-box, then they will all be safe in one place and not get confused with the pile of rubbish you're going to send to the trash.

Once you take a piece of paper out of the in-box, what do you do? Toss, File or Act!

Your out-box contains items that should be mailed or delivered to someone else in the office. That box should be emptied at least twice a day: once before lunch and once before you're ready to leave the office for the day.

Can't this be kept on disk?

Quite a bit of your office information can and should be kept on disk. However, one word of warning before we go any further: Back up everything! Too many hours have been spent bemoaning lost files or (worse) retyping information that was saved on the hard drive but not on disk.

One of the best timesavers ever invented is the battery backup system for computers. If your power goes off or someone unwittingly unplugs something, your computer will stay on and you won't lose the work you've been doing. Surge protectors also help, but they won't always keep you on during those surges for more than a couple of minutes. If your system must stay online, you have to provide an alternate source of energy. Even when gasoline or diesel-driven generators are available, you must have a battery-operated backup if you really need to stay online without any interruption whatsoever.

Watch Out!
Don't begin using your in-box as a receptacle for everything that comes into the office or it will lose its efficiency. Go through the mail before you put it in your in-box—and toss what you don't need *first*.

Depending on the size of your computer system and how often you anticipate power failure, batteries can provide the total requirement or enough energy to shut your system down before you lose anything of significance or the energy necessary to give you time to connect to an alternate source.

Since your computer's hard drive is basically an extra-large filing cabinet, you should be able to keep quite a bit of information there. Just remember to keep disks of whatever you save on the hard drive.

Some of the info you might want to think about transferring to the computer includes:

- Mailing lists

- Form letters

- Calendars

- Weekly/Daily/Monthly Schedules and To-Do Lists

- Budgets/Checkbooks/Bills

- Personnel files (make sure you create a code so no one but you can get into these)

  Clean off the hard drive to make more space:

- Delete old programs you don't use anymore.

- Don't keep more than one screensaver (they're incredible space hogs). You can always get a new one off the Net when you get bored with the one you have.

- Put files you still need but don't use every day into a zip file.

- Delete backup files (the ones that end with .bk! or .bak).

- Dump old files onto disks (don't forget to label them) and file them in a disksaver box (alphabetically).

Unofficially...
Bill Gates, computer mogul and one of the richest men in the world, doesn't allow anyone to bring paper into his meetings.

Amazing how many magazines/newspapers you can read in the bathroom

For those of you who still don't have time to read all the mail/news generated by our paper-loving society, create a shelf in each of your bathrooms and stock it with those materials you can read in bits and pieces. One piece of advice though: Once you've read a magazine or newspaper, dump it in the recycling bin instead of back into that shelf unit.

Just the facts

- It takes planning and communication to schedule an office reorganization and there are professionals you can hire to help.

- If you open your mail while standing next to a trash barrel, you can save the time of reading junk mail.

- If you use both paper and computer filing systems, create a list of subject guidelines so you'll file items consistently.

- Make sure you check all paper-clipped items so that you don't throw important papers away inadvertently.

- Remember to keep important documents in a permanent place and, preferably, in a fireproof file.

Watch Out!
Even though we have the ability to keep almost everything on computer, more than 2 trillion pieces of paper are generated by offices every year and it costs more than $100 in labor to find a piece of paper when it's lost. Better to keep documents on disk or to send an e-mail.

GET THE SCOOP ON...
How to utilize different types of calendars ▪
How to figure out which daily planner will
work best for you ▪ How to save time on the
computer ▪ How to make your phone a timesaving device ▪ How to create family meals
in less time

The Handy Tools That Really Help Beat the Clock

Chapter 16

No matter how organized our mindset is, we still need some tools to help us manage the busy hours of our day. Unfortunately, some of those 'timesavers' are even more time-consuming than just the basics. And what about technology? Has it actually saved us time or are we wasting more time than ever?

Yes, we're more productive, but are we actually saving time? You need to seriously evaluate your own habits and see if you're spending more time than necessary learning new technology or transferring files from one place to another. Are you spending hours surfing on the Net only to come up empty-handed? Would it be better for you to keep a hand-written day-planner than to try to transfer all your meetings, appointments, and chores to a computer-ized schedule?

66
Any sufficiently advanced technology is indistinguishable from magic.
—Arthur C. Clarke
99

Only you can answer these questions, but in this chapter, we'll offer some ideas and options on how to maximize your time through the use of 'timesaving' tools. It's up to you to decide which are the best for you—and which will fit into your budget...since technology doesn't come cheap!

Calendars

It's a given that we all need to keep a calendar. I, personally, have four on the walls in my home, two in my office (one desk and one wall), and one that I keep in my wallet/day-planner. As long as I can keep each one for a different purpose, I'm fine, but when I try to figure out whether I have student appointments when I'm not in my office at school, I am lost. There's something to be said for taking down all the calendars except for one.

One is best

Recently, a dear friend was faced with trying to organize her parents' life. One of the first things she said to me was: "Just getting them ready for doctors' appointments is a chore. The other day when I was at their house, I realized they had seven calendars! It's no wonder my mother is confused about which day I'm taking her to the doctor."

The first thing I told my friend was that she had to put everything—all her parents' appointments with doctors, for hospital tests, to see the accountant—on one calendar and to hang that calendar by the phone. The second thing I told her was to make sure that calendar had big blocks so that she could fit everything on it and her parents would be able to see it clearly. Third, she'd probably have to take all the daily appointments and write them on an erasable board on the refrigerator or someplace where they would see them on a regular basis. Amazingly, once she had the calendars organized, her parents felt more comfortable and in control of their lives. It was almost as if she'd given them a big "de-stressor pill." And, as a result, she'd also become less stressed.

Whenever possible, cut yourself down to one calendar. Or at least one for every purpose. I have a 90-day organizer calendar made of vinyl hanging on my home office wall. I write on it with an erasable marker and use that particular calendar *only* for deadlines. Since it's a three-month spread, I can see what's coming up and whether or not I'm on time for book or school deadlines. I also can see at a glance whether I'm on task and what to expect on certain weekends. The beauty of this calendar is that it's erasable, so when I'm finished with the deadlines for that 3-month period, I can erase it and start over on the next three months. There have been times in the past when I've used a yearly calendar, and that might be something you should consider for yourself. Small businesses often need to consider certain seasonal considerations and should be able to look at, for example, sales figures to compare production from one year to the next.

Monthly calendars take care of more immediate concerns and one should be hung in the home (preferably a place where all members of the family can see it) and used to mark specific occasions that won't change (i.e. birthdays, anniversaries, parties, special school occasions, sports events, and holidays).

Weekly calendars focus on what's happening on particular days and when placed in a spot where family members can mark down their own

Moneysaver
Write down expenses in your appointment calendar. Notes in an appointment calendar are acceptable to the IRS when it comes to tax time if you lose your receipts and will also give you an immediate idea of what you're spending on business lunches and travel.

appointments, they work well to organize the type of family that might not see each other often enough to keep track of everyone's schedules. An erasable calendar with a marker hanging on it by a string is great for Junior to remind everyone of his soccer game, Mom to let the family know which night she'll be working late, Dad's note that he'll be out of the state on business, and for the family to share certain responsibilities.

In the office, a desk calendar is best for appointments. Whether your day is broken down into morning/afternoon segments, hourly, or minute-by-minute segments, determines what type of calendar you use.

Paper, Vinyl, or Computer?

If you're using a paper calendar, write your appointments in pencil since they often change and it wastes time to white-out penned comments. It's also wise to add phone numbers to the notations about your appointments, as well as the names of the people you are going to meet or details about what job might be due at that particular time.

Vinyl calendars serve a purpose for those people who want to reuse their calendars. They're also great because they're erasable. If you're the type of person whose appointments change on a regular basis, use vinyl. They're also great for families with kids because they can be reused. And each member of the family can write in their engagements in a different-colored marker. Colored markers can also work in the office when you have several people working on different facets of one project. Let each choose their own color and you'll be able to keep track of who's doing what. This way, no one treads on anyone's toes and you'll also know if someone needs help.

If you're keeping your appointments on your computer, there are many fine programs that will help you keep yourself organized. A contact manager helps you keep track of all your appointments, your to-do list, your addresses, and to keep notes as well. Some of them include alarms that you can set, say, if you need to call someone in twenty minutes—and you can even program them to dial the numbers for you.

Timesaver
Address book software that's included on your desktop or laptop can dial the phone for you—saving you precious moments.

Some contact manager programs include:

- ACT! Made by Symantec Corporation and available in Windows, DOS, and Mac versions. Can be programmed to come on your computer screen as soon as you boot up every day. Included are features to help you import information for your address book and everything you might have already entered in your current contact manager.

- Consultant 2.5. Made by Chronos for Macintosh software. Features a full-featured contact manager, a calendar that offers multiple views, and automatic word completion so you save time on keystrokes. Also has pop-up alarms to notify you of upcoming events.

Keeping control

Wouldn't you like to have control over where the time goes? All you need to do is organize. Whether it means remembering to write something down on a calendar or getting an organizer on your desktop or laptop—or an electronic palm-pilot, all you need to do is tell yourself: I'm going to take control and keep it.

Getting in the habit of writing everything down means repeating that credo: I'm going to take control and keep it.

Unofficially...
Donald Trump, businessman extraordinaire, made a practice of repeating a person's name several times in order to remember it. Deals were his business and personal deals were made largely on the basis of his extraordinary memory for names.

Once you have done something three times, it becomes habit. So, say it once again: I'm going to take control of my time and keep it.

Write everything down and check it

You just got a phone call from the manager of your firm. He wants you to call Mr. Hemphill and check on the supplies for the Monroe firm, then e-mail Ms. Voller about the job for CompBass, and report back to him by Thursday on the status. Easiest way to accomplish all the above?

1. Write it down in your planner (or on your palm pilot/or in your contact manager).

2. Set some deadlines for yourself right away.

3. Repeat what the manager has asked you to do so that you'll get the details right.

4. Then get to work!

Day-Planners

Whether you choose to call your planners Franklin™ Planners, Filofaxes™, Day-Timers™, Day Planners, Day-Runners™, At-A-Glance, Rolodex, most every American we know has one. They come with leather, recycled rubber, cardboard, plastic, or vinyl covers, and in various shapes, sizes, and with daily, weekly, monthly, and annually divided schedules. Some are divided into segments devoted to special dates that won't change, addresses, travel expenses, notes, voice/mail records, business card holders, CD-ROM Disk/computer diskette holders, and even a segment to keep track of your health and fitness routine.

For more information about where to order organizers call Day Runner at 800-643-9923 or Day-Timer at 800-225-5055 or download sample versions from their Web pages so you can sample the products before you buy: www.dayrunner.com *or* www.daytimer.com

There are so many ways to use these time organizers that the Day-Timer™ people have even created a set of training tapes to help people learn how to "use the Day-Timer System to plan and prioritize multiple tasks." The four-cassette program is available at most office supply houses for approximately $120. If you can afford the time to listen to the program, you'll be the most organized person on your block. Suggestion: Listen to the tapes while you're driving and you'll accomplish two tasks at once.

Each time organizer provides a pen or pen holder, and we suggest you keep that pen in the same place all the time. People waste more time looking for pens than is necessary, but if you get into the habit of sliding it back into its holder, you'll save not only time but irritation.

Depending on your business and personal needs, you should design an organizer to meet your particular whims. Here are a few suggestions on what *not* to do:

■ Don't keep every business card that's handed to you. If you'll contact that person again, enter their name, phone number, address (both street and e-mail) in your address book immediately and toss the card. Or, file the card on a Rolodex in your office and keep the written info in your organizer. If you're going to keep the card, it's a good idea to write on the back of it where and when you met the person.

■ Don't keep a section in your organizer that you'll never use. Toss it or give it to someone else who might use it.

Bright Idea
Link to a planner that has computer calendar software online. You can type out your lists, address books, and calendars and print them to fit your planner.

Moneysaver
Buy a three-ring
binder planner.
That way, at the
end of the year,
you can remove
the calendar sec-
tion and simply
replace it with a
new one rather
than buying a
whole new
planner.

▪ Don't write all your appointments in pen. Keep a pencil in your organizer for that purpose and use it.

▪ Don't keep the same info in your organizer that you'll keep at home or in the office. Your organizer should be the one place where all your scheduling and addresses, as well as info on your finances, are kept. *However,* be careful that you have copies of the most important documents just in case your organizer is lost or stolen. Too many people put their lives into their day planners, only to find they can't survive without them.

▪ Don't file information in your day planner, then forget about it and end up with a bulging organizer filled with useless pieces of paper. Go through the cards and notes you collect on a regular basis, and toss them when the project is finished (or file them in your office).

▪ Don't forget the organizer is meant to simplify your life, not complicate it!

Daily, weekly, or monthly?

Your organizer should help you schedule your work time in advance, which should take some of the stress of time management off your shoulders. If you tend to have hourly appointments or deadlines, then consider an organizer broken down into that format. If your jobs are due on a weekly basis, you might not need the daily planner. And if you have long-term commitments, get a monthly planner.

Here's how it works:

▪ Use your to-do list in your planner. Write down the tasks you need to accomplish prior to the date they are due. When your boss tells you a report is due on Friday, you check your planner, see that you're jammed on Tuesday and Thursday, so schedule the work for the report on Wednesday. Write it down!

- As each job is finished, cross it off your list and move the rest of the work you need to do up.

- If you don't finish your daily tasks, move them to another time when you can complete them.

- Once you've made that phone call or written that letter, X through the task and move on (and remember to congratulate yourself for managing that piece of time so well!).

- Remember to block out time to eat and relax. When my day is filled with student appointments every ten minutes, I remind myself to block out 'break time' to eat or just to take a walk down the hall or outside. By doing so, I'm sure I won't get backed up, which lessens the stress on me and also gives me ample time to 'refuel my engines' by getting a bite to eat. You also need to schedule time for your family, friends, and vacations. Cross out those days completely so that you won't be tempted to squeeze in a quick appointment.

- If there's a birthday or anniversary coming up, don't just slide the person's name in on the actual date, but make a point of writing that special occasion in a week earlier so you won't forget to send a card or buy a gift.

- Remember to give your assistant or family member a copy of the most important dates on your calendar so they'll be able to keep up with you.

Unofficially...
Presidents have traditionally had their secretaries remind them of important birthdays and anniversaries so they wouldn't slip by without either a personal phone call or a card to those colleagues closest to them.

Use a pencil!

A lot of time-management guides will tell you not to use a pencil when writing your to-do lists, and we agree. The to-do lists are things you must accomplish and writing them in pen cements them, makes you cross out each task as you finish it. But if you write your appointments in pencil, it's much easier to make changes. We also suggest you write your address names in pen, but the addresses themselves (and phone, fax, and e-mail addresses) in pencil since we are such a transient society. Most people move an average of once every three to five years, and a lot of us move even more frequently than that. In addition, we are all likely to add a new number or change telephone options, as well as e-mail servers, so putting that information in pencil saves time and pages in your address book.

Electronic day-planners and/or calendars

New electronic planners come on the market every day. Some are designed as calendars, some as address books, some have word processing programs, some are calculators, while still others balance your finances. One of the best places to find out which ones are best for you is the Pickled Palm Pilot Web site (http://www.pickled.com). The Web site is easy-to-navigate and offers information on software to help you enhance what you already have and even introduces 'small hackers' to help you add to existing programs, graphics, games, and language translators.

For those of us who simply need something to organize information, an electronic planner might take the place of handwritten calendars and address books.

The Multi-Task 1.0 allows you to handle to-do lists in about half the time (as well as working multiple tasks). Rolodex, Sharp, Franklin, Casio, Texas Instruments, and Sony also make various types of 'personal information organizers' or 'databank organizers.' The best bet is to get one with a good-sized memory. Even if you think you might not use it, better to have too much memory than not enough. More memory space also usually allows a computerized device to operate a bit more quickly. Another thing to consider is a back-up battery, a large display screen, and a backlit screen so you'll be able to see it no matter where you are.

Most organizers include an address book, a keypad, calculator, and clock. Some also offer an alarm, which can come in handy when you're traveling. Still others offer games (which are time-wasters, not savers!) and currency converters (not only a time-saver, but a money saver).

Building in time

Use your calendar or datebook as a way to build in time for special events or for yourself. Making an appointment to get your hair done requires you to block out at least an hour or more. Going to a party might mean at least three hours, and Junior's soccer game might require a whole afternoon.

When you're building your schedule, think of how much time each event will require out of your day and block it out immediately. Don't just write in the hair appointment at 2 p.m. Consider how much time it'll take Rocky to do your hair, how much time it'll take to travel there and back, and consider a little extra time in case he's running late.

Bright Idea
Computerized calendars often offer additional money savers like the ability to print out copies of your schedule. It'll save you the money you might spend on a day-planner.

Don't forget to build in travel time to other appointments. Give yourself at least twenty minutes extra just in case you have traffic problems.

And make sure you give yourself some time to relax! Sometimes making an appointment with yourself to do that is the only way busy people get valuable moments of regenerative time.

Making to-do lists and checking them twice

As stated many times in this book, to-do lists are your friends. Whether you choose to keep it in your planner, on your computer, on a pad on your desk, or on a vinyl message board on your refrigerator, make your to-do list a priority that you attend to first thing in the morning. Don't forget to delete the items you do as you do them and move the more important items up on the list.

Computers

The greatest timesaving device ever invented is the computer. To take millions of pieces of information and condense them to one little box is truly amazing. How writers and researchers worked before the advent of the computer programs we now have and the access to the Internet is astounding. Yet, Shakespeare did create hundreds of works by pen and bookkeepers balanced corporate accounting with ledgers and pencils. Do we utilize computers to their full extent now, or are we wasting time swimming in the vast sea of programs and knowledge now offered to us?

Our bet is you could use a few timesaving tips when logging on to your computer—and that as soon as this book is published, there will be many more ways to save time via new products, so keep your eyes open and your finger on the pulse!

The newest in hardware and software

One of the biggest time-wasters on computers is when a virus hits and you're down for the count, so our first piece of advice when adding software to your system is to invest in a decent virus scan program like Norton AntiVirus. A program that detects viruses and allows you the opportunity to not only spot them before they destroy you but to eradicate them is worth its weight in gold. McAfee also makes an Office Utility Suite that includes a virus scan that checks out all documents in your e-mail and anything downloaded from the Net automatically, a 'first aid' program that fixes hardware programs and notifies you if your hard drive is ready to fail so you can save documents before it happens, 'nuts & bolts,' which can help you rescue files, 'guard dog,' which keeps your work personal, and several other components that keep your computer updated and 'healthy'. You can check out all of McAfee's products and test versions of some of its programs at its Web site: www.mcafee.com.

For those people who either don't type quickly or would prefer to dictate because of hand problems or time constraints, there are several good programs (like Dragon Naturally Speaking Preferred 3, L&H Voice Xpress Professional, and Via Voice 98 Executive) that allow you to create documents simply by talking into a microphone. The first and probably best is Dragon Naturally Speaking. They also have created a handheld recorder called VoiceIt that you can use while on the road or at any other place besides in front of your computer. For more information, visit their Web site: www.insyncit.com/dragonsys/

Bright Idea
Make sure you back up everything! Set your computer's backup option for every 5 minutes so your work will be automatically saved. It'll save you hours of heartache later on.

Timesaving steps on the Net

The Internet, designed by the government and military, is the world's biggest library. Some of the info online is static, meaning it doesn't change, while other information is in a constant state of flux, changing daily, hourly, and sometimes by the moment. Every day, millions more pieces of information are loaded onto the Net. Is it any surprise that it's actually harder to do research now than it was two or three years ago? How can you save time researching on the Net? There are actually a number of ways and some of them change depending on which browser you're using, but here are a few simple steps you can take.

66

The best minds are not in government. If any were, business would steal them away.
—Ronald Reaga

99

1. Use a search engine specific to your needs. For example, Alta Vista searches the entire Web and comes up with thousands of hits, while InfoSeek deals with more academic information.

2. Be as specific as possible when giving the search engine words for which to search. If you're looking for a new computer and enter the word 'computer,' everything with that word in the line will come up as a possibility and you'll literally be swimming in information.

3. Use Boolean logic. Boolean operators such as AND, OR, or NOT limit your search and help you find exactly what you're looking for rather than thousands of things you don't need.

4. Refine your query. When you do a search and the results come up, most browsers give you the option to refine your search. You can go through the list and get rid of the hits that have nothing to do with your subject, then re-search and get a tighter list.

5. Time yourself. Give yourself a set amount of time to search so that you don't waste hours surfing instead of doing the job you set out to do.

6. Bookmark it. If you find something of interest that you might return to later, bookmark it so you won't waste time searching for it again.

7. History. Utilize the Ctrl H command to find out all the sites you've already visited. When searching for something you know you've seen before, it's the easiest and quickest way to find it.

Six easy steps to saving time on e-mail

1. Check your e-mail only when you log on and log off your computer.

2. Use group messages whenever you have to repeat the same thing to a number of people.

3. Cut and paste your messages when you must repeat part of the same message, but want to personalize it.

4. Delete unnecessary messages in your in-box without reading them.

5. Set a kitchen timer next to the computer and give yourself a maximum amount of time to answer your e-mail. When the bell rings, stop. No matter what you're doing.

6. Notify senders of unwanted e-mail that you wish to be removed from their list. If you find yourself getting tons of junk mail, it has to be because someone is giving out your e-mail address.

66
Until you value yourself, you won't value your time. Until you value your time, you will not do anything with it.
—M. Scott Peck
99

Organize your files and programs

1. Always file your disks alphabetically.
2. Don't keep any disks or programs that are undated or unused.
3. Bookmark the sites for upgrading programs you own. It's a quick way to get the fastest version of the program already on your computer.
4. Use key words for similar files. If you write articles, filing them by title is fine, but if you add 'art' to the end of the title, you'll know right away what it is.
5. Delete any programs you don't use. The extra space will make your computer work more quickly and you won't have to search through unnecessary files when looking for something you *really* need.

Make your computer save time for you

By investing in programs that make it easy to do your taxes, you'll save days (possibly weeks) at income tax time. You should get a program like this before taxes are due so that you can be prepared when the time comes.

Banks offer accounts that you can check online. They also offer checking-account management programs that will automatically deduct checks paid and figure your balance. Not only does this save you from going to the bank and waiting in line, but it's more trustworthy than adding and subtracting in your head.

If you need certain types of information on a regular basis, include updates on your homepage. Mine allows me to design my homepage so that the items I want to see first are right up top. You can add

Moneysaver
The Quicken accounting program offers many features that can help the average American balance their budget quickly.

news and weather, horoscopes, sports facts, stock market reports, or whatever.

Telephones

Telephones can either waste your time or buy you some, but you need to know how to handle them. A friend of mine spends most of her day online watching the stock market. Since she has one only line, everyone who calls her gets her answering service. My advice to her: Get two lines.

If you have a business, whether it's at home or in a small office, two lines are the minimum you need to keep the business running properly. One should be dedicated to your computer; the other can handle incoming calls and faxes. You can also include a fax program on your computer.

Some basic things to consider for saving phone time:

1. Install at least two lines in your home.

2. Get a phone with buttons for two or more lines.

3. Add conference calling, call holding, and speed dialing to your phone. (But remember to turn off call holding/call waiting when on a business call so that you're not interrupted.)

4. Get a speakerphone or a cordless so you can move around while you talk.

5. At least one of your telephones needs to be cordless.

6. If you're on the phone a lot, get a telephone headset to free your hands and save you from a stiff neck.

7. Get an answering machine and turn it on when you're in the middle of a big project so you won't be interrupted. When creating a message

Bright Idea
Stand up when talking on the phone. You'll get some exercise and won't stay on the phone as long as you would if you were sitting in a comfortable chair.

> **❝**
> A friendship can weather most things and thrive in thin soil; but it needs a little mulch of letters and phone calls and small, silly presents every so often—just to save it from drying out completely.
> —Pam Brown
> **❞**

on your machine, add information about when it's best to call you.

8. Use voice mail so you can pick up messages from any location—and screen your calls. It's also an advantage because if your telephone is out of order, you'll still receive your messages. In addition, voice mail will take messages while you're on the phone (a reason why some like voice mail better than call holding/waiting).

9. Hire an answering service so that customers/family/friends will talk to a 'real' person.

10. Decide who in the office/home will answer the phone and how.

The easier it is for customers, family, and friends to contact you, the more smoothly your life will flow and the more time you'll save.

How do you save time while on the phone? First, organize yourself. Second, plan. Third, put a smile on your face and remember your voice will sound as welcoming as that smile. Fourth, prepare!

Before you make that call, ask yourself the following questions:

- Why am I calling this person?

- What do I expect to accomplish?

- What do I need to ask?

- What do I need to tell them?

- How much time shall I spend on this task?

- If my contact isn't there, what message do I want to leave? Or, can anyone else there answer my question?

Once you've answered these questions, it's time for a mini list.

- Subject(s) to discuss.

- Important questions/deadlines/information.

- Info you need on hand.

Prepare for the call by having your files and other notes on hand before you pick up the phone, then think about the best time to make the call.

- During lunch isn't a good idea because you probably won't get the person. However, if you call close to lunch hour or quitting time, your phone calls will be shorter and to the point.

- Calling early in the morning or late in the day is wise because many people come in early or work late to catch the 'quiet' hours of the day. However, use this technique only when you have to, as you may discover that certain people don't want to be disturbed if they come early or stay late.

- Monday mornings and Friday afternoons are the worst times to call.

After the call:

- Note in your organizer or on your computer what was said, who'll you need to contact, and what the next action will be.

- If there's something else to do, add it to your to-do list.

- If you need to call someone else, make the call right away or enter their number on your contact manager.

While you're on hold, fold a load

How much time do you waste on hold? We sit at our desks or in our chair at home, tapping a pencil, getting frustrated and listening to canned music. By the time the person we're holding for comes back

Moneysaver
Make sure your long distance service offers you the best rates on in-state long distance charges. Often the companies will give you low weekend rates, but they're also available during the week—if you ask for them!

66

Men have
become the tools
of their tools.
—Henry David
Thoreau

99

on the line, we've not only wasted valuable time but we're steaming.

Here are a few things to do during those 'short time bites.'

- Fold a load of laundry.
- File whatever's in your filing basket.
- Dust the living room.
- Read the article you marked in last week's business newspaper.
- Balance your checkbook.
- Correct your child's math homework.
- Chop up some veggies for tomorrow night's soup and put them in a plastic bag so you can just grab them later.
- Write a note to your aunt.
- Do some quick research on the Net.
- Water the plants.

Voice mail?

Voice mail offers many options for the busy person:

1. It allows you to scan calls before returning them.
2. It offers you automatic dialing.
3. You can save, delete, or replay calls.

Does it save time? Only if you respond to the calls immediately. If you save them, then have to replay them in order to reply, you're wasting time. If it stops people from interrupting you while you're immersed in an important project, it saves time. If you don't check your calls and someone needs to get to you immediately, you can be chasing that person forever—and lose a sale, a contact, or information about what's going on with your child at school.

How do you utilize voice mail to your advantage?

■ Listen to your voice mail whenever you want. If you're a night person, you can take your time to listen to those messages and prepare how you'll work with them the next day.

■ Record a basic message that gives the listener specific details about when you check your messages and who they can contact if they need answers right away.

■ When leaving a voice mail message for someone else, spell your name and repeat your phone number at least twice. Also, tell the caller what day and time you're calling. Give the listener an idea of when you'll be available for a call back.

■ If you get a lot of messages, you might be able to speed up the playback option so you can listen to them more quickly. The callers might sound like Minnie Mouse, but you'll save time.

■ Transfer voice mail messages that don't pertain to you or copy them to other people who might need to listen to them.

Cellular, speakerphones, and cordless wonders

Cell phones have definitely served as timesavers for busy people. You don't have to go digging in your pocket for change, then find a phone booth that's working. Your family/friends/business associates can contact you no matter where you are, and you can even forward calls from your other phones.

Some suggestions for cell phone users:

■ Utilize a phone service that gives you unlimited time for one monthly fee. Watch out for the ones who charge for every second of the minute!

Unofficially...
Recent movies have pointed to the possibility that satellites circling the earth can pick up on anything being said on a cell phone.

■ If your company offers voice mail, use it. There are times you don't want to be available on your cell phone (i.e. while you're in the theater!) and voice mail will store your calls for you until you can get to them.

■ Don't give your cell phone number to everyone if you have to pay for incoming calls.

■ Don't forget to jot down messages into your calendar.

■ Check with your company to see whether you can use your cell phone while you're on the road. Your roaming charges should be included on your bill only when you travel. If you're a frequent traveler, this service can be invaluable.

One warning: If you're using your cell phone (or car phone) while in transit, make only the most important calls and make them short! Yes, it's great to have a cell phone when you're caught in traffic, but if you try to let your colleagues/family know you're going to be late and you're using the phone while trying to negotiate driving, you could end up being very late! As in 'six-feet-under' late. Take a lesson from those who have had accidents while driving and talking on the phone. Pull over for a second or use the car/cell phone only while at stoplights.

Speakerphones are invaluable for those who want to include several people in conversations. They're also great when you're trying to work on several projects at once and need your hands free.

Here are some ways to utilize the values of speakerphones:

■ Use a speakerphone when trying to get files or information for the person on the other line instead of putting them on hold. You can talk while looking.

■ When it's necessary to include someone in a conference, use a speakerphone for the other members of the group and tie in your missing person.

■ When the family is calling Grandma on a holiday, use the speakerphone instead of handing the phone from person to person. Not only does this save time, but it also saves on your phone bill!

And set aside a particular time of day for making all your phone calls. Think about scheduling this chore when you are at your least stressed. When you make the call, let the person know you just have a few moments, and don't forget to smile!

When is e-mail better?

If you're a night owl and tend to shy away from the phone, e-mail might be a timesaving way of communicating. I'm often amazed to see the time stamp on some of the e-mail I receive. I'd certainly be quite upset to get a phone call at 3 a.m., but by sending me an e-mail at that time, my colleagues/ friends/family have accomplished their task of communicating with me and I can attend to answering their e-mail whenever I have time.

However, here are some time-wasters to consider:

■ **Jokes.** Reading ten to twenty jokes from well-meaning friends wastes more time than junk mail sent via snail mail. Delete them without reading them and don't send them!

■ **Subscription mailing lists.** Subscribe only if the list gives you information you absolutely should

Moneysaver
When you want to order a catalog or need information about a product/ conference/event, check to see whether you can e-mail your request before spending the money on mailing it via the post office.

have. File it in an e-mail folder to read later if
you don't have time to read it immediately upon
logging on.

■ **Listservers.** Being connected to a hundred people is wonderful for those who need some
communication with the outside world and welcome pithy messages from others with the same
interests, but listservers can be overwhelming.
Receiving 50-60 messages a day can literally con-
sume hours of your valuable time.

■ **E-mail alarms or announcements.** Do you really
need to know each time you get a piece of mail?
If you hear the alarm, you'll automatically check
it out, which is time-consuming. Make it a habit
to check your e-mail upon logging on your computer and logging off—and at no other time
unless you have a spare moment. Otherwise,
e-mail becomes an interruption, instead of a
convenience.

"
Good communi-
cation is as stim-
ulating as black
coffee, and just
as hard to sleep
after.
—Anne Morrow
Lindbergh
"

The etiquette of call waiting

If you're planning on making an important phone
call and finally reach the person you've been trying
to connect with for a week, the worst thing you can
do is attend to the call-waiting signal. Do you turn it
off before making the call or ignore it? It's up to
you, but remember that answering the other call will
waste time and, more than likely, offend the person
to whom you're talking.

An option? Get voice mail so you don't have to
be interrupted. Instead of hearing the annoying
call-waiting buzz, the caller is switched to voice mail
with a polite message that you're either 'busy or on
another call and will get back to them momentarily.'

Cooking, cleaning, and house upkeep

Don't we all wish we could snap our fingers and rid our houses of the dust and clutter that accumulate more quickly than weeds on the lawn? Unfortunately, when we go into high gear and time becomes a problem, the first thing we do is neglect the housework. I don't know about you, but cockroaches aren't my friends, so housecleaning has to be a priority. How do you save yourself from the roach crew moving in? Take advantage of those little bits of time to get that housecleaning, cooking, and lawn cutting done, then move on to the next chore—sometimes doing several simultaneously!

It amazes me when I hear about those families with six kids, those working mothers who make their kids' clothes and pack them all wonderful lunches, those corporate dads whose landscaping is the pride of the neighborhood, those writers who produce a book every three months and throw fabulously successful dinner parties. What do all these people have in common? They are time-management specialists who have learned the value of the small moment.

Microwave miracles

Who says you need to spend at least an hour an evening preparing dinner for your family? Or that a full, nutritious breakfast consists of eggs and homemade biscuits? Think microwave!

Here are some timesaving and totally nutritious ways to utilize the convenience of the 'nuker' most Americans have on their kitchen counters.

- **Coffee.** Why waste time making a whole pot when you're going to have time for only a cup? Either reheat some you made earlier or have a cup of instant. One minute.

Timesaver
Takeout menus from favorite restaurants should be kept near the phone. When your family really has no time, call for pizza or Chinese food and have it delivered.

- **Baked potatoes.** What usually takes an hour in the oven takes only about five minutes in the microwave.

- **Leftovers.** For those wise enough to make large amounts of food on the weekends, leftovers can be heated quickly in a microwave and are perfect for kids who have to make do before parents get home from work.

- **Defrosting.** Did you forget to take out that chicken for supper? Pop it in the microwave, program it for defrost and in less than half an hour, the chicken will be ready to cook.

- **Dinners/lunches/breakfasts.** The microwaveable meals cost a bit more than the actual ingredients, but in time saved, they're worth their weight in gold.

The weekend chef

One way to feed your family great meals all week is to get a few pots a'boilin' on the weekend or your days off. It's easy to make a pot of tomato sauce at the same time that you've got a stew or boiled dinner going. You can use the morning to chop your veggies and get them going during the day. Check on them, give them a stir and a taste while you're cleaning the house or helping the kids with their school projects.

Some 'dinners' you can make on the weekend to stretch all week:

- **Tomato sauce.** Use it for spaghetti one night, meatball sandwiches another, then over chicken or meatloaf, also great on veggies. And if you have any left over, it can be easily frozen.

- **Baked macaroni.** Make twice as much as you normally would and package it up in small

Unofficially...
Several large families recently interviewed by a writer for an article on cooking for groups reported they couldn't find a way to satisfy everyone, so ultimately each member ended up heating a microwave meal for themselves.

containers the kids can pop into the microwave.
It's great as a side dish or as the main entree.

▪ **Turkey.** Bake a turkey on the weekend and,
well, you know the many things you can create during the week! Turkey's not just for
Thanksgiving.

▪ **Vegetables.** Chop up a bunch of veggies on the
weekend and put them into sandwich bags.
They can go in lunch bags for snacks and can
also be cooked for side dishes through the
week.

▪ **Soups.** They can boil while you're doing other
things and you can freeze them in little packets,
then throw them in the microwave. Also, if you
make bean or veggie soups, you can change the
taste by adding leftover meats later.

Suggested books for quick meals:

▪ *Cook Your Meals: The Lazy Way* by Sharon Bower

▪ *Recipes 1-2-3 Menu Cookbook: Morning, Noon, and
Night: More Fabulous Food Using Only 3 Ingredients*
by Rozanne Gold and Tom Eckerle

▪ *Microwave Gourmet: The Only Microwave Cookbook
You Will Ever Need* by Barbara Kafka

▪ *Frozen Assets: How to Cook for a Day and Eat for a
Month* by Deborah Taylor-Hough

▪ *Feed Your Kids Right: The Lazy Way* by Virginia
Van Vynckt

Dusting doesn't pay rent

Most people believe they absolutely have to clean on
their days off, spending all of their free hours pushing brooms, vacuum cleaners, and dust cloths. Why
not do the dusting in those moments when you're
on hold and spend your off hours rejuvenating

Bright Idea
Store canned
goods by
category so that
you can plan
meals and find
things more
easily.

yourself? One of the things I've learned to save time is to clean something when it looks dirty. Right at that moment. You don't have to wait for Saturdays.

And if the house is a little dusty, does it really matter? Take care of your priorities. Pay attention to the work you need to accomplish. Play with the kids. Have a date with your significant other. The dusting doesn't pay rent.

The best household tools

Musts for the person interested in saving time with household tools:

- **Dust-buster.** A hand-held vacuum cleaner cleans up spills and dust without you dragging out the 50-pound stand-up vacuum cleaner.

- **Microwave.** For many reasons, but mostly because it saves time.

- **Crockpot.** Dinners can be cooked while you're at work.

- **Compactors.** Saves you time emptying the barrels and is much better for the environment.

- **Blender/Chopper.** Makes healthy shakes, chops vegetables in a third of the time, creates tasty desserts in moments.

- **Electric screwdrivers.** Drills that unscrew or screw things together in seconds not only save time but energy.

A recent Good Housekeeping report on time-savers stated that money wrappers save no time whatsoever, that microwave bacon trays waste almost four minutes more than cooking the bacon on towels, palm organizers aren't as quick as looking up phone numbers in daytimers, and nail-drying machines only save you approximately two minutes in time (why not just buy instant-dry nail polish?).

Moneysaving
Barter for someone's housekeeping talents or schedule each member of the house for a different chore each week. Either way, this saves money on what you really want to do: hire a housekeeper!

One book offers lots of help: *Helpful Household Hints: The Ultimate 90s Guide to Housekeeping* by June King.

Organized closets/organized lives

We talked about organizing closets in other sections of this book, but there are plenty of other places in the house where organizers can take the clutter away, provide you with extra space, and save the time you spend looking for that hammer or for the parts you need to make the bicycle work.

Yes, it's not easy to get every member of your household to remember to put things back in the same place, but if you could organize where you store items, you'll find them every time rather than playing the hide-and-seek game.

Check out Closet Masters items for everything from closet racks to garage storage for bikes, tools and sports items—and office organizers. The California Closet Company is another firm that specializes in helping people organize to save both space and time.

What to watch out for: closet organizers that take too much time to put together. Some of them have been tested by *Good Housekeeping*; see its April, 1999 issue.

Just the facts

- A vinyl calendar that's erasable gives you the option of adding every member of the household's appointments in different colors.

- Day-planners are designed in daily, weekly, or monthly at-a-glance schedules so that you can use the one that best suits your personal needs.

- Building in time for lunch or relaxation can actually save time.

Bright Idea
When getting a closet organized, take it step by step. One shelf at a time. Don't empty the whole thing or it'll be impossible to figure out what needs to be thrown away and what should be saved.

- A cordless phone allows you the freedom of accomplishing small tasks while you're on hold or conversing with a friend.

- A pot of tomato sauce cooked on your day off will translate into meals all week long.

GET THE SCOOP ON...
How to find the best seminars/courses ▪ How to
make the most of travel time ▪
How to save time in the car ▪ How to hire help

The "Thinking" Tools You Need to Save Time

F or the truly busy professional who spends a lot of time on the road or away from home, there are special considerations. Perhaps you are a newly promoted executive or a salesperson who travels out of a suitcase, or maybe you simply have a long commute to and from work—whatever the case, you need to utilize the long periods of time away from desk and office. Maybe you have a love of travel but have discovered the trip becomes too stressful when you can't organize yourself.

This chapter is for those of you who have not learned to manage "moving" time. By that, I mean the time spent away from the physical tools you have in your familiar work spaces. Under certain circumstances, we need some "thinking" tools, like the ones described in this chapter.

Seminars/courses on managing time

There are many time-management experts from whom you can learn. Our suggestion is to utilize the suggestions and contacts in this volume first, then if you need more, check out the time-management seminars listed. Since some people learn by listening, others by seeing, and still others by practice, you might be best served by taking a seminar. However, before you spend hundreds of dollars, sit down and question yourself about whether you truly need a seminar and whether you can afford to spend that much money to learn something that might already be included in this book or a number of others available at your local bookstore.

Unofficially
At a recent sales convention, several top execs were overheard discussing why they used particular computer servers. One said the reason he uses one of the top servers is because he can access his e-mail from anywhere in the world.

Choose the one specifically for you

Just as we are all individuals, we all have specific reasons for needing to manage our time. The corporate executive who is trying to climb the ladder to business ownership has different needs than the parents of six who are trying to manage jobs and child care; the nurse who craves the ability to juggle the paperwork and the student who's stressed at the end of the semester also have different needs.

Before you sign up for a seminar, take a moment to research the speaker or organization giving the course. A five-minute phone call or quick list of e-mailed questions will show you whether the course is the right one for you.

There are hundreds, perhaps thousands, of speakers and organizations willing to help people learn how to manage their time. Besides the author of this book, here are a few that we have found:

- Common Sense Solutions, located in Edmonton, Alberta, Canada. They help individuals and staff members with a number of business-related problems, including time management. They also offer online mentoring and appear to specialize in Web page design. Check out their Web site: www.comsensesolutions.com

- Nationally recognized expert on organization, Ronni Eisenberg, runs workshops and lectures on time management for both corporations and individuals. You can write to her at P.O. Box 3272, Westport, CT 06880. Or, visit her Web site at http://www.reisenberg.com

- Lisa Kanarek, author and authority on organizing home and office, specializes in showing people how to organize their office and deal with the paper blizzard. Contact her through her Web site: http://www.westward.com/people/kanarek.htm

- Knowledge Management seminars, run by Stephen Goodfellow and staffed by specialists in various corporate aspects, come to your company. They offer management and corporate-world training and are specialists in technology. They also offer CD, audio, and slide presentations. Phone number 888-624-6319 and Web site address: www.accesskm.com

- Dr. Donald Wetmore of the Productivity Institute, a college professor, attorney, and time-management professional with twenty-five years of experience, is the author of *Beat the Clock*. Based in Huntington, Connecticut, he offers seminars at your location for $495 and states he has a 100% money-back guarantee if you're not satisfied. His phone is 800-969-3773, and his Web site address is www.world-wide.com

- Management and leadership skills training is offered in a day-long seminar by John Maddy, president of Greater Horizons, Inc. in Camanche, Iowa. His phone number is 800-944-0766 and Web address is www.greaterhorizons.com

❝

Technology is a
way of organiz-
ing the universe
so that man
doesn't have to
experience it.

—Max Frisch

❞

▪ Ken Daugherty, a trainer and speaker, specializes in executive seminars. He's the owner of
Leadership Management Development Center,
Inc. in Winter Haven, Florida and his phone
number is 941-318-9339.

Each of the time-management seminars, workshops, and speakers we've researched charges
anywhere from $25 per hour to thousands for a
speaking engagement. Since each specializes, you
need to discern what your specific needs are, then
check out one of the organizations/speakers above,
or the phone book in your area for the experts who
are closest to you.

Costs and effectiveness

The effectiveness of seminars, workshops, or time-
management training is measured directly by
whether you are able to utilize the suggestions made
to you. A lecture may prove inspiring for that
moment, but when a person tries to implement
those tips in the office or home, the follow-through
might be missing. Nothing will work unless you
make it a habit. And making something a habit
means you need to repeat it at least three times. So,
write down the tips you believe will work for you,
then remember to use them, make a mental note of
how much time they save, then use them again,
make a mental note, and use them again. By that
time, your mindset should be changed and you can
evaluate whether the time spent in the seminar/
workshop or listening to the lecture was effective.

But, first, get a book like this that suits your
needs. Spending less than $25 is the wisest invest-
ment to make at first. *Then* consider the more
expensive seminars.

Are they worth your time and money?

If you want to train a group of people or if you've invested the time and energy into reading a book, then have failed in getting your message across to your colleagues, employees, or family members, it might be time to bring an expert to your group. They'll save you time, and in the long run, if they train your workers, they might save you money.

One thing for sure is that if you've already tried to train the people around you and you find you're still not accomplishing everything you need to within your time frame, it might be time to let someone else take over—and relieve you of the stress.

Utilizing travel time

With so many of us traveling a distance to a job or on the road with our business, we might find it frustrating to spend so many hours in our cars, on the train, in an airplane or bus. Those are empty hours that we can definitely use to save ourselves a little time and energy, but how?

If you are in transit to work, you might want to consider joining a commuter club that will allow you to drive once a week rather than every day. Use the time you're commuting to quietly sip your coffee and reflect, catch up on the news of the day, or prepare your to-do list.

When you're on the road constantly, your car or your motel room becomes your office, and you need to make sure you're able to reach everyone you want to and to keep up with the work at hand.

Whichever scenario might be your case, there are plenty of ways to save time while commuting or traveling, and if you're well-prepared and knowledgeable before you get into that vehicle, you'll be

Bright Idea
Make a list of things that can be packed two or three days prior to leaving, and also make a list of things you won't be able to pack until the last moment. Those last-minute items are the most important—and often left behind.

able to utilize what you once thought were wasted hours.

Prepare everything you need in advance

The first and most important rule to consider when travelling is to prepare in advance. Getting to your destination only to discover you've forgotten something important is the result of a lack of forethought. The old Boy Scout motto (Be Prepared) is imperative.

For most business travelers, time is of the essence. You don't want to waste precious hours (or even moments) in airports or hotels, and the best way to save time is to think about all you need to do before you walk out the front door of your home.

For the vacationer, the same rule applies. And the same rule applies if travel to you means the daily ride back and forth to work.

Reservations and research for travelers

Timesaver
Try to take the earliest flight of the day. They're less crowded and less likely to be delayed.

One of the many sites for travelers on the Web is http://www.travelsecrets.com/tricks/ and it offers tips on everything from how to beat Montezuma's Revenge to secrets for getting the best seat on a flight, and even tips about where to find the best gambling casinos in the world! Everything you could possibly want to know is all in that one site—and even seasoned travelers can learn something.

There are also *Consumer Report* books on getting the best travel deals. These books are prepared every year by the experts and offer tips on how to get the best discounts on airfare, hotels, car rentals, and tourist attractions.

Other sources for those who want to make their own reservations quickly online:

■ Air Fare.com

- Bestfares.com

- Priceline.com

- On Line Vacation Mall

All airlines, train services, and buses have their own 800 numbers, but be prepared to wait on hold for quite a while. You're really better off calling a travel agent, spelling out what you need, and letting them take care of the details. By delegating that work, you save yourself a lot of time and worry. The agent will get the best deal possible for you.

Make sure you have the following information at your fingertips before calling:

- The full names of everyone traveling.

- The dates and times you wish to travel (and any options—prepare to be flexible).

- Passport identification (if necessary).

- Credit card information.

- Frequent flier card information.

Once you get the reservations you want, be sure you get a confirmation number and double-check your ticket to make sure all the information is correct. Make sure you have seat assignments and boarding passes for every leg of the trip. If you don't, you'll have to wait in line at each airport—a major time-waster!

Don't leave home without it!

Before you leave, don't forget to leave a detailed itinerary of where you'll be, complete with dates, phone numbers and addresses, with folks at home and at your office/business. Who knows what might happen when you're away? The cat could have kittens, the house could burn down, and your company could get sold to Bill Gates. Leave an itinerary with someone at home, as well as with a good friend and someone at the office. The itinerary should include:

- Airline name, flight times and numbers, as well as destinations.

- Hotel names and phone numbers, as well as dates when you'll be arriving and departing.

- Your e-mail or fax address, if you'll be using a computer to keep in touch while away.

Other things you will need to think about are:
Money. How much do you take with you? Figure out a budget for meals according to what the average costs are for the area you'll be visiting (the travel books and Web sites all give approximates for different budget, moderate, and first-class restaurants). Consider how many additional activities you'll plan and their approximate cost, then add an average of 25% per day for unforeseen expenses.

When you have summarized your budget, check to see what the exchange rate is if you are travelling to a foreign country. Remember that the rate published online or in the newspaper is usually a bank rate and many countries have exchange offices located in airports or in shops on the street—and you can often make a deal.

One of the many online sites that can help you with currency conversion is www.ThomasCook.com, and you can check with them about any other money questions you have while traveling. In addition, the many personal organizers discussed in Chapter 16 also offer a conversion program, so if you take one of the organizers on your trip, you can easily figure out the exchange rate while deciding what to eat or buy.

"
Very funny, Scotty. Now beam down my clothes.
—As seen on a bumper sticker
"

To save time, exchange some money for foreign currency before you leave the United States so that you'll have some cash for taxi fares and tips once you arrive in the country of your choice. Don't change all your money in the States or in the same place in the country you're visiting because the rate does change daily and you can often get a better deal once you're actually on foreign soil.

Don't bring all cash when you travel. Split your money up in three or four different ways: some foreign cash, some U.S. cash, traveler's cheques, and credit cards. Store your monies in different places on your person and if you're traveling with someone else, have them hold some as well. If you're using a credit card that allows you to withdraw cash, always check the exchange rate of the establishment where you're using it.

Bring copies of your credit cards and traveler's cheques. Have someone else carry the copies or store them someplace other than where you have the originals. Traveler's cheques are easy to replace, but credit cards aren't, so make sure if you lose either, you immediately notify the police.

It's actually cheaper to use your check card when paying for a meal or service rather than using it to withdraw cash because the banks tack on an extra service charge for each cash withdrawal. Also, be careful if the cash machine is out in the open. Better to have someone stand with you while you make your transaction. Many travelers have been ripped off while at cash machines. And there's nothing that wastes time more than losing your source of money while on a trip—whether at home or abroad.

Remember: Some countries will not accept credit cards and travelers' cheques, while others will charge you for the use of either. Best to check with your travel agent before you leave home, or connect to one of the online travel sites for up-to-date information.

Weather. Just because it's snowing where you are doesn't mean it's going to be where you're going. However, the snowstorm that hits Minnesota when you're trying to get out of Florida might make an impact on whether the flight you're taking is delayed. (With that in mind, make sure you arrive at the airport/train or bus station at least an hour in advance, so that if secondary arrangements need to be made, you can do so.)

Check the Weather Channel for at least a week in advance. Also, consider the weather in foreign countries before you start planning the kind of clothes you'll take with you. The Sunday newspaper travel section usually has average temperatures in the major cities around the world. For more in-depth weather information, you can check travel guides or get on the Net and peruse Web sites like Armchair World, Lonely Planet, or Fodor's. They have search engines within the sites and can give you an average weather forecast for most regions of the world. Knowing what to expect ahead of time will save time in packing and will also save money (i.e. if May is the month when the south of France is likely to get its highest rainfall, packing an umbrella would be wise—and you wouldn't have to buy one when you get there).

Electricity. Most countries outside the U.S. use a different voltage, so it's best to pick up a voltage converter and plugs before you leave. TravelSmith sells an adapter kit made by Franzus that will give you four adapter plugs and a converter that will work anywhere in the world. You'll need power aids if you're traveling with a hair dryer, electric shaver, or any kind of device that is powered by electricity. If you bring your own adapter kit, not only will you save time by not having to hunt for one there, but you will be able to run anything you need to use at any time in any place.

While we're at it, battery-powered devices are extremely useful when traveling. If you tend to do a lot of reading, there are several battery-powered booklights that clip right onto your book or the bed. They can be used to supplement the low lighting supplied in airplanes and can be used in any hotel room or even out in the wilderness. Most are light, foldable, and compact. We received ours as a gift for subscribing to a magazine, but you can get a powerful one from TravelSmith or one like the Itty Bitty Book Light sold by Levenger (catalog call 800-544-0880 or check levenger.com on the Web). Battery-powered clocks, radios, and CD or tape players are also a wise addition to your list of things to pack.

Medications. Before you leave home, check with your health insurance to see whether you'll be covered if you're traveling out of the state or country. Taking the time to find out this information before you go anywhere can mean the difference between getting medical attention when you need it or being left without. And we don't even want to think about what will happen if you're not treated for an injury or illness while traveling. If, for some reason, you do get sick or hurt, you can contact the American consul if you're in a foreign country, but best to have checked out your insurance before leaving than wait for an emergency.

Bright Idea
Carry at least one extension cord if you are bringing electrical devices in case the outlet is not convenient. If bringing your computer, pack an extension phone line cord and use your Swiss army knife's screwdriver to remove wall plates so you can connect everything.

If you're taking prescription medications, the best way to pack them to save time is to dole them out in a plastic container that separates the pills by the day (available at local supermarkets and drugstores). However, if you're travelling internationally, it's often safer to carry your prescription medicines in their original containers to avoid any misunderstandings with customs officers.

In addition to prescription meds, it's always a good idea to bring some aspirin, anti-diarrhea medicine, adhesive bandages, and something for stomach distress—all in small, tightly closed containers. What do you need to make you comfortable? Some people need very little, while others need to feel at home no matter where they are. If you consider this question before you start packing, you'll find it saves both time and money when on the road.

Conveniences. Instead of packing a travel iron, consider a steamer. They're quicker and more likely to get a piece of clothing spruced up—especially one that might be burnt if the iron isn't working correctly.

Personally, my household needs to have coffee in the morning, so we've gotten into the habit of packing a small package of instant coffee mixes, sugar, powdered cream and an electric heating coil (available at supermarkets and hardware stores) that slips into a cup of water and will heat it within seconds. (Remember to bring your electrical conversion kit if traveling abroad or the immersion heater won't work—and don't forget to put it in the water before plugging it in!).

A Swiss army knife is an invaluable traveling tool. Even when you're in a civilized area, you can always use the gadgets the knife offers—if only to open that fabulous bottle of wine you packed for a romantic lunch in the Tuscan countryside. Nothing is more irritating than sitting down after a long walk only to realize you've forgotten the corkscrew!

Language. Most travel guides give you a quick overview of the phrases you will probably need to know to get along in a foreign country, but I always buy a pocket-sized version of the language and practice on the plane on the way to my destination. Often, someone will overhear me and offer to help, which is an added plus in many ways: You get the right inflection from someone who's a native and you have the added opportunity of finding out a little more about the country.

For those of you who are business travelers, a Palm Pilot, or other handheld organizer, often includes a translation device that can save time and help with transactions you might not have otherwise been able to complete—without knowing the right phrases.

It's also helpful to listen to some foreign language tapes that will give you an idea of basic phrases used on a regular basis (i.e. Where is the nearest toilet? How can I get to my hotel? How much money do you need? Hello. Goodbye. Thank you. —and the ever important: I'm lost.). Foreign language tapes are available at your local library for rental and you can listen to them while you're running errands in your car or via personal cassette players while you're doing house or garden work before your trip.

Luggage and Packing. Most airlines have regulations about how much luggage you are allowed to bring. When you're making reservations, ask about the number of pieces you're allowed to check-in, as well

Watch Out!
Make sure you store the Swiss army knife in your checked luggage. If you put it in your carry-on luggage, it will be confiscated. Anything that might be used as a weapon (i.e. pepper spray, darts, knives) will not be allowed as a carry-on item.

as the measurements for carry-on luggage. Remember that American luggage regulations are not necessarily the same as standards in other parts of the world. If you have a travel agent, ask him/her what to expect. The charges for overweight baggage are usually more than what the items are actually worth.

The best way to save time while traveling is to pack lightly. Though most of us can't think of going without all possible combinations of clothes and accessories, wise and well-seasoned travelers have learned to pack everything they need in their carry-on. Not only does it save time while checking in, but it will also negate the possibility of the airline losing your luggage.

How you pack, as well as what you pack, can save you time and heartache. One simple tip that saves both time and space is to take clothes that don't need to be ironed and instead of folding them into your suitcase, roll them. Military personnel who need to look cleaned and pressed at all times have known this for years. Make use of all those little spaces by leaving smaller items for last, then slip rolled-up socks into shoes or in the corners of your suitcase; bras and underwear roll up very tightly and often can be wedged into the spaces left by larger pieces of clothing or can be used to pad breakable items.

What do you really need to take with you? Remember that most people who see you on a trip won't know what you wore the day before. You'll meet different people all the time, so with a little imagination and coordinated clothing, you can get away with very few outfits on a trip of a week or more. And there's no need for carrying bulky

Unofficially...
Beryl Markham, Amelia Earhart, and Charles Lindbergh, three of the greatest pilots of our time, always checked and rechecked their travel bags to ensure they'd brought only what was necessary—and each time they checked, they'd leave one additional nonessential item behind.

sweaters and coats if you remember to layer your clothing.

Some suggestions:

1. Consider clothing made of materials that don't wrinkle (jersey and lycra dresses, skirts, slacks, and shirts are indispensable). The TravelSmith Outfitting Guide and Catalog is a wonderful source for traveling clothes that are wrinkle-proof (Call 800-950-1600 for a catalog.).

2. Jackets with lots of pockets and zip-off sleeves are not only adaptable for weather changes but will give you more storage space for carrying items you've bought or things like cameras and film.

3. Bring only clothes that match so you can switch them around to create different outfits.

4. Remember that you can wash most of your underwear in the hotel room.

5. Take only the essential toiletries and bring small bottles of each (most grocery and drug stores sell sample sizes of lotion, toothpaste, shampoo and deodorant, as well as fold-up toothbrushes and hairbrushes, which will take up less space). Pack them in zip-lock plastic bags so that if they open during the trip, the liquids won't stain your clothes. You can always use the plastic bags to hold wet bathing suits during the trip.

6. Don't bring new shoes. One thing that wastes time and causes anguish during trips is blisters. You don't want your vacation or business travels ruined by that easily avoidable irritation. Take the time to break in your shoes before you leave. Or, simply bring shoes that are comfortable and go with just about everything you own.

Watch Out!
Don't allow one member of the group or family to carry all of the passports. If you travel with a tour group and the leader controls the passports, be sure you have copies in at least two other places.

One pair of flats or sneakers and a pair of low heels are enough for most women; men can wear loafers with just about everything.

Identification. When traveling to a foreign country, you will probably need a passport. Some countries will let you travel there with simply a birth certificate and a picture ID, but you're safer with a passport. In order to get a passport, you need two photos (2" × 2" in color against a light background). Some pharmacies and one-hour photo labs now offer passport photo services in-house. Get yours done while you're waiting to pick up the family prescriptions. The cost for a ten-year passport is $65 and you can obtain one at any of the following: a passport agency, a state or federal court, or a post office. When you go to the agency to apply, make sure you bring the photos, your money, your birth certificate, and a picture ID.

Apply for your passport at least two months prior to leaving for a foreign country. If you need one quicker, call the passport agency closest to you to see if they can issue it or whether you need to go elsewhere.

You also should always bring identification with you when travelling within the country. All airlines ask for a photo ID before they allow you to check in at the gate.

Reservations and the trip itself. There are so many online services now, you can practically name your own price for airline and hotel reservations, but going online to do a search is often more time-consuming that simply looking up dates and times of flights and other travel information in the OAG Travel Guide. They have a Web site, as well as many printed publications to help the frequent traveler save wasted time spent on hold with airlines. If you have the flight info you need at hand, you can make reservations more quickly. OAG also gives you city information and is in a partnership with Lotus Organizer to offer you access to travel databases from your office computer or personal organizer.

Always make copies of your passport and traveling papers and keep several in different places just in case you lost the original (I lost mine in Greece and it would have been a lot easier to get it replaced had I thought to make copies. As a result, I missed the last two days of my trip and all I saw of Athens was the inside of the U.S. Embassy.).

Communication. While you're away, remember that the most expensive way to keep in touch is by using the phone in your room. They usually add hefty surcharges to your room bill, sometimes even if you use a telephone credit card. If you can, use a phone booth in the hotel lobby where you can spread out your papers and make calls. Or ask the front desk if the hotel charges if you use a telephone credit card. Some telephone credit cards (like AT&T) offer users an 800 number that you can dial from other phones to access their service. This will save you the connecting fee.

If you're using a computer to keep in touch via e-mail, you still might have to pay a connection fee from a hotel room to connect to your server. Check with the hotel before you get online to save yourself the huge fees. You might also want to check before making reservations with the hotel to see if they have modem-ready telephones in the rooms.

Shopping. When making purchases while away from home, keep all the receipts. Most customs officers will ask for proof of purchase to see whether you're

Moneysaver
It's often cheaper to make long distance calls from a pay phone than from a hotel room. Quite a few hotels add an extra charge when customers make long distance calls on calling cards.

bringing in items that shouldn't be taken out of the country or whether you should be charged duty.

You should also bring proof of purchase for the personal items you're bringing with you (such as cameras, watches, computers, video recorders) so Customs officers don't subject those items to duty when you return to the States.

Safety. Most airport detectors recognize Mace or pepper spray canisters and personnel won't allow you to carry them. Something you are allowed, however, is a police whistle. Women, especially, should always carry one and use it whenever threatened.

Remember the following to remain safe:

- Don't open your hotel room door for anyone you don't know—no matter how convincing they are. Call the front desk or the hotel's security office to check on the person's identity first.

- Don't take your hotel room key/card out of your pocket until you're right in front of your room door, and it doesn't hurt to check over your shoulder before going in your room. Don't get caught unaware!

- Try to get a room located far from the exit doors. Most travelers think those rooms are safer in case of a fire, and they're probably right, but they also offer criminals a quicker exit/ getaway and it's been proven that rooms near exits are more likely to be robbed.

- Don't ever leave your door propped open for any reason. You might as well hang an invitation on the door for strangers to come in.

- When you leave the room, put all valuables away, preferably in a locked suitcase.

- Conduct all your business in a restaurant or the lobby, not in your hotel room.

▪ Avoid isolated places, badly lit streets or parking lots, and keep your eyes open for loiterers or strangers who appear to be following you or watching you. If you find yourself in an uncomfortable situation, find a well-lit store or public place. If that's not possible, scream. The worst thing that can happen is you'll be embarrassed if you're wrong about the person you believe to be a danger.

Bright Idea
Because lots of luggage looks alike, it's easy to take the wrong bag. Tie a bright ribbon around the handle or add a distinctive sticker that is immediately noticeable.

Maps and how not to waste time getting lost or sitting in traffic

We've all taken a wrong turn somewhere or received poor directions and ended up arriving late at an important meeting or function. How do you make sure you don't waste valuable minutes or hours aimlessly wandering strange streets in search of your destination? Preparation!

When you know you have an appointment somewhere you've never been before, take a moment before you get into the car and prepare a route.

▪ Spread that map out on a table.

▪ Find your destination.

▪ Look at the various ways you can reach it.

▪ If possible, call ahead to see if there are specific exit numbers or street addresses you should know.

▪ Most importantly, allow yourself at least fifteen minutes extra time to reach that location. Better to be a few minutes early—you can take out that piece of office correspondence or the book you have tucked in your bag/briefcase and relax before your appointment time, rather than tearing your hair out while in traffic.

If you have long-term plans for travel, get maps from your local AAA office. A membership in the American Automobile Association is probably the best investment a car owner can make. Not only will they cover towing if you're stuck with car problems, but they will offer travel information and free mapping. You can call your local office or check their Web site www.aaa.com to find out what region you are in.

Or use one of the mapping services provided on the Web. All have 'zooming' options that will allow you to see the major roads in and out of a city, as well as the small side streets, adjusting your focus until you find your desired location.

Some of the computerized mapping services include:

- Thomas Bros. Maps, the Thomas street guides at http://www.thomas.com

- Map Quest, all the maps you need across the world, http://www.mapquest.com

- For more, check out this link page which claims to provide all the maps "there is on the net" [sic]. http://www.algonet.se/~cristar/index. htm

One of the best inventions ever to be implemented is the new computerized maps some luxury cars include. What better place to put a map that saves you time and helps you find your way? Though only the new, more expensive cars offer this feature right now, it's been predicted that every car will have a computerized mapping device in the future.

In addition, keep a road atlas in your car at all times. Several maps are actually better than just one:

- A country road atlas like the ones put out by Mobil, AAA, or the travel guides

Moneysaver
Ask your company to add AAA to your benefits. If you're self-employed, take the membership fee off your taxes at the end of the year.

- A state map of the state(s) where you live or travel most often
- City guides of the larger metropolitan regions in your area
- A street guide of the city in which you live

If you keep these on hand in your car, you'll never be far from where you need to be, and the danger of stopping and asking a stranger for directions is eliminated. Besides, if you don't have a car phone or are miles from the nearest pay phone, the maps can be invaluable.

The beauty of audio tapes and learning while you drive

If you must be in the car all the time and are finding that your anxiety level is at an all-time high because you're wasting time traveling from one place to another, why not make that drive time worthwhile?

- Listen to audiotapes of the books you're not getting a chance to read (check Barnes & Noble online or its stores for hundreds of choices of both novels and nonfiction texts you can "read" while driving).

- Learn that language you haven't had a chance to learn. (Nothing makes you more valuable as an employee than knowing more than one language.) Berlitz has been teaching people how to speak another language with the use of audiotapes for many years and can offer courses in everything from French to Swahili. Check out their Web page at www.berlitz.com

- Listen to self-enhancement tapes. Everything from "how to sell to anyone" to "how to buy your dream house" and "how to lose weight

Unofficially...
A friend checks out audiotapes at the library, so she can listen to them once and return them. While she's there, she treats the kids to a few of their own. It keeps them all occupied while in the car—and they're learning, too!

without actually trying" has been put on tape. If you want to better yourself, take those hours you waste traveling and put them to good use. Though most bookstores have a great selection of these tapes, they're also available through special catalogs like Shambhala Publications.

■ Tape important meetings or conversations and listen to them again in the car in order to remember the finer points.

■ If you're a student, tape the class lessons or important lectures and listen to them while going to and from school. It'll be like building in extra hours of study time without worrying about cramming them into your already busy schedule.

■ In addition to listening to tapes, consider carrying a handheld tape recorder with you. You can record notes you don't want to forget or correspondence. Voice-activated recorders also save you the time and repetitive motion of turning the recorder on and off. The best invention, however, is the voice-recognition software that has come on the market in the past couple of years. Dragon Systems now has a handheld recorder that is portable—the beauty of this gadget is you can take those wasted hours in the car, utilize them, and not have to think about doubling the time and translating your spoken words into typed ones because the program does it for you!

Car phones—a necessity or a danger?

We all have mixed emotions about cell phones. We hate getting behind that chatty person who isn't paying attention to the lights because they're on their phone, but the thought of breaking down on a lonely highway is less frightening if you know you can pull out the car phone/cell phone and call for help. And the time these phones save is incredible! Going to be late for dinner? You can call. Lost? Call the person waiting for you or the local police for directions. Desperately need to contact someone for information? A quick phone call will get it for you.

Is the car your second office or your refuge?

The decision as to whether your car serves as an office or a refuge from ringing phones and demanding people is yours. However, once you make that decision, how can you best utilize the time spent in that automobile?

If you're always on the road and your car is your office away from the office, make it the most efficient one you can. Before you pull away from the curb, make sure your "office" is stocked with supplies.

Do you have:

- A portable copier—and enough paper and toner to last the trip? Before you leave is a good time to check to see whether the machine is working properly. A quick two-minute check can save you hours of frustration later.

- A portable fax machine? Is there an extra roll of paper in case you run out?

- A stapler, paper clips, stationery, pens, stamps? Restock each time you hit the home office so that you won't run out while on the road.

- Laptop or portable computer? Charge the battery while in your home office or hotel room. Keep an additional battery always on hand. Extra disks are a must and they should all be

Timesaver
Usually, a new cell phone company will give you additional air time if you sign up for its program. Save hours spent researching cell phones by simply calling the company you are already with on your home or office phone service.

labeled so you can find important documentation quickly.

■ Portable printer? Again, paper needs to be handy and make sure you have an extra ink cassette. (Idea: Get a combination printer/fax/ copier and you'll save yourself the energy of carrying all three.)

■ Portable cell phone? Make sure you have the right roaming modes for the areas into which you're traveling. Nothing is more frustrating than hitting a dead cell.

■ Pager? If you think you might be out of reach on your cell phone, you can add a pager to your office-away-from-the-office so you're always reachable.

■ File boxes? Rubbermaid makes lightweight milk crates or file boxes that will help you keep yourself organized and keep important papers from sliding all over the place. Get one that has a handle for easier carrying—and stock up on file folders so you can keep your projects organized.

One last piece of advice for the traveler: Whenever you leave your vehicle, cover your expensive equipment with a towel or sheet you can keep in the car. Not only will that stop potential thieves, but it will also help protect the valuable equipment from the sun. And don't forget to check your hotel room at least twice before you leave it. Many a traveling exec has left behind their palm-top organizer or cell phone in their rush to get to the next appointment.

Just the facts

■ Time-management seminars can often be held right in your office. Let the consultant know exactly what you need.

- Packing efficiently can often save hours, as well as space.

- Take extras of your medication in case you run out or are stranded by unexpected events.

- Travel time is empty time unless you utilize it by listening to tapes or catching up on dictation.

- Hiring temporary help to catch up during the busy season can save you from losing valuable customers.

- Listen to self-enhancement tapes. If you want to better yourself, take those hours you waste traveling and put them to good use.

- Tape important meetings or conversations and listen to them again in the car in order to remember the finer points.

- If you're a student, tape the class lessons or important lectures and listen to them while going to and from school.

- Sometimes, hiring someone can save you both time and money.

GET THE SCOOP ON...
How to clean off your desktop ▪ How to control
your input and output ▪ How to organize your
workspace ▪ How to find the right desk, chair,
and lighting to increase productivity

Your Workspace

Chapter 18

How many times have you had something at
your fingertips only to lose it seconds
later? If you could add up all the moments
it took you to find something, you'd find hours,
perhaps days, that you'd lost simply because you
couldn't put your hand on an item within seconds.
And think about the credibility you lose in front of
colleagues!

Most of us spend a minimum of five hours a day
in an office, yet we don't take the time to make it
streamlined and efficient. We'll spend hours—even
days—outfitting a car with all the modern conveniences to makes it suitable for our needs, but
suggest spending an extra $25-100 on a chair that
adjusts to make us more comfortable and we raise
our eyebrows. And what about that special desk
where you can spread your spreadsheets, or a
computer screen that's large enough to be viewed
several feet away? That's pure luxury.

"
A complex sys-
tem that works
is invariably
found to have
evolved from a
simple system
that worked.
—John Gall
"

Well, it's not. Luxuries are things you don't need. You do need an office and office space that is conducive to the type of work you do, and once you get it, not only will you be more productive, but you'll take less time to produce. No, this won't cost your life savings. All it might take is a little time to rearrange and do some cleaning up.

What are you losing if you're not organized?

- Deadlines. If you can't find something and miss the deadline because of it, you might lose your job—or at the very least, money!

- Time. Looking for items wastes time—and while you're looking, you find something else and start thinking about that, totally forgetting what you were looking for to begin with!

- Customers. If you can't find something and keep someone waiting as a result, sooner or later that customer is going to find someone who knows where everything is.

- Money. All of the above costs you money.

Think of it this way. An organized space will:

- Save time because you'll be able to find things easily.

- Save money because you'll save time (and as we all know, time is money).

- Increase productivity, effectiveness, and creativity because it will lower your frustration level.

- Win the confidence of co-workers and customers.

Does a messy desk really signify genius?

How many times have you heard this? Or what about the person who says, "It might look messy, but I know where everything is and can put my hand on it in a second." To that we say, "Horse puckey!" If you're one of those people who thinks Felix Unger was an nut and Oscar Madison is your idol, we have something else to say: It's time to come out from under that pile of mail from the 1970s and see the way things are done today.

There are many reasons why people exist with messy workspaces, and you might not like some of them, but let's list them here. Be honest with yourself. If you fit into one of them, you might not admit it to anyone else, but admit it to yourself. Then we'll be ready to rearrange things so you'll be more time-efficient.

People with messy workspaces often can't see the mess because they're...

▪ Used to someone else picking up after them; never learning to organized themselves.

▪ Not able to see the real condition of their desks/offices because they're absentminded, scatterbrained, or on what we affectionately call "intellectual overload."

▪ Depressed. Maybe they can't see the mess around them, or maybe they simply don't care.

▪ Rebels or nonconformists. "If everyone says I need to clean up and organize, that's okay for them, but I'm not going to. Period."

What do you do? Easy. Stop making excuses and start taking responsibility. If you want to find time in your day, the first place to look is under the mess on your desk.

Exactly what's causing the problem anyway?
Before you begin to clean off and organize, you need to figure out what's causing your inability to manage your office time. Then, zero in on the

Timesaver
Answer as much of your mail as possible within half an hour after you've opened it. Then file the mail you've answered.

specifics. It might be as easy as changing your desk arrangement, or it might mean an overhaul in the way you handle your incoming projects.

Here's a little test to determine your weaknesses:

Rank	Activity
	Keeping up with daily tasks.
	Finding what you want on your desktop.
	Focusing on tasks.
	Finishing tasks.
	Saying no and delegating.

Rank yourself from 1 to 5, with 5 being the weakest.

When you look at this test, can you see a pattern? Are you doing anything to strengthen these weaknesses? One of the first things you can do to save time and help you keep on task is to create a workable space where everything is easy to find.

Only the most important projects get desktop space
Right now, look at your desk. Do you see piles of unfinished work? Do you have a system of some kind? Be honest! Now, let's divide all those papers, files, notes, projects, and envelopes into piles according to when you use them. Utilize the chart below and see where each piece of paper falls.

CATEGORIZING THE STUFF ON YOUR DESK

Daily	Weekly	Monthly	Yearly	Some-times	Never
———	———	———	———	———	———
———	———	———	———	———	———
———	———	———	———	———	———
———	———	———	———	———	———

List each piece in one of these categories. Hint: A piece of paper should never fall into more than one.

Watch Out!
If you begin asking people not to move the piles on your desk, it's a sign you have too many piles and it's time to throw most of them away.

First step: Toss the whole pile that falls into the "never used" category. That's right. Into the barrel it goes. And most of the "sometimes pile" can go there too. The yearly pile gets filed. The monthly pile can go on your master list or get referred to others. Now you're down to just the daily and weekly piles. The daily items go into your to-do basket, and the weekly piles get noted on your master list.

Now, clean off the piles that you're not working on. All that should be left is your in-box and the jobs you're attending to at this very moment.

The hardest part of cleaning off the desk is making the decision to do something about those piles. Here are some general guidelines that should help you put it all to work.

- Handle each piece of paper only once.

- Before creating a new piece of paper, ask yourself if you have to do it. Is there another way you can pass on your message (e-mail? phone?)?

- Divide large tasks into small steps. One step at a time is the best way to conquer the mountain.

- Act! Beginning a job takes you closer to completing it.

- Remember: Not deciding is actually deciding.

- Shoot for a smooth desk flow. Don't let everything stop on top of your desk. It should *move.*

- Work on one thing at a time and finish it!

- Keep your desktop clean or everything that's on it will appear to be demanding your attention all at once.

- Create a daily to-do list and as you finish each chore, cross it off. Your goal is to reach the bottom of the list.

Moneysaver
Use a paper shredder instead of barrels in your office. You'll save money on trash (and trash bags) and ensure everyone's privacy.

Bright Idea
Remember: Only
20% of the paper
that crosses your
desk is worth-
while and needs
to be acted
upon. The rest
can be filed, for-
warded, or put
into the
trash can.

In-boxes and Out-boxes

Your in-box/out-box should be the only thing
(besides necessary tools) on your desktop. It should
contain only those items requiring same-day attention. For example:

■ Messages from your superiors.

■ Lists of people you need to call.

■ Items upon which you need to act.

■ Items for signature.

■ Correspondence that needs to be answered.

Once you've acted upon each piece of paper in
your in-box, it should be transferred to your out-
box, filed, or thrown away. Nothing should stay on
your desk once you're finished working on it.

Here's how to maintain the flow. The in-box
should be in the left corner of your desk. The center of your desk is your workspace and the right corner is where your out-box should be (and to the
right of the desk on the floor, is your waste can).

Secondary filing systems

Besides the filing cabinets that inhabit every office,
you should have a secondary system where you can
keep the projects on which you're currently working. Ideally, this system should be in your desk
drawer. Most office desks have one drawer that is
specifically designed to be a filing drawer where you
can insert hanging file folders and label them so
that they're easily identified. However, if you don't
have such a desk, there are several other options.

■ Stacking bins (usually designed for clothing or
   kids' toys) are perfect to hold magazines or
   larger projects. Most of them are also see-
   through, an added benefit.

- Plastic desktop file folders are small boxes, usually open on top, where you can file papers you need right away. Once you have used them, transfer them to a permanent file or discard them.

- Wire desktop file holders are simple and designed to hold a minimum of files. This is not meant to be a permanent receptacle for your files, so make sure you move them once you've acted upon them.

- Portable files. File carts on wheels are useful for people who need to move files from one place to another, or who might need to move the files out of the way when they need desk space.

- Cardboard file boxes. The least attractive and least permanent of the temporary file holders, these are inexpensive and are made in a number of different sizes. These can also be used to archive items that you can store in an area outside the office (but remember, they can get moist and destroy everything inside, so put them in a dry place).

The importance of having your tools within arm's reach

If your most important tools are within arm's reach, you'll always have them when you want them instead of digging through drawers or file cabinets to get them. Every time you use one, return it to its original place. And if the stapler is empty, refill it right away. If a pen runs out of ink, toss it. Don't tell yourself you'll refill it when you get time to buy refills. The refills are often the same price as a new pen anyway.

Timesaver
Sort through your desktop files on a regular basis to see whether there are papers you don't need anymore and can toss or move them to a permanent reference file.

It's been proven that office workers spend an average of 1-3 hours a week looking for items they use more than ten times a day.

Everything in its place—all the time

When an office space and everything on your desk is set up correctly, you should be able to reach whatever you want with a minimum of movement. Here are some things to consider before you start thinking about rearranging, buying a new desk, chair, files, and lighting.

■ Remember that convenience is most important. You need to reach the things you use on a regular basis. Everything else can be filed or stored.

■ Break your office down into quadrants or circles. The quadrant that is your desk (or the circle, whichever you prefer) is the most important space. Consider what type of worker you are: Do you need only a small amount of desk space because you do most of your work on the computer and very little writing? Or, do you need to spread out architectural plans or spreadsheets? Your central workspace should be whatever works for you. More about this in the section about desks.

■ Shoot for professionalism. Remember that people who visit your office don't see you first; they see your desk and its surroundings. If you're a psychiatrist, your office should reflect the warmth you want your patients to see in you. If you run a Fortune 500 company, streamlined accoutrements are probably more your style. If you're an accountant and your desktop is strewn with computer printouts, some stained with coffee cup rings from the cup you forgot to empty

Bright Idea
Keep the paper for your computer printer or copy machine right underneath it or in a drawer/shelf above.

this morning, and your lunch containers have not been thrown away, chances are your clients aren't going to feel comfortable having you manage their money.

■ Think about color. Yes, we're talking about time management, but have you ever thought that a simple color switch can also make you more productive? It's been proven that blue and green promote serenity and coolness; white increases the impact of light; black is usually too drastic and depressing; and beige tones can be boring, while red/yellow/orange are warm and often bring on anger or anxiety.

■ Consider the level of sound in your office. If you have no control over the noise coming from other offices around you, perhaps a simple solution would be to cover two of your walls (even cubicle walls) with large corkboards. They not only serve as places where you can hang your calendar and to-do list, but also tend to muffle sound. Some professors we know also tune in a small radio to a classical station or install a mini-fountain that offers a calming, soothing water-fall noise to offset the tensions students feel when they walk into the office.

Now that the overall tone for the office is set, it's time to think about the items you need to have on your desk and within reach. The first rule is: Everything has its place and it goes right back into that place when you're finished using it. You heard this from your mother, right? Well, she probably knew a bit about organization from raising a family. When you put things back into the same place, it makes them easier to find—and yes, it saves time!

Unofficially...
Rosie O'Donnell,
the talk show
host, thinks
organization is
so important
that the items
on her television
desk are not only
grouped by cate-
gory but also by
height, so she
can put her hand
on whatever she
needs simply by
shifting her line
of sight.

Desktop organizers are sold by every office product company. They differ according to the needs of the person, but we've found the most useful are the ones that lift off the desk, giving you additional storage space above the desk itself.

If you have an organizer that is not attached to your desk, chances are you can store all your working materials, reference books, diskettes for your computer and other "have-to-haves" in that organizer. If you don't, use your desk drawers and smaller containers to keep everything handy.

Here are the essentials you need to have on your desktop. Everything else is shelved elsewhere, stored or filed.

- Telephone. If you can get one that stores the numbers you dial on a regular basis, you'll save yourself time, but you'll also forget the numbers. A cordless phone can free you to walk around the office, do your filing, or other jobs while talking.

- In-box/out-box. (Keep your "to be filed" box on top of the filing cabinet or out of reach.)

- Writing utensil cup or container. Holds several pencils (sharpened every morning), pens (toss when they're used up), a highlighter, felt-tipped pen for writing labels.

- Calendar and address book. An erasable one for the wall is best and a daily one, broken down into hours, is good for the desk. Keep it small so you can take it with you when you leave for the day—and if your addresses/phone numbers are contained in the same book, it's easier. *Also* don't forget to write in appointments, addresses and phone number in pencil—easier to change that way.

- Stapler/staple remover
- Tape dispenser
- Cup of paper clips and binder clips
- Scissors (put them in the cup with the pens)
- Dictionary/thesaurus
- Guides for computer and management manuals you need to refer to on a regular basis (if you don't refer to them at least once a week, find someplace else to put them)

If your computer takes up part of your desk, you might want to consider a pull-out shelf for the keyboard—and that's part of the desk we're going to discuss next.

The right kind of desk and chair

If you're going to make the best use of your time, sometimes being comfortable is equal to being productive. This is the case when considering the right kind of desk and chair. Everyone has their own habits and needs. Personally, I like the L- to or U-shaped desk because I want to be able to reach everything around me. Others need solid desktop space.

Here are your options. You make the choice as to which one is right for you.

- Stand-up desks. Great for people with back problems, and for those who can do computer work standing up. A good source for this type of desk is Amish Country Furniture Sales (888) 384-7883 (www.standupdesks.com).

- Hutch desks. These take up little space and are perfect for the technology-oriented worker. One source for this type of desk is Workspace Resource, an online source for office furniture

Unofficially...
Thomas Jefferson built a stand-up desk for himself in 1776 after suffering from back pain.

and accessories, that has just about any piece of furniture you can want and access to all the major manufacturers. (www.workspace-resources.com)

- Executive desks. With a large flat surface, these desks are perfect for people who regularly meet in their office with others. Some very nice ones are made by Hon, a manufacturer that sells through most office furniture stores such as Business Products Express (www.bexpress.com) (888) 225-1524

- Single pedestal credenza. A flattop desk with one drawer on the side, these are often paired with double pedestal desks to create an L- or U-shaped desk for more desktop room. Made by most manufacturers and sold by such companies as Office Furniture Brokers, (217) 485-5345 (www.officefurniturebrokers. com).

- Double pedestal credenza. A desk commonly found in most offices, with one box drawer and one file drawer in each pedestal. Sold by just about everyone who offers office equipment, including Interior Office Solutions, (888) 262-2343 (www.intsol.org).

- Computer workstations. These come in all sizes, shapes, and categories. Most have shelf units above the computer station so you can store CDs, manuals, supplies, and books. Some also come with sliding keyboard trays, sliding printer trays, and file drawers. All major office supply stores, including places like Sears and Best Buy sell them. The one I have also came with a little side station where I put my phone/fax, answering machine, and large Oxford dictionary, as well as all my office supplies.

■ Armoires. No, not the kind you put your clothes in. Office armoires not only hold all your office equipment and computer, but they close up, leaving your mess inside. Perfect for the person who doesn't have an office where they can close the door. And they're available just about anywhere they sell furniture.

When considering the right chair for you, think about how long you'll be sitting in it every day. If you're going to spend hours in one place, you want to make sure it's not only comfortable, but mobile and adjustable. Here are some of the aspects you need to consider when purchasing a chair:

■ Does it fit your body? Truthfully, if the arms of the chair lock you in, you need a larger chair!

■ Does the seat height adjust? Your elbows should be even with your keyboard and your feet should rest on the floor (flat).

■ Does the backrest adjust up and down? Fit it into the curve of your lower back so that you sit up straight, arms resting at your sides.

■ Does the seat cushion slope forward slightly? It needs to so the strain is off the back of your legs.

■ If your chair has arms, are they adjustable? You should be able to change the height and slope of each arm so that your body's comfortable.

■ Does the chair have casters? A movable chair allows you easy access to everything in your office.

■ Is it ergonomic? For those of us with back or neck problems, ergonomic chairs ease the pain

66

The better work men do is always done under stress and at great personal cost.
—William Carlos Williams

99

of working in the same position for more than a couple of hours at a time.

■ Does the chair fit comfortably under your desktop? No matter how good the brand of chair is, if it doesn't fit, it's worthless.

■ Does it have a high back? A back that cuts into the middle of your spine gives you little or no support.

■ Does it make you smile when you sit in it? No kidding, you need to be happy in that chair.

Some of the manufacturers that make office chairs are:

■ Boss—executive-type chairs.

■ Hag—utilitarian office chairs, nice colors and styles.

■ La-Z-Boy—just as comfortable as their parlor furniture.

■ Krug—stylish, 50s wood and steel chairs. More for sitting at a table than working at a desk.

■ Tuohy—like an overstuffed armchair on wheels.

■ Hon—everything from leather executive chairs to clerk stools.

■ Globe Business Furniture—some special chairs for big and tall users, as well as other styles.

■ United Chair—has a series of ergonomic task chairs.

Do you need cubbyholes or flat work space?

As you can see, there are many different types of desks and workspaces. Depending on your habits, you'll need something to fit your needs.

Watch Out!
If your hands are tilting backward, you're not at the right height for your keyboard and will be asking for problems later on.

Some things to consider:

- Do you use a computer? You probably need a desk with storage space above.

- Do you often have to unroll plans, blueprints, or computer printouts? Then, at least part of your office space has to include a long, flat surface.

- Do you cover most of your desk with books, tools, CDs, and disks? Then perhaps a desk with cubbyholes would be best for you.

- Are books a necessity in your business? Then install a bookcase behind your desk so you can simply swivel to get at them.

- Do you need both a desk for your computer and flat space to spread out the documents on which you're working? Perhaps you'd be better off working in a "corridor." Put your desk with its computer and accessories in front of you and install a flat-topped credenza behind you. Keep the credenza clear of all papers except the ones on which you're working and you'll always have flat space when you need it.

How's your lighting?

One of the most important factors to consider when setting up your office space is where your lighting is coming from. Most people think it should be above their heads, but that isn't true. The light should focus on the papers, books, plans that you need to see—not on you! A lamp that reflects in your computer screen is definitely misplaced.

Try to use lighting that is as close to natural light as possible. It's healthier and causes less glare. Nothing makes the eyes tire faster than glare.

Bright Idea
Use soft glare
60-watt light
bulbs in all your
office lamps.
Several lamps are
better than one,
especially if you
work in different
areas of the
office.

Decorating the desk and office

One word of caution: *Don't* decorate the desk. You'll only add to the clutter we've just worked so hard to get rid of. Hang any photos you can on the wall or just use one family photo in a small frame for the top of your desk or computer. Mine is less than 3 × 5, but I have all three family members' smiling faces and it's just enough to remind me they're in my life.

Food belongs in your office kitchen or the tote bag you bring with you every day, not in your desk. Trophies can be stored on bookshelves or the credenza behind your desk, but if they start taking up workspace, get rid of them. Who are you trying to impress anyway? Plants are lovely and might make you smile, but if they are in the way of important papers, move them. And if watering them means you also water files and calendars or part of your in-box, get rid of them. Keep them at home where you can nurture them. One plant is enough. The only way you should have any more is if you have a wide windowsill where they're out of the way.

Just the facts

- Most mail can be opened while standing next to a trash can to save time.

- Desktops should be clear except for what you're working on at the moment.

- Every tool you use daily should be within arm's reach.

- Your desk and chair are crucial to your productivity and should be chosen carefully.

- A standing desk can help back problems.

Time-Management Seminar Guide

The American Management Association (AMA-COM), 135 West 50th Street, New York, NY 10020. (800) 262-9699. This company offers classes in time management, as well as all types of other management skills, all over the United States.

George E. Baker, a retired military officer who has offered leadership and management courses to over 10,000 people, is president and CEO of The Productivity Institute in Little Rock, Arkansas. The firm specializes in both individual and organizational productivity improvement training and consulting and can be contacted at: 3 Johnson Ranch Road, Little Rock, AR 72212, (800) 393-1704, (501) 868-1702. http://www.tpi-qdg.com

Hal Burrows, co-author of the *One Minute Manager* books, has run two Fortune 500 companies and has many years of experience as owner/operator of his own consulting firm. He's been speaking to companies and managers at all levels since 1973 and

presents two seminars: Managing Management
Time, and Managing Negotiations Under Pressure.
He and co-authors Ken Blanchard and William
Oncken can be contacted for presentations, semi-
nars, consultations, and other learning materials at:
Blanchard Training and Development, Inc., 125
State Place, Escondido, CA 92025.

Change Dynamics, a company that offers management seminars to employers, employees, and teams.
Its programs are highly interactive sessions of three
to four hours that are either instructor-led or self-
paced. The courses build skills to translate business
strategies into performance capabilities. The
address: Change Dynamics, 211 Melrose Avenue,
Mill Valley, CA 94941, (800) 342-7560 or (415) 389-
6100, Fax: (415) 389-9933. E-mail: train@best.com

Merrill and Donna Douglas, consultants who run
the Time Management Center in Marietta, Georgia,
conduct time-management seminars, and authored
Time Management for Teams and *Manage Your Time,
Your Work and Yourself,* both published by the
American Management Association. Contact them
at: 1401 Johnson Ferry Road, Suite 328-D6,
Marietta, GA 30062, (404) 973-3977.

The Dynamics Group, a company that helps managers focus on particular leadership skills such as
dealing with people, coaching, sales, career goals,
and others. Seminars and workshops are available
and you can call for a free, no-obligation session by
contacting The Dynamics Group, One Westbrook
Corporate Center, Suite 300, Westchester, IL 60154,
(708) 246-2002. http://www.thedynamicsgroup.
com/coaching.htm

Ronni Eisenberg and Kate Kelly, authors of five
books on how to manage time and organize your

life, run workshops and lecture on the subject for major corporations and business associations. Eisenberg also does one-on-one consulting regarding getting organized in the workplace. Contact them at: Ronni Eisenberg & Associates, P.O. Box 3272, Westport, CT 06880.

Keith Ellis, a consultant who advertises that he will consult with clients by phone, thus saving travel and expenses. He has over 25 years of expertise in goal setting, time management, and leadership. Call (800) 738-5267, e-mail him at consultant@selfhelp. com, or visit his Web site at http://selfhelp.com

Dr. B. Eugene Griessman, author of *Time Tactics of Very Successful People*, has taught at prominent universities throughout the world, has been management consultant to major corporations, has written six books, and has created award-winning television productions for TBS. He is available for private workshops, keynote, or special presentations, and can be contacted at (800) 749-GOAL.

Innovative Business Technologies, a company that offers its expertise in teaching you or your group about: Communications, Leadership Development, Youth Development, Performance Management, Personal Development, Team Building, Coping & Stress, Customer Relations, Leadership, Diversity, Learning Approaches, Values, Conflict Resolution, Change Management, Motivation, Innovation, Time Mastery, Sales, Educators, Counseling/ Coaching. For more information, please contact: Innovative Business Technologies, Inc., P.O. Box 448, Cordova, TN 38088-0448, (888) 818-2281, (901) 751-1280 (Memphis), or (615) 223-7008 (Nashville). E-mail: BTpearl@aol.com

Terri Wildemann, owner and coach of Image Plus, offers training programs and products on topics such as Customer Service, Telephone Courtesy, Image Management, Leadership, Team Building, and more. She can be reached at: Image Plus...® Associates, (401) 847-9291; Fax: (401) 846-0678; or by e-mail: Success@Image-Plus.com.

Glossary

80/20 Principle Vilfredo Pareto, an Italian economist, discovered a truth about time and workers' input/output that remains solid to this day. A hundred years ago, he did a study on income and wealth patterns. What he discovered is that there is a "predictable imbalance" that shows up in every area of life. Called the 80/20 Rule or the Pareto Time Principle, it directly relates to time management in that it states that 80% of time spent poorly equals 20% of desired results, while 20% of time spent wisely nets 80% of the desired results.

ABC Analysis An analysis strategy to figure out which tasks are urgent, which are important, and which can be left to free time.

- It's figured that 15% of the most important tasks (A tasks) are actually worth 65% of the goal.

- B tasks make up approximately 20% of the total and are worth 20% of the value in managerial tasks.

- And C tasks make up the largest percent of the tasks (thus take up the most time) at 65%, but contribute to only 15% of the value.

Attention Deficit Disorder A disorder characterized by inability to stay on task, distractedness, and hyperactivity.

Biorhythm The biological cycle that affects a person's emotional, physical, and intellectual energy levels.

Checklist The list that a time manager uses to keep focused on goals for the day, week, month, or year.

Dayplanner A scheduling device often set up in calendar form. It can be in notebook or computer form.

Delegation Handing over tasks to someone else. Used by time managers when they are unable to finish everything on their to-do list.

Dovetailing The ability to join together two or more tasks.

Eisenhower Principle Former President Dwight D. Eisenhower took the ABC Analysis one step further, by adding a W that stands for wastebasket. When determining how to meet his goals, he divided his tasks into four categories:

- Immediate/Important: The tasks that need to be tended to right away.

- Immediate/Less Important: The jobs that are demanding, but can wait a moment.

- Less Immediate/Important: Those tasks that can wait, but will become problematic if put off too long.

- Less Immediate/Less Important: The chores that can be relegated to the wastepaper basket or given to someone else without a worry. These are often the tasks that make a person feel overworked and underpaid.

Goal-setting The ability to put a time limit on something one wishes to attain.

Law of the Slight Edge Small changes, over time, make a big difference.

Myers-Briggs A well-known personality test, commonly used by schools and mental health professionals, to determine a person's style and talents.

Outsourcing A 1990s word for delegating, it means that you farm out work to outside sources rather than delegating it to office staff.

Palm organizer A device used to help a time manager keep track of deadlines, duties, addresses, etc., on a handheld computerized unit.

Parkinson's Law Work expands to accommodate the time you have to do it in. For example, if your deadline is a month from now, it will take you a month to finish the task. If the same job is given a week's deadline, it'll take you a week to finish the task. In other words, we pay attention to deadlines.

Personality tests The standardized tests created by psychologists to determine what type of personality subjects have.

Prioritize To decide which task/problem should be taken care of first.

Proactive To take the first step toward getting something accomplished.

Procrastination The act of putting off doing something until later.

Re-prioritize To rethink priorities/goals and to juggle activities to accommodate any surprises or interruptions.

SMART   An acronym coined to help people figure out their objectives. The letters stand for Specific, Measurable, Achievable, Realistic, and Timed.

Spam   Junk mail sent through the Internet.

Time budget   The amount of time you have to accomplish the tasks you wish to do.

Timeline   The schedule of time within which you intend to accomplish your goals.

Time manager   A person who has control over their time, goals, and is organized enough to get everything done by deadline.

Time management   The act of organizing one's self in order to accommodate deadlines and create both work and personal time in one's life.

To-do list   The list of items you wish to accomplish that you create every day/week/month and will complete during the specified period of time.

Type A personality   People who are impetuous, quick to act, extremely competitive, often hostile, and angry. This personality type often has high levels of stress and is prone to health problems such as heart attacks, stroke, headaches, ulcers, and other disabilities.

Type B personality   People who take time to smell the roses, are generally not aggressive, and often miss out on opportunities because they don't take action. These people are usually quite healthy and happy, though they might tend to be a little lackadaisical.

Resource Guide

Academic Timesavers:

Books specific to saving time in school:
Awesome Student Planner and Assistant. Nickle Press, 1995. Helps students ages 9-12 plan school assignments.

College time management courses:
AHEAD
Programming for College Students with Learning Disabilities
P.O. Box 21192
Columbus, Ohio 43221

Davis and Elkins College
Elkins, WV
Online list of time management techniques:
http://www.osb.org/advising/help/23tmt.html

Edinboro College
Time Management and Academic Survival Tips
Online information: http://www.edinboro.edu/cwis/acaff/suppserv/tips

The Harvard Course in Reading and Study Strategies
Bureau of Study Counsel
Harvard University
5 Linden Street
Cambridge, MA 02138
617-495-2581
Online info:
http://www.fas.harvard.edu/~sc/Rcinfo.htm

Memory Skills for Improving Comprehension
Online information: http://www.alarice.com

Multimedia program designed to address problems remembering written content. Six free multimedia exams, plus tracking software. $29.95

Counseling Center
Division of Student Affairs
University of Buffalo
120 Richmond Quadrangle
Buffalo, NY 14261
716-645-2720

Online Counseling Center:
http://ub-counseling.buffalo.edu/Stress/procrast.html

University of Minnesota/Duluth
Student Handbook
Study Skills Survey
Online information: http://www.d.umn.edu/student/loon/acad/strat/self_test.html

Virginia Tech
Division of Student Affairs
Cook Counseling Center
Time Scheduling Information
Online information:
http://www.ucc.vt.edu/stdysk/htimesch.html

Business timesavers:

Attention Deficit Disorder information:
Attention Deficit Disorder Association
(http://www.attn-deficit-disorder.com)
or write to:
The A.D.D. Family... From Heartache to Triumph!
c/o New Net Media, Inc.
1355 S Boulder Rd. Suite F-259
Louisville, CO 80027

Books specific to business timesaving techniques:
The Banker's Handbook of Letters and Letter-Writing: A Complete Collection of Timesaving Letters that Work by Jeffrey L. Seglin. Probus Publishing, 1992.

Be Decisive: A Six Step Formula for Making Your Best Decisions Everytime by Lori Ann Smith. Change Your Life Books, 1999.

Beyond Time Management: Business with a Purpose by Robert J. Wright, Robert A. Wright. Butterworth-Heinemann, 1996.

The Business Traveler's Survival Guide: How to Get Work Done While On the Road by June Langhoff. Aegis Publishing Group, 1997.

Chuck Carlson's 60-Second Investor: 201 Tips, Tools and Tactics for the Time-Strapped Investor by Charles B. Carlson. McGraw-Hill, 1997.

Competing Against Time: How Time-Based Competition is Reshaping Global Markets by George Stalk and Thomas M. Hout. Free Press, 1990.

Developing Products in Half the Time by Preston G. Smith, Donald G. Reinertsen. John Wiley & Sons, 1997.

The Disney Way: Harnessing the Management Secrets of Disney in Your Company by Bill Capodagli, Lynn Jackson.

Economy for Women: The Complete Guide to Saving Time and Money by Diana Hunter. Consumer Press Inc. 1992.

Effective Project Management: How to Plan, Manage, and Deliver Projects on Time and Within Budget by Robert Wysocki. John Wiley & Sons, 1995.

Everyday Math for the Building Trades: A Time-Saving Field Guide by James Gerhart. McGraw-Hill, 1996.

Excel 97 for Busy People: The Book to Use When There's No Time to Lose by Ron Mansfield. Osborne McGraw-Hill, 1997.

Find the Job You've Always Wanted in Half the Time with Half the Effort by Jeffrey J. Mayer. NTC/ Contemporary Publishing, 1993.

The Five Rituals of Wealth: Proven Strategies for Turning the Little You Have Into More Than Enough by Tony Robbins, Tod Barnhart. Harperbusiness, 1996.

The Warren Buffett Way by Robert G. Hagstrom. John Wiley & Sons, 1995.

Car Office Accessories:

A2Z Mobile Office Solutions
Accessories for Mobile People
800-347-6222/fax 304-296-5284
Outside U.S. 304-296-8800
http://www.a2zsolutions.com

Chairs:

Note: These chairs are available in most office furniture stores.

Boss—Executive-type chairs.

Globe Business Furniture—Some special chairs for big and tall users, as well as other styles.

Hag—Utilitarian office chairs, nice colors and styles.

Hon—Everything from leather executive chairs to clerk stools.

Krug—Stylish, 50s wood and steel chairs. More for sitting at a table than working at a desk.

La-Z-Boy—Just as comfortable as their parlor furniture.

Tuohy—Like an overstuffed armchair on wheels.

United Chair—Has a series of ergonomic task chairs.

Day-planners and organizers:

Cambridge ® Day Planners

www.meadweb.com

DayRunners ™

Call for info or sample products online:

800-643-9923

www.dayrunner.com

Day-Timers ™

Call for info or sample products online:

800-225-5055

www.daytimers.com

Filofaxes ™

800-635-4321

www.thedailyplanner.com

Franklin ™ Planners

800-655-1492

www.franklinquest.com

Rolodex (regular and electronic)

800-266-5626

www.franklin.com

Desks:

Double-pedestal credenza. A desk commonly found in most offices, with one box drawer and one file drawer in each pedestal. Sold by just about everyone who offers office equipment, including Interior Office Solutions, (888)262-2343 (www.intsol.org).

Executive desks. With a large flat surface, these desks are perfect for people who regularly meet in their office with others. Some very nice ones are made by *Hon*, a manufacturer sold through most office furniture stores such as Business Products Express (www.bexpress.com) (888)225-1524. **Hutch desks.** These take up little space and are perfect for the technology-oriented worker. One source for this type of desk is Workspace Resource, an online source for office furniture and accessories, that has just about any piece of furniture you can want, plus access to all the major manufacturers. (www.workspace-resources.com) **Single-pedestal credenza.** A flattop desk with one drawer on the side, these are often paired with double-pedestal desks to create an L- or U-shaped desk for more desktop room. These credenzas are made by most manufacturers and sold by such companies as Office Furniture Brokers, (217) 485-5345 (www.officefurniturebrokers.com). **Stand-up Desks.** Great for people with back problems, and for those who can do computer work standing up. A good source for this type of desk is Amish Country Furniture Sales (888) 384-7883 (www.standupdesks.com).

Office furniture:

Best Buy (800)648-0113 (www.bestbuy.com)
Circuit City (800)395-4377 (www.circuitcity.com)
Levenger's (800)544-0880 (www.levenger.com)
Office Depot (800)685-8800
Office Max (800)788-8080 (www.officemax.com)
Office World, Inc. (800)541-5059
(www.officeworld.com)
Staples (800)333-3330 (www.staples.com)
Value America (888) 510-VALU
(www.valueamerica.com)

Office supply and timesaver tools:
Levenger/Tools for Serious Readers
420 S. Congress Avenue
Delray Beach, FL 33445-4696
(800)544-0880
Online: www.levenger.com
Reading and office timesavers for the discerning buyer: pens, leather cases, binders, desks, bookcases, special pens, traveling desks, storage units, special laptop organizers, briefcases, etc.

Palm III Electronic Organizer
One of the best places to find out which ones are best for you is to visit the Pickled Palm Pilot Web site (http://www.pickled.com)

Racks for organizing
One rack with different levels and file pockets, preferably see-through, will be enough for you to keep everything you need close by. One such rack is made by WolffWire Corporation (800)748-0190 e-mail: exdesign@carrinter.net

Computer timesavers

Books specifically designed to save time on the computer:
America Online for Busy People: The Book to Use When There's No Time to Lose by David Einstein.
The Internet and the World Wide Web: A Time-Saving Guide for New Users by Mark Kressin. Prentice-Hall Computer books, 1997.

Antivirus Programs:
Norton AntiVirus. A program that detects viruses and allows you the opportunity to not only spot them before they destroy you but to eradicate them.
McAfee. Makes an Office Utility Suite that includes a virus scan that automatically checks all documents

in your e-mail and downloaded from the Net; a 'first aid' program that fixes hardware programs and notifies you if your hard drive is ready to fail so you can save documents before it happens; 'nuts & bolts,' which can help you rescue files; 'guard dog,' which keeps your work personal; and several other components that keep your computer updated and 'healthy.' Web site: www.mcafee.com

Contact manager programs:

ACT! Made by Symantec Corporation and available in Windows, DOS, and Mac versions.
Can be programmed to come on your computer screen as soon as you boot up every day. Included are features to help you import information for your address book and everything you might have already entered in your current contact manager.

Consultant 2.5. Made by Chronos for Macintosh software. Features a full-featured contact manager, a calendar that offers multiple views, and automatic word completion so you save time on keystrokes. Also has pop-up alarms to notify you of upcoming events.

Voice recognition programs:

Dragon Naturally Speaking Preferred 3
www.insyncit.com/dragonsys/
L&H Voice Xpress Professional
www.l&h.com
Via Voice 98 Executive
www.software.ibm.com/is/voicetype

Home timesavers:

Books specific to saving time in the home:

Clutter's Last Stand: It's Time to De-Junk Your Life! by Writer's Digest Books.

Easy One-Dish Meals: Time-Saving, Nourishing, One-Pot Dinners from the Stovetop, Oven and Salad Bowl (Prevention's Quick and Healthy Low-Fat Cooking) by Jean Rogers, ed. Rodale Press, 1999.

The Family Manager's Everyday Survival Guide by Kathy Peel. Ballantine, 1998.

Frozen Assets: How to Cook for a Day and Eat for a Month by Deborah Taylor-Hough.

Great Garden Shortcuts: 100s of All-New Tips & Techniques That Guarantee You'll Save Time, Save Money, Save Work by Joan Benjamin and Erin Hynes, editors.

Helpful Hints for Hurried Homemakers: Time and Money-Saving Shortcuts by Dorsey Connors. Bonus Books, 1988.

Helpful Household Hints: The Ultimate 90s Guide to Housekeeping by June King.

Is There Life After Housework? by Don Aslett. Writer's Digest Books, 1992.

Microwave Gourmet: The Only Microwave Cookbook You Will Ever Need by Barbara Kafka.

Recipes 1-2-3 Menu Cookbook: Morning, Noon, and Night: More Fabulous Food Using Only 3 Ingredients by Rozanne Gold and Tom Eckerle.

Closet organizers:
Closet Masters
10626 York Rd.
Cockeysville, MD
e-mail: clomas@erols.com
http://www.closet-masters.com

The California Closet Company
http://www.everythingforthehome.com

Housekeeping timesavers
Improvements/Quick and Clever Problem Solvers
Catalog Service
Hanover, PA 17333-0084
(800)642-2112
Online: www.improvementscatalog.com
Timesaving and moneysaving storage units and household goods, such as shoe racks, hideaway hampers, spacesavers for desks and kitchens, organizers for letters and bills, closet organizers, garment storage, bathroom organizers, furnace filters, and many other home organizing devices.

Personal timesavers:

Aromatherapy and herbal remedies:
Frontier Cooperative Herbs—Aromatherapy, culinary spices, organic coffee and natural remedies
http://frontierherb.com
(800) 669-3275

MotherNature.com—Large site with natural medicines, aromatherapy, vitamins, minerals, bath and body products, books, etc.
Mother Nature Barn
Old Bedford Road
Concord, MA
(800)517-9020
http://www.mothernature.com

Sunrise Herb—Catalog of aromatherapy products, personal care products, natural herbal remedies, and more. Shop online or call for catalog.
Sunrise Herb
4808 Dreams End Drive
Louisville, Kentucky 40291
http://www.sunrize.com
(888)880-0384

Books specific to personal timesaving, fitness, health, creativity.

The 10-Minute L.E.A.P.: Lifetime Exercise Adherence Plan by Richard L. Brown. Regan Books, 1998.

12-Minute Total Body Workout by Joyce L. Vedral. Warner, 1993.

American Heart Association Fitting in Fitness: Hundreds of Simple Ways to Put More Physical Activity into Your Life by American Heart Association. Times, 1997.

A Room of One's Own by Virginia Woolf. Harcourt Brace, 1990.

The Art of Doing Nothing: Simple Ways to Make Time for Yourself by Veronique Vienne. Clarkson Potter, 1998.

Beyond Time Management: Life Balancing Connections by Jane Allen Petrick, Ph.D. Informed Decisions International, 1998.

Bible Gems for Busy People: Devotions for Quality Time with God by Richard Howard. Beacon Hill Press, 1996.

Brain Fitness. Anti-Aging Strategies for Achieving Super Mind Power by Bob Goldman. Doubleday, 1998.

Breathless: Transform Your Time-Starved Days Into a Life Well Lived by Gary R. Collins. Tyndale House, 1998.

The Essential Guide to the New Adolescence: How to Raise an Emotionally Healthy Teenager by Ava L. Siegler, Ph.D. E.P. Dutton, 1997.

Healthy Eating: For Extremely Busy People Who Don't Have Time for It ("KISS" for Health) by Christine H. Farlow. Farlow Publishers, 1998.

If You Can't Make Time, Don't Make Children; How to Spend More Time with Your Kids by Steve Smith, Cay W. Smith. Smith Publishers, 1996.

Running for Dummies by Florence Griffith Joyner, John Hanc, and Jackie Joyner-Kersee.

The Unofficial Guide to Child Care by Ann Douglas. Macmillan, 1998.

The Unofficial Guide to Having a Baby by John R. Sussman, Ann Douglas. Macmillan, 1999.

Child care:

Child Care Aware (800) 424-2246 http://www. childcarerr.org/childcareaware/index.htm Nationwide campaign that trains child care providers, educates parents on what quality child care should be like and how to search for it.

Fitness:

All types personal exercise videos:
Collage Exercise Video Specialists
Guide to Exercise Videos
5390 Main St., NE, Dept R 34
Minneapolis, MN 55421
(800) 433-6769
http://www.collagevideo.com

Tae Bo: Billy Blanks Tae Bo videotapes
Tae Bo
7095 Hollywood Blvd.
Hollywood, CA 90028
(800) 637-6632
http://www.taebo.com

Tai Chi: Tai Chi Strength and Conditioning
videotapes created by
Boston Kung-Fu Tai-Chi Institute
361 Newbury Street
Boston, MA 02115
(617) 262-0600
http://www.taichi.com

Erle Montague's Taiji World
videotapes and personal training
http://www.216.156.11.240/videos
e-mail: taiji@moontagu.com

Wai Lana Yoga
PO Box 6146
Malibu, CA 90264
(800)228-5145
http://www.wailana.com
e-mail: info@wailana.com

Junk mail (getting rid of it!):

Zero Junk Mail—will stop all unsolicited brochures, newsletters, sales material by contacting the direct mail organizations to get your name taken off their lists.
(www.zerojunkmail.com)

Mail Preference Service
Direct Marketing Association
PO Box 9008
Farmingdale, NY 11735-9008

Junkbusters Spamoff—SM will build a "no e-mail solicitations" block for your Web page that should stop most of the unwanted junk mail.

Petsitters:

The National Association of Professional Pet Sitters offers info on local sitters and will give you names and numbers when you call 1-800-296-PETS 24 hours a day, 7 days a week.

Professional organizers:

National Association of Professional Organizers
1033 LaPosada Drive, Suite 220
Austin, TX 78752.

Relaxation tapes:
Light Unlimited Publishing—Relaxation tapes, CDs, and books by Jon Shore; guided meditation retreats and lectures in chalet in Colorado mountains; relaxation training and stress reduction; children's relaxation; childbirth preparation; onsite and retreats.

Jon Shore
13652 Shore Drive
Conifer, Colorado 80433
(303)816-9247 or (303)816-9458
http://www.jonshore.com
  e-mail: budanatr@jonshore.com

Psychological Wellness Associates, LLC—Mental health professionals who provide psychotherapy, counseling, biofeedback therapy and guided relaxation tapes.

Frank McManus, Ph.D., Barbara Kelly, and Robert Mabel,Ph.D
Psychological Wellness Associates, LLC
PO Box 5025
Deptford, NJ 08096
http://www.psycwellness.com

Sounds Natural: Relaxation Tapes—Some tapes can be made to order
http://www.onml.demon.co.uk/index.htm
e-mail: pete@onml.demon.co.uk

Suki Productions—Guided imagery and other relaxation tapes (some can be personalized); alternative medicine therapies; Chinese medicine; Japanese water fountains; Zen clocks; Cancer guide.
http://www.sukiproductions.com/index.htm
e-mail: info@sukiproductions.com

Troutlily Music—Relaxation tapes and bedtime music for children and adults

http://www.troutlily.com
e-mail: troutlily@wmsnet.com

Shoppers:
Online Personal Shopper
http://www.wsin.com/pershop.html
iMall Personal Shopper
http://bonnieandclyde.hypermart.net/
features.html
Executive Personal Shopper
http://www.hasslefreegifts.com
eBay Personal Shopper
http://ebay.com
Bloomingdale's and most large department stores
offer personal shoppers. Contact your local outlet
to get particulars.

Teaching Timesavers:

Books specific to teachers' and librarians' timesaving:

Elementary School Librarian's Survival Guide: Ready-to-use Tips, Techniques, and Materials to Help You Save Time and Work in Virtually Every Aspect by Barbara Farley Bannister et. Center for Applied Research in Education, 1993.

Workshops/online information:
Yale Working at Teaching Office
432-1198
Online Workshop Manual:
http://www.yale.edu/wat/guide.html

Travel timesavers:

Books specific to helping travelers save time:
Author's note: Any of the Frommer's, Lonely Planet, and Fodor's guides will help you save time by

giving you information about the places you intend to visit.

10 Minute Guide to Travel Planning on the Net by Thomas Pack. Que Education & Training, 1997.

The Cheapskate's Unauthorized Guide to Walt Disney World: Time-Saving Techniques and the Best Values in Lodging, Food & Shopping by Michael Lewis, Debbi Lacey. Citadel Press, 1997.

Don't Waste Your Time in the B.C. Coast Mountains: An Opinionated Hiking Guide to Help You Get the Most from this Magnificent Wilderness by Kathy Copeland. Wilderness Press, 1997.

Fodor's Net Travel: Your Guide to Sun, Fun, Fantasy & Adventure Using the Internet and Online Sources by Mary Goodwin, Kristin Miller, Shaun Witten. Wolff New Media, 1996.

Catalogs for travel-related items:
TravelSmith
Outfitting Guide and Catalog
60 Leveroni Court
Novato, CA 94949
(800)950-1600
Great for suitcases, travel kits, wrinkle-free travel clothing, organizer bags, passport wallets, packable tripods/cameras/binoculars, etc.

Recommended Reading List

(These books have been reviewed and used for research, thus deemed useful for the time manager.)

General Reading

Berner, Jeff. *The Joy of Working from Home: Making a Life While Making a Living.* San Francisco: Berrett-Koehler Publishers, Inc., 1994.

Blanchard, Kenneth, and Spencer Johnson. *The One Minute Manager.* New York: Morrow, 1982.

Blanchard, Kenneth, and William Oncken, Jr., and Hal Burrows. *The One Minute Manager Meets the Monkey.* New York: Blanchard Family Partnership, 1989.

Branscomb, H. Eric. *Casting Your Net: A Student's Guide to Research on the Internet.* Boston: Allyn and Bacon, 1998.

Bruno, James E. *It's About Time: Leading School Reform in an Era of Time Scarcity.* Thousand Oaks, California: Corwin Press, Inc., 1997.

Carter, Carol, et al. *Keys to Effective Learning*. Upper Saddle River, New Jersey: Prentice Hall, 1998.

Cooper, Mildred and Kenneth H. Cooper, M.D. *Aerobics for Women*. New York: Bantam Books, 1972.

Covey, Stephen R., et al. *First Things First: To Live, to Love, to Learn, to Leave a Legacy*. New York: Simon & Schuster, 1994.

Covey, Stephen R., et al. *The Seven Habits of Highly Effective People*. New York: Simon & Schuster, 1989.

Dalai Lama and Howard C. Cutler, M.C. *The Art of Happiness*. New York: Penguin/Putnam, 1998.

Downing, George. *The Massage Book*. New York: Random House, 1972.

Eisenberg, Ronni with Kate Kelly. *Organize Your Family!* New York: Hyperion, 1993.

Eisenberg, Ronni with Kate Kelly. *Organize Your Home!* New York: Hyperion, 1994.

Fonda, Jane. *Jane Fonda's Workout Book*. New York: Simon & Schuster, 1981.

Fonda, Jane. *Women Coming of Age*. New York: Simon & Schuster, 1984.

Forsyth, Patrick. *First Things First: How to Manage Your Time for Maximum Performance*. London: Pitman Publishing, 1994.

Frank, Dr. Stanley D. *Remember Everything You Read: The Evelyn Wood Seven-Day Speed Reading and Learning Program*. New York: Times Books, 1990.

Goldfein, Donna. *Every Woman's Guide to Time Management*. Millbrae, California: Les Femmes Publishing, 1977.

Griessman, B. Eugene. *Time Tactics of Very Successful People*. New York: McGraw-Hill, Inc., 1994.

Grizzard, Lewis. *They Tore Out My Heart and Stomped That Sucker Flat*. New York: Warner Books, 1982.

Hardin, Carlette Jackson. *A College Yearbook: Making It Through The First Year*, 2nd Ed. Needham Heights, MA: Ginn Press, 1988.

Hemphill, Barbara. *Taming the Office Tiger*. Washington, D.C.: Kiplinger Books, 1996.

Hemphill, Barbara. *Taming the Paper Tiger, Fourth Edition*. Washington, D.C.: Kiplinger Books, 1997.

Hobbs, Charles R. *Time Power*. New York: Harper & Row Publishers, 1987.

Hottenstein, David S. *Intensive Scheduling: Restructuring America's Secondary Schools Through Time Management*. Thousand Oaks, California: Corwin Press, Inc., 1998.

Hunt, Diana and Pam Hait. *The Tao of Time*. New York: Simon & Schuster, 1990.

Huyvaert, Sarah H. *Time Is of the Essence: Learning in Schools*. Boston: Allyn and Bacon, 1998.

Kahn, Norma. *More Learning in Less Time: A Guide to Effective Study*, Rev. Ed. Upper Montclair, New Jersey: Boynton/Cook Publishers, Inc. 1984.

Kanar, Carol C. *The Confident Student*. Boston: Houghton Mifflin Company, 1991.

Koch, Richard. *The 80/20 Principle: The Secret of Achieving More With Less*. New York: Bantam Doubleday Dell, 1998.

Kornhauser, Arthur W. *How to Study: Suggestions for High School and College Students,* 3rd Ed. Revised by Diane M. Enerson. Chicago and London: The University of Chicago Press, 1993.

Lakein, Alan. *How To Get Control of Your Time and Your Life*. New York: Penguin Books, 1974.

Mackenzie, Alec. *The Time Trap.* New York: AMACOM, 1990.

Mayer, Jeffrey J. *Time Management for Dummies: Briefcase Edition.* Foster City, CA: IDG Books Worldwide, Inc., 1995.

Miller, David K. and T. Earl Allen. *Fitness: A Lifetime Commitment.* New York: MacMillan, 1986.

Murray, Michael and Joseph Pizzorno, M.D. *Encyclopedia of Natural Medicine: Revised 2nd Edition.* Rocklin, California: Prima Publishing, 1998.

Nickell, Paulena and Jean Muir Dorsey. *Management in Family Living.* New York: John Wiley & Sons, Inc., 1967.

Ornish, Dr. Dean. *Program for Reversing Heart Disease.* New York: Ballantine Books, 1996.

Pehrsson, Robert S., Ed.D and Peter R. Denner, Ph.D. *Semantic Organizers: A Study Strategy for Special Needs Learners.* Rockville, Maryland: Aspen Publications, Inc., 1989.

Perkins, Ed with Walt Leonard and Editors of Consumer Reports Travel Letter. *Consumer Reports Best Travel Deals: 1997 Edition.* New York: Consumers Union of the United States, 1997.

Pleck, Joseph H. *Working Wives/Working Husbands.* Beverly Hills: Sage Publications, 1985.

Rechtschaffen, Stephan. *Time Shifting: Creating More Time to Enjoy Your Life.* New York: Doubleday, 1996.

Robinson, John P. and Geoffrey Godbey. *Time for Life: Surprising Ways Americans Use Their Time.* University Park, Pennsylvania: Pennsylvania State University, 1997.

Ronsard, Nichole. *Cellulite: Those Lumps, Bumps and Bulges You Couldn't Lose Before.* New York: Bantam Books, 1973.

Schlenger, Sunny and Roberta Roesch. *How to Be Organized in Spite of Yourself.* New York: Signet, 1990.

Seiwert, Lothar J. *Time is Money: Save It.* Homewood, Illinois: Dow Jones-Irwin, 1989.

Siebert, Al and Bernadine Gilpin. *The Adult Student's Guide to Survival and Success! Time For College.* Portland, Oregon: Practical Psychology Press, 1989.

Snowdon, Les and Maggie Humphreys. *Walk Aerobics.* Woodstock, New York: The Overlook Press, 1992.

Somer, Elizabeth. *Age-Proof Your Body.* New York: William Morrow and Company, Inc., 1998.

Strohmer, Joanne C. and Clare Carhart. *Time-Saving Tips for Teachers.* Thousand Oaks, California: Corwin Press, Inc., 1997.

Stull, Andrew T. *English on the Internet 1997-1998: A Student's Guide.* Upper Saddle River, New Jersey: Prentice Hall, 1998.

Taylor, Robert B., M.D. *Dr. Taylor's Self Help Medical Guide.* New York: Signet, 1977.

Tribole, Evelyn. *Eating on the Run.* Champaign, Illinois: Life Enforcement Publications, 1987.

Van Ness, Ross. *Eliminating Procrastination Without Putting It Off.* Bloomington, Indiana: Phi Delta Kappa Educational Foundation, 1988.

Wenig, Lynne. *The A to Z of Time Management.* St. Leonards, Australia: Allen & Unwin, 1993.

Winston, Stephanie. *Getting Organized: Updated and Revised.* New York: Warner Books, 1991.

Woodhull, Angela V. *The New Time Manager.* Hampshire, England: Gower Publishing, 1997.

Suggested biographies, autobiographies, and memoirs of the great time managers and other inspirational people

(These books are simply suggestions for further research; most have not been personally read by the author. By reading about the lives of others who have been successful, you can often adapt some of their "tricks of the trade" to your own lives.)

Ash, Mary Kay. *Mary Kay You Can Have It All: Lifetime Wisdom from America's Foremost Woman Entrepreneur.* Prima Publishing, 1995.

Ashe, Arthur, and Frank Deford. *Arthur Ashe: Portrait in Motion.* Carroll & Graf, 1993.

Bibb, Porter. *Ted Turner: It Ain't As Easy As It Looks: A Biography.* Johnson, 1997.

Bonher, Kate, et al. *Trump: The Art of the Comeback.* Times, 1997.

Brown, Helen Gurley. *Having It All: Love, Success, Sex, Money, Even If You're Starting with Nothing.* New York: Simon & Schuster, 1982.

Bruetz, Connie. *Master of the Game: Steve Ross and the Creation of Time Warner.* Penguin, 1995.

Carnegie, Dale. *Dale Carnegie's Lifetime Plan for Success: How to Win Friends and Influence People; How to Stop Worrying and Start Living.* Galahad, 1998.

Caroli, Betty Boyd. *The Roosevelt Women.* New York: Basic Books, 1998.

Cher, and Jeff Coplon. *The First Time.* New York: Simon & Schuster, 1998.

Chernow, Ron. *Titan: The Life of John D. Rockefeller, Sr.* New York: Random House, 1998.

Clark, Jim and Owen Edwards. *Netscape Time.* New York: St. Martins, 1999.

Cosby, Bill. *Congratulations! Now What?: A Book for Graduates.* New York: Hyperion, 1999.

Dalai Lama. *Freedom in Exile: The Autobiography of the Dalai Lama.* San Francisco: Harper, 1991.

Davies, P.C.W. *About Time: Einstein's Unfinished Revolution.* Touchstone, 1996.

Decker, Jeffrey Louis. *Made in America: Self-Styled Success from Horatio Alger to Oprah Winfrey.* University of Minnesota Press, 1997.

Delany, Elizabeth, et al. *Having Our Say: The Delany Sisters First Hundred Years.* Delta, 1997.

Gates, Bill. *Business @ the Speed of Thought: Using a Digital Nervous System.* Collins Hemingway, Warner, 1999.

Gilbert, Martin. *Churchill: A Life.* New York: Henry Holt, 1992.

Haney, Lynn. *Naked at the Feast: A Biography of Josephine Baker.* Parkwest Publications, 1996.

Heilbrun, Carolyn G. *The Education of a Woman: The Life of Gloria Steinem.* New York: Ballantine, 1996.

Hemingway, Ernest, and Matthew Joseph Bruccoli. *Conversations with Ernest Hemingway.* University Press of Mississippi, 1986.

Hilton, Conrad. *Be My Guest.* Prentice-Hall, 1984.

Iacocca, Lee. *Iacocca: An Autobiography.* Bantam, 1986.

Jackson, Tim. *Richard Branson, Virgin King; Inside Richard Branson's Business Empire.* Prima, 1996.

Jordan, Michael, and Mark Vancil. *For the Love of the Game: My Story.* Crown Publishers, 1998.

King, Billie Jean. *The Autobiography of Billie Jean King.* Longinotti-Buitoni, Gian Luigi. *Selling Dreams.* Simon & Schuster, 1999.

Lowe, Janet C., and Oprah Winfrey. *Oprah Winfrey Speaks.* John Wiley & Sons, 1998.

McBride, Joseph. *Steven Spielberg: A Biography.* DaCapo Press, 1999.

O'Neill, Jennifer. *Surviving Myself.* William Morrow & Company, 1999.

Parish, James Robert. *Rosie: Rosie O'Donnell's Biography.* Carroll & Graf, 1998.

Sasson, Hellen, and John Redziewcz, eds. *Between Friends: Perspectives on John Kenneth Galbraith.* New York: Houghton Mifflin & Co., 1999.

Shawcross, William. *Murdoch: The Making of a Media Empire.* Touchstone, 1997.

Stahl, Lesley. *Reporting Live.* New York: Simon & Schuster, 1999.

Strouse, Jean. *Morgan: American Financier.* New York: Random House, 1999.

Taraborrelli, J. Randy. *Sinatra: A Complete Life.* Birch Lane Press, 1997.

Thomas, Helen. *Front Row at the White House: My Life and Times.* New York: Scribner, 1999.

Unseld, Joachim, and Paul F. Dvorak. *Franz Kafka: A Writer's Life.* Ariadne Press, 1997.

Von Franz, Marie-Louise. *C.S. Jung: His Myth in Our Time.* Inner City Books, 1998.

Wall, Joseph Frazier. *Andrew Carnegie.* Pittsburgh: University of Pittsburgh Press, 1989.

Wallis, Michael, and Wilma Pearl Mankiller. *Mankiller.* Griffin Trade Paperback, 1999.

The *Unofficial Guide*™ Reader Questionnaire

If you would like to express your opinion about managing time or this guide, please complete this questionnaire and mail it to:

The *Unofficial Guide*™ Reader Questionnaire
IDG\ Lifestyle Group
1633 Broadway, floor 7
New York, NY 10019-6785

Gender: ___ M   ___ F

Age: ___ Under 30   ___ 31–40   ___ 41–50
___ Over 50

Education: ___ High school   ___ College
___ Graduate/Professional

What is your occupation?
_____

How did you hear about this guide?
___ Friend or relative
___ Newspaper, magazine, or Internet
___ Radio or TV
___ Recommended at bookstore
___ Recommended by librarian
___ Picked it up on my own
___ Familiar with the *Unofficial Guide*™ travel series

Did you go to the bookstore specifically for a book on starting a business online?   Yes ___   No ___

Have you used any other Unofficial Guides™?
Yes ___   No ___

If Yes, which ones?
_____
_____
_____

What other book(s) on managing time have you purchased? _____
_____
_____

Was this book:
___ more helpful than other(s)
___ less helpful than other(s)

Do you think this book was worth its price?
Yes ___ No ___

Did this book cover all topics related to managing time adequately?
Yes ___ No ___

Please explain your answer:
_____
_____
_____

Were there any specific sections in this book that were of particular help to you? Yes ___ No ___

Please explain your answer:
_____
_____
_____

On a scale of 1 to 10, with 10 being the best rating, how would you rate this guide? ___

What other titles would you like to see published in the *Unofficial Guide*™ series?
_____
_____

***Are Unofficial Guides*™ readily available in your area?** Yes ___ No ___

Other comments:
_____
_____
_____
_____

Get the inside scoop...with the *Unofficial Guides*™!

Health and Fitness

The Unofficial Guide to Alternative Medicine
ISBN: 0-02-862526-9 Price: $15.95

The Unofficial Guide to Conquering Impotence
ISBN: 0-02-862870-5 Price: $15.95

The Unofficial Guide to Coping with Menopause
ISBN: 0-02-862694-x Price: $15.95

The Unofficial Guide to Cosmetic Surgery
ISBN: 0-02-862522-6 Price: $15.95

The Unofficial Guide to Dieting Safely
ISBN: 0-02-862521-8 Price: $15.95

The Unofficial Guide to Having a Baby
ISBN: 0-02-862695-8 Price: $15.95

The Unofficial Guide to Living with Diabetes
ISBN: 0-02-862919-1 Price: $15.95

The Unofficial Guide to Overcoming Arthritis
ISBN: 0-02-862714-8 Price: $15.95

The Unofficial Guide to Overcoming Infertility
ISBN: 0-02-862916-7 Price: $15.95

Career Planning

The Unofficial Guide to Acing the Interview
ISBN: 0-02-862924-8 Price: $15.95

The Unofficial Guide to Earning What You Deserve
ISBN: 0-02-862523-4 Price: $15.95

The Unofficial Guide to Hiring and Firing People
ISBN: 0-02-862523-4 Price: $15.95

Business and Personal Finance

The Unofficial Guide to Investing
ISBN: 0-02-862458-0 Price: $15.95

The Unofficial Guide to Investing in Mutual Funds
ISBN: 0-02-862920-5 Price: $15.95

*The Unofficial Guide to Managing Your Personal
Finances*
ISBN: 0-02-862921-3 Price: $15.95

The Unofficial Guide to Starting a Small Business
ISBN: 0-02-862525-0 Price: $15.95

Home and Automotive

The Unofficial Guide to Buying a Home
ISBN: 0-02-862461-0 Price: $15.95

The Unofficial Guide to Buying or Leasing a Car
ISBN: 0-02-862524-2 Price: $15.95

The Unofficial Guide to Hiring Contractors
ISBN: 0-02-862460-2 Price: $15.95

Family and Relationships

The Unofficial Guide to Childcare
ISBN: 0-02-862457-2 Price: $15.95

The Unofficial Guide to Dating Again
ISBN: 0-02-862454-8 Price: $15.95

The Unofficial Guide to Divorce
ISBN: 0-02-862455-6 Price: $15.95

The Unofficial Guide to Eldercare
ISBN: 0-02-862456-4 Price: $15.95

The Unofficial Guide to Planning Your Wedding
ISBN: 0-02-862459-9 Price: $15.95

Hobbies and Recreation

The Unofficial Guide to Finding Rare Antiques
ISBN: 0-02-862922-1 Price: $15.95

The Unofficial Guide to Casino Gambling
ISBN: 0-02-862917-5 Price: $15.95

All books in the *Unofficial Guide* series are available
at your local bookseller, or by calling 1-800-428-5331.